# RICARD O'SULLIVAN BURKE

*Ricard O'Sullivan Burke in American Civil War uniform*

# O'Sullivan Burke
# FENIAN

*Mary C. Lynch*
*Seamus O'Donoghue*

*Published by*
EBONY JANE PRESS
Coolalta, Carrigadrohid,
Co. Cork, Ireland.



**ISBN 0 9536582 0 1**

This publication has been supported by the West Cork LEADER Co-Op.

***Printed by Litho Press, Midleton, Co. Cork.***

This book is dedicated to the memory of Catherine Burke Walsh, mother of co-author, Mary Lynch, who kept alive the memory of her grand uncle, Ricard and instilled in her daughter the desire to publish his life story.

# CONTENTS



## PART TWO

# ACKNOWLEDGMENTS

This book would not have been possible without the help of many people.

We wish to thank the West Cork LEADER who are supporting the publication of this book.

We particularly want to thank Deirdre Clancy, M.A., Chief Advising Examiner, Dept. of Education who through discussion, advice and, at times, criticism, helped us enormously; our sincere thanks to Tim Cadogan, Niamh Cronin and Denis Murphy, Cork County Reference Library who were always so approachable and helpful; our thanks also to Anthony Greene for his advice which was available at all times; Donal O'Flynn who did much of the photographic work; Kate Caniffe, Chicago, who did a lot of the preliminary research; Jane O'Donovan who acted as chauffeur and guide during our American research trip; Michael Kenny, National Museum, Staff of the National Archives, Dublin; Kevin Browne and Staff of the National Library, Dublin; James Abbott, Assistant Commissioner of Police, Suffolk County, New York; Islington Public Library; Broadmoor Criminal Lunatic Asylum; Paul Rose; Peter Quinlivan; Walter McGrath; Brother W. P. Allen (R.I.P.) who compiled the writings of Ricard O'Sullivan Burke; Patricia McCarthy, Cork Archives; Paddy Connolly, Bandon; George Hayes, Kinsale; Staff, Harold Washington Library, Chicago; Dr. Colin A Lennon, Lecturer, History Department, National University of Ireland, Maynooth; National Archives Trust Fund, Washington; Ellis Island Immigration Museum, New York; Staff, Bro. Allen Library, O'Connell Schools, Dublin; and our many friends who gave us such great assistance.

A special word of thanks to our respective spouses, Jim Lynch and Lil O'Donoghue, for their encouragement, support and, particularly, their patience during this project.

# SOURCES

## PRIMARY SOURCES

The Cork Examiner.
The Nation.
The Irishman.
Waterford Citizen.
Cork County Eagle.
New York Herald.
Cork Herald.
Boston Pilot.
Freeman's Journal.
London Express.
Chicago Daily Tribune.
Gaelic American.
New York Times.
Cork New Evening Post.
Morning Star.

## SECONDARY SOURCES

The Fenian Movement, edited by T. W. Moody.
My Years in English Jails. Jeremiah O'Donovan Rossa.
Report of the Devon Commission.
The Fenians in England. Patrick Quinlivan and Paul Rose.
The Bold Fenian men. Robert Kee.
Manchester Martyrs. Paul Rose.
The Fenian Movement in the United States, 1856 - 1886. W. D. Darcy.
The Irish Militia. McAnally.
Pitchcap and Triangle. Dr. J. M. Barry.
New Irish Library.
Charles Stewart Parnell. F. S. L. Lyons.
Recollections of an Irish Rebel. John Devoy.
The Fenians. Michael Kenny.

William Roantree, Kildare Historical Journal. Michael Kenny.
Waterford Fenians, Decies Historical Journal. Patrick McCarthy.
The Irish Sword, 1967.
Fenian Memories. Mark Ryan.
Doherty Papers, Bandon.
Green Brigades - The Irish and the American Civil War. Conference at University of Massachusetts, Amherst. Role of the Irish in the Confederate Army, Dr. David Gleeson, Armstrong Atlantic State University and The Irish Brigade, Professor Lawrence Kohl, University of Alabama.
Encyclopaedia Britannica.
The Irish in Chicago. Edited by Lawrence J. McCaffrey, Ellen Skerrett, Ml. F. Funchion and Charles Fanning.
Chicago's Irish Nationalists, 1881 - 1890. Michael F. Funchion, South Dakota State University
A Cork Felon. Walter McGrath.
Patrick Cleburne; Confederate General. Purdue & Purdue.
The Great Shame. Thomas Keneally.

# INTRODUCTION

Ricard O'Sullivan Burke was, according to John Devoy, by long odds the most remarkable man the Fenian movement produced and also one of the ablest. The story of his life is, in large part, the history of the Fenians and reads more like a romance than a record of actual facts. In his gloomy prison cell he solaced his long lonely hours by penning down his experiences. And surely they are strange, chequered, strong in contrast, brimful of picturesque life, filled with buyont Celtic humour, a very panorama of wildest most romantic adventure.

Truth is stranger than fiction and surely the eventful history of this Irishman's career is strange indeed. This splendid young Gael, brimming over with vitality, was driven, in his youth, from the land where his fathers had been able to live and thrive and die. Like many another young Irishman cast on the waves of the world in America, Ricard Burke at once set himself to work to build a new world for himself. He had a good education, did not dread work, and was thoroughly in earnest whenever he set to work. His temperament invited him to the side of adventure and he has left us a vivid record of his life as a sailor and an adventurer.

But the soldier's life was more to his taste than the sailor's. He thirsted for adventure and he had some desire, perhaps, to learn the soldier's trade with some possible ulterior motive. He enrolled as a volunteer in a cavalry corps, a sort of guerilla band, and fought in one of those petty South American wars. He was a splendid horseman and made his mark in the campaign.

He settled down in the City of Santiago and made rapid progress in that majestic Castilian language. He spoke French tolerably well and was fluent in both Irish and English. He was an accomplished artist and, unfortunately, all that remains of his many drawings is a self-portrait. He enlivened many a party and celebration with his music. His writings include his autobiography and sketches, real and imaginary, entitled "Christmas Holidays in Prison" which contain prose and poetry.

Some further writings were lost and others never saw the light of day.

When the guns booming across the harbour of Charleston gave the call to arms, Burke hurried to the side of the soldiers of the Union. His regiment, though not distinctively, was almost exclusively Irish. He served throughout the war and was mustered out at the close of hostilities as a colonel, having worked his way upward through every grade with honourable certificates of fidelity, courage and efficiency.

His career, subsequently, became part and parcel of a larger history as Burke took a leading role in Fenian affairs in Ireland, England and America. A key to the character of this amazing man can be gleaned from a passage from the last letter written previous to his trial. "If I go, and I suppose I shall, depend upon it that I will do what we all hold dear, no injury morally or otherwise. I have not an atom of regret."

*Mary C. Lynch.*
*Seamus O'Donoghue.*

# FOREWORD

From a very early age, long before I had any deep interest in Irish history, I was aware of the existence of Ricard O'Sullivan Burke. For almost two decades, from six years of age onwards, I spent each entire summer in Coachford, Co. Cork, with my uncle, Tim Gleeson, and his wife, who was the Mary Burke mentioned in Chapter One of this book. Much time was spent in the house of her sister, Catherine Walsh (nee Burke), which was then Burke's Hotel in Coachford, and I can recall my childish curiosity being piqued by a large framed photograph that graced the wall of the breakfastroom in that establishment. The subject was attired in the full military regalia of a Colonel of the Federal Army in the American Civil War, and questioning elicited the proud reply: "that is our great-uncle, Colonel Ricard O'Sullivan Burke." Sadly, the photograph has long since disappeared and I seem now to be the only person left who remembers it ever being there.

When, therefore, many years later, my kinswoman, Mary Lynch, consulted me about her plan to publish a life of Ricard O'Sullivan Burke, incorporating material that had been in her family for generations, I felt both nostalgic and grateful; nostalgic for the long-ago summer idylls, grateful to be invited to play even a small part in this worthwhile project. Over the past two years I have watched with admiration the energy, enthusiasm and formidable research activities of Mary and her co-author, Seamus O'Donoghue (also a native of Coachford) as they carefully welded their material into a compact readable unit.

On the one hand, no longer will those whose favourite literary pastime is the identification of characters that feature in that most widely read of works, James Joyce's Ulysses, have to search further than this book for the full story of "Colonel Ricard Burke, tanist of his Sept" mentioned in the first section of that work. For here it is in its entirety. On the other hand, for those whose whole primary interest is Irish history, it is to be hoped that this publication will serve as an inspiration to others in possession of similar material to heed the old African admonition: "let those who come after see that their names are not forgotten."

*Deirdre M. Clancy, M.A.*
*May 1999*

## CHAPTER 1

# THE BURKES OF CLOUNYREAGUE

" 'Where's Rick?' said my father feebly. 'Bring the boy round to my bedside.'

"The nurse conducted me out of the retired corner of the sick room where I was vainly striving to smother my passionate sobs, and taking my hand placed it in his. It was moist and feverish.

" 'It's you, my son, speak,' he murmured painfully as he grasped me with what little strength he had left and drew me nearer to the eyes over which the film of death was gathering.

"I couldn't answer for emotion.

" 'Are you there?'

" 'Yes, sir,' I gasped with effort, for he was indeed very dear to me - a good father, and I was a favourite child.

" 'I'm going, my son, going to a better land. My hours are numbered in this world. I have little to leave you but an honest name. Keep it honest. Fear God, love Ireland and your brothers and sisters.'

"The sorrowful parting was made to each and all of us in turn; the neighbours dropped in to bid their neighbour, 'one of the good old stock,' as they called him, with the old blood in his veins, a last adieu; and then the priest came and shrived him, and the Litany for the Dying was repeated by a sombre group around a white bed; the coffin-maker with his rule; the candles were lit, and there was a wake, and two days after a caoin and a long, melancholy procession to a grassy churchyard and the smoothing of green turf over a new grave - and I realised I was fatherless.

"The scene will for ever remain imprinted in my memory. I was sensitive, affectionate, high-spirited. 'I leave you my honest name.' What nobler legacy could I have! I was prouder of it than if he had left me broad acres and thousands in bank.

"For young as I was I had the Gaelic haughtiness of race, I knew the history of my family, I had spent days poring over its traditions until my mind had been filled with the ambition to lift it if I could

*The birthplace of O'Sullivan Burke*

to its former high estate, at all events to keep its name honest as my father had charged me from his death-bed.

"The Burkes are no novel importation in Ireland. Norman by extraction they have, like the Geraldines, adapted themselves to the people amongst whom they settled, intermarried with the Celts, and became in course of time Hiberniores ipsis Hibernis, more Irish than the Irish themselves. Whether as De Burgho, Bourke or Burke they have always played a more or less conspicuous part in the history of the country; their annals, from William, Earl of Ulster, dead 1333, down to our own unchivalric age (for has not Edmund of the ilk declared that the age of chivalry is past?) bristle with 'rebelly' Tibbets, and Ricks, and Redmonds. Some of them, however, were wiser in wordy sense, in their generation, and accepted the situation. Of these at this writing flourish still a Burke, Marquis of Clanrickard, a Burke, Earl of

Mayo, and a Burke who is Ulster King at Arms and surveys the practical work-a-day world from the heights of a genealogical eyrie in the Bermingham Tower of Dublin Castle."

This is the opening chapter of an autobiography of Ricard O'Sullivan Burke written in 1867/68 while in jail awaiting trial on a treason-felony charge. It came to be written as a result of a chance meeting in a cafe in Paris in the summer of 1867 between an Irish journalist, John Augustus O'Shea, and a gentleman who called himself Livingstone. According to O'Shea, this gentleman was genial, agreeable, and had a certain bold bonhomie and soldierly frankness of mien and manner which O'Shea admired. He lost sight of him after a few weeks. It subsequently transpired that Livingstone and a prisoner in custody in an English jail were identical. This prisoner was Ricard O'Sullivan Burke. He wrote to O'Shea and this letter led to a correspondence out of which grew the autobiography. "Unhappily for the completeness of my undertaking my journals are wanting. Ah! if I had only been able to save my old diaries - for like a sentimental goose, I used to indulge in that weakness once - how easy it would be to read off the log of my wanderings today! But they are gone to Davy Jones's locker long since. All, except one. And that I became disgusted with because of its sameness. It was the diary I kept while in Uncle Sam's army. If the chances of active service during the greatest civil war in history failed to give it charm or throw a glow of life into its pages, what think you must have been the interest of those I tried to rescue from the jaws of old ocean when we went down off Peru."

(John Augustus O'Shea was born in 1839 in Nenagh, Co. Tipperary. Having received his elementary education in his native town, he was sent to the Catholic University then recently established in Dublin. In 1859 he went to London and sought work as a journalist. His love of adventure led him to become a special correspondent. He covered the Austro-Prussian war and also the Franco-German war. He was for twenty years on the staff of the "Standard" newspaper. When he left that newspaper he wrote occasional articles for various newspapers and he was long a regular member of the staff of the "Universe" an Irish Catholic paper. He died on March 13th 1905.)

*The Round Tower at Kinneigh*

Ricard O'Sullivan Burke was the son of Denis and Margaret Burke of Clounyreague, Kinneigh, near Ballineen in West Cork. Margaret Burke was a daughter of Timothy and Mary O'Sullivan of Slieveowen in the neighbouring parish of Kilmichael. The O'Sullivans of Slieveowen were Catholic leaseholders or middle landlords claiming descent from O'Sullivans More of Kerry. A ms. History of Kerry written by a Friar O'Sullivan of Muckross Abbey about 1750 records that a branch of the O'Sullivans More settled in the Bandon district where its members were in good stations of life for a time. It is thought this refers to the O'Sullivans of Slieveowen - Ricard's maternal ancestors.

*Burke's Hill, Kinneigh*

In the early part of the last century Denis Burke lived a farm in Clounyreague - a townland adjacent to the Round Tower of Kinneigh. This was rented from Lord Bandon and was held without a lease. The road leading by this holding to Kinneigh is still known as "Burke's Hill", thus commemorating the family which lived there over one hundred years ago. The Burke holding consisted of 66 acres 3 rds and 20 sq, pers. and the yearly rent was £46 - 3 - 1. This was increased to £49 - 6 - 2 in 1838.

Denis and Margaret Burke had twelve children including Ricard.

**Denis:**
He went to America.

**Edmond:**
He emigrated to New York where he married an Irish girl, Ellen Harrington. One son, Dionysius (Denis), married Catherine Hennessy and they had nine sons and one daughter - Alonzo, Dionysius W., Edmond, Ricard O'Sullivan, John, Richard, Eoin, Thomas, William , Isabelle. Isabelle married James McGuone. One of their daughters, Catherine, married John Abbot and they had six children including James Abbott who is Assistant Commissioner of Police, Suffolk County, New York.

**Daniel:**
Born on August 26, 1819. Probably lived in the Dunmanway area all his life and is buried in Kinneigh.

**Ellen:**
Born on November 17, 1821

**Catherine:**
Known as Kate. She was married to William Barry, had two daughters and lived in England at 6, Harriet Str., Lower Marsh, Lambeth.

**Cornelius (Con):**
He also used the double barrel name, O'Sullivan Burke. In 1869 he opened a candle factory in Upper Distillery yard in Bandon and he had a similar establishment in the South Terrace in Cork. Had one daughter.

*Cornelius Burke - brother of Ricard*

**Eoin:**
Born May 30, 1824.

**Bridget:**

She was Mrs. Baldwin and spent the last years of her life living in Coachford in a house adjacent to Burke's Hotel. Her grand-daughter, Molly Murphy, died in 1942.

**Richard:**

*Richard Burke - brother of Ricard*

Born March 30, 1829. He came to Coachford and worked in Clonmoyle Mills. He married Coachford hotelier, Catherine Hayes, and the establishment became known as Burke's Hotel - a noted landmark in the area. He played a very prominent part in the public life of Coachford. He had four children, Mary, who died at an early age, Denis, who lost his life at the age of 12 in an accident on the Cork/Macroom railway near Ballincollig in 1878, Ellen, who suffered serious injuries in the same accident, never married and was postmistress in Coachford post office and Thomas Richard, who succeeded to the ownership of the family business. Thomas married Jane Oldfield and had two daughters, Catherine (Kitty) and Mary. Catherine married George Walsh and had two children, Tom who until recently carried on the family business in Coachford and Mary (Lynch) who is co-author of this book. Mary married Jim Lynch and had six children, two of whom, Mary and Jane are now running the family business - the sixth generation to do so. Thomas Richard's other daughter, Mary, married Timothy Gleeson and had two daughters, Maura and Grace, both of whom have four children. Denis Burke's wife, Margaret, spent the last years of her life in Coachford being cared for by her son, Richard.

**Morgan:**
Born on August 28, 1832. He went to America and was never heard of again.

**Mary:**
Born on February 3, 1835. She went to Australia.

**Ricard:**
The youngest - born on January 24th, 1838 - and subject of this book.

***Authors' Note:*** Though the christian names are very similar, Ricard Burke and Richard Burke were brothers.

*Mary Burke - sister of Ricard*

*Ricard's Grandnieces, Catherine Burke and Molly Murphy, Coachford.*

*Thomas R., Ellen and Denis Burke – niece and nephews of Ricard*

*Dionysius Burke – nephew of Ricard*

*Catherine and Mary Burke – grand nieces of Ricard*

*Burke headstone in Aghinagh Cemetery*

## CANDLE WORKS,

UPPER DISTILLERY, BANDON.

### To the Candle Merchants and Consumers of the County.

ADVERTIZER is now making and ready to supply CANDLES, produced from the following materials, BLEACHED and UNBLEACHED WAX, PARAFFIN, STEARINE and SPERM, in sizes of 4, 6, and 8 to the lb. A trial is only wanted to prove the value of those Candles. They will be sent *free* by Rail, and a LIBERAL DISCOUNT given to Customers.

A Price List sent on application to

**CORNELIUS O'S. BURKE,**

*Candle Works, Upper Distillery, Bandon.*

(2.10.69-6t)

*(From West Cork and Carbery Eagle and County Advertiser)*

**THE ROCKSAVAGE PATENT CANDLE WORKS, SOUTH TERRACE, CORK.**

I, Advertiser, (CORNELIUS O'S. BURKE), at the Special Request of my friends in the City of Cork, removed from Upper Distillery, Bandon, to the above address, where I can supply the Trade with a variety of high-class and other Candles, as cheaply as any other Maker. I call particular attention to my Class of Large Christmas Candles from half to two and a-half lb. each, of an improved Wax Mixture, very cheap and calculated to supplant PALMER's Patent Spiral Candle Tubes for Altar purposes, and to which I refer the favourable notice of the Clergy. A Partner wanted with Capital between Two and Three Thousand to assist Advertiser in Establishing a Patent obtained by him for the Manufacture of Soap and Candles. A Prospectus of the Investment can be had on application to Advertiser. (7429)

*(From Cork Examiner)*

# CHAPTER 2

# RICARD'S EARLY LIFE

Ricard, in his autobiography, describes his father and the misfortune that befell him.

"He was a prosperous tenant-farmer at Kinneigh, near Ballyneen, in the County of Cork. An active intelligent man, and, unfortunately for himself, a man of advanced politics. He loved his neighbour and served his kind in his sphere; the beggar was never sent away empty-handed from his door, and he was vainer of an honest vote for the good of Ireland as he conscientiously thought than the cobweb-covered blazonings of heraldry. His landlord was the Earl of Bandon, a nobleman of strong Conservative opinions. Feargus O'Connor, the Chartist agitator, offered himself as a candidate for Cork, there was a bitter election and party feelings ran high. My father was an ardent supporter of O'Connor, his landlord was not."

**Feargus O'Connor**

The O'Connors or Conners of Connorville in West Cork held, at one time, a high social position. The first member of the family to take up residence in West Cork was a Mrs. O'Connor who, when her husband had been brutally killed by Cromwell's soldiers, fled to Bandon with her infant son, Cornelius. There, Cornelius was duly trained in the religious and political principles then prevalent in that town and the surname was changed into the English sounding Conner. In due time Cornelius married and became the father of "Daniel Conner, of Bandon-bridge, merchant" who made considerable purchases of land.

This Daniel was the father of numerous children. One son, Roger, married Anne Longfield, sister of Richard, Viscount Longueville. He had five sons and Roger told them that their true name was O'Connor and that the surname "Conner" had been adopted for political motives in the previous century. The two younger sons, Roger and Arthur, thenceforth, decided to call themselves O'Connor. Both Roger and Arthur, were involved with the United Irishmen and imprisoned for a while in Cork gaol on a charge of high treason. Roger's second wife was Wilhelmina, daughter of Nicholas Bowen of Bowenscourt, whom he married in August, 1788. and by her had several children among whom was Feargus O'Connor.

Feargus inherited a similar revolutionary outlook from his father and uncle. In 1832 he was elected to the British House of Commons for the Cork constituency as a well-known activist in local Anti-Tithes protests and as an ardent advocate of Repeal. His strong "Socialist" sympathies caused him to align closely with the British Radicals in Westminster. Here he defended and attempted to further the interests of the urban and rural poor. In 1835 Feargus retained his seat but was subsequently unseated for lacking the necessary £600 freehold requirement, and so turned his attentions to Britain.

For the next twelve years Feargus functioned outside of parliament, involving himself deeply in working class politics. He founded the English Chartist movement, the first nationally orchestrated working class political movement in world history, and became its leader. He was a charismatic figure in the same vein as Jim Larkin but, at the height of his notoriety, wielded a far greater influence. The economic hardships eased and frustration and demoralisation crept into the movement and Chartism petered out. Before the movement was spent, however, O'Connor instigated a novel land scheme. The Chartist Land Co-operative, formed in 1845, purchased land and settled working class families in small holdings. The land plan ran into financial difficulties and in 1851 the co-operative was declared bankrupt.

As the Chartist movement declined, Feargus, deserted by the thousands with whom he once was popular and assailed on all sides with the clamorous outcry of crowds whose money had been swallowed up in ill starred Land Scheme, sought refuge from despair by drinking heavily. Eventually he was pronounced insane and he died on August 31, 1855. Over 40,000 mourners followed the coffin when his remains were interred. Some of his

Chartist disciples erected a statue in memory of their Chief at Nottingham for which town he was a member of parliament from 1847 to 1852.

Because of his support for Feargus O'Connor, tradition has it that Denis Burke was evicted from his holding. However true that is, Burke was issued with a notice to quit on May 1, 1842 and there were some arrears in rent due. Burke, however, did not go peacefully and meekly and Lord Bandon's agent noted in the rent book: "Notice to quit being then given. This ground forcibly held after 1st of May for a few weeks."

Whether the Burkes left peacefully then or force was used, Ricard does not record this in his autobiography. However he has very strong views on the results of the eviction. "From that eviction I date a natural dislike of all aristocracies in general, the Irish aristocracy in particular. It was the ruin of our fortunes, the scattering of our family. The private tutor under whom I had received the rudiments of my education had to be dismissed, my three brothers and my sister had to emigrate to England, and I, being too young to face fortune in a strange land, had to remain at home to shift for myself."

Presumably the Burkes went to live in Dunmanway. In a letter, dated December 9, 1870, written to Ricard in prison, a friend, David Coffey, of 46 Dunbar St, writes: "Great changes in Dunmanway since you left. You recollect the Long Bridge near where you lived in your youthful days. Your poor father and I spent some happy hours together." Ricard attended Dunmanway Model School which at that time was not long in operation. John Devoy states that the schoolmaster was a Carlow man named Murphy - a pronounced loyalist. He was later transferred to Dublin where he taught Devoy. When, in later years, his two pupils were sentenced to penal servitude he expressed sorrow - not for them - but for his own misfortune in having taught two such rebels.

Burke was a bright and intelligent boy. In the Model Schools he showed some precocious talent in sketching. Later in life he was an accomplished artist. "Being a lad of self-reliant disposition I

## Facsimile of David Coffey's letter.

No. 46 Duncan St, Cork. Dec. 9th 1870 ~

My dear Friend

You will, I'm convinced, think it a most unusual and strange thing to be addressed by a person whom you never saw. But I was well acquainted with your Parents from a very early age, and the different members of your once numerous family, John, Jenny and Mrs Barry excepted. Your brother Dick lately visited you at the 'Broad Moor Asylum'. He was giving me some particulars about you. I was glad to know from him the Officials of that Establ. were rather lenient and kind towards you. Rumours are prevalent in our City for the last month, that the Political prisoners will soon get their discharge. Petitions to that effect have been drawn up generally by the Corporations of Ireland to the Government, including persons of all shades of opinion. Our prime Minister Gladstone, and those serving under him are well-intentioned towards the Country and I have the strongest hopes before the Great Festival of Christmas come round that the Prison doors will be thrown open, and the sons and Parents, brothers, sisters, friends and acquaintances will meet in harmony again! —

Your brother Dick requested of me to write to you, which I readily do, he said, it would be courteously received at the 'B. M. & A.' and handed to you. When you return, with God's assistance, you will find the members of your Family thus circumstanced: Your br. Dick in Coachford, doing an excellent Business in a miscellaneous way; respected and loved by all around him. As long as I know him, the qualities of his mind are good, kind, and charitable. He is blest with a wife, who is, certainly, 'a crown to her Husband'; and an interesting progeny. Your Mother, who is now old and feeble, lives with Dick, and is well and tenderly cared for. Your brother "Con" is now established in his peculiar Business near the "South Terrace", in our City. He is the first person that Manufactured Wax, Parafine &c Candles in the City of Cork. He is very clever in his Business, and he has taken out Patents for same. Con's wife often speaks of you; they have an interesting, nice young woman, a daughter, who recollects you. The "S. Terrace, Wax, Paraf Estab" is now arresting the attention of the Citizens; and, I am most happy to announce to you, your brother Con holds well with our Citizens. Your brother Morgan, (since he left Dublin for America) we never heard from. ~~Ann~~, Your sister, Bridget, (Mrs Baldwin) is well, and fulfills the Duties of her Station in Life. You may recollect, some years ago, when your brother, Con, was living in Glasgow, you spent some time with him there, I used to correspond with him. On one of those occasions, you acted as amanuensis for Con, and replied to me. This circumstance, most likely, now, you dont remember. The Model S. in Dunmanway must [illegible] to you, now and again. Here you evinced some precocious Talent in "Sketching"; Mrs Hall of Dunmanway, has, I'm informed, some of your early attempts. When you were in the habit formerly of writing those interesting and humorous Letters on the Dublin Teleg. I always read them with much pleasure.

Your Uncle Con at Shanacashel is in capital condition. He is secondly married and has 3 children. Your Uncle Jerry of Sleveen is dead over 3 years. You must be aware before this, of the death of your Aunt Wall of Crookstown, and Aunt Leary — Great changes in Dunmanway since you left it. You recollect the "Long Bridge", near which you lived in your youthful days. Your poor Father and I often spent some happy hours together. I take it for granted, you must have heard long since of the terrible war going on between France and Prussia, for the last five or six months. Paris is for the last two months invested by the Prussians. What the

What the result will be, cannot well be determined. Some think Paris will be Bombarded, others that it will be starved out. The remarkable event of the Emperor's Surrender at Sedan must have reached your ears. He is for the last few months a Prisoner in his Palatial residence at Wilhelmshöhe in the Electorate of Hesse Cassel and ... the dull waters of the Elbe! Six months ago [his] voice could command the attention of Europe. "Sic transit gloria Mundi". It would be entirely out of place here to go into all the details of this terrible and destructive War. Our past Summer and Autumn were highly favourable: not a single day to interrupt the work of harvest. Con, his wife, and daughter desire me convey to you their remembrance and warm affection. How I should like to see you this winter's evening, at their cosy Fire side, and hospitable Board! But brighter times will shortly come. Hope on: hope ever! ——
... Bridget, Mrs Baldwin ... you ... will speak ... Mrs O'Sullivan (a Cousin of your Mother's) with whom I lodge here for the last 20 years, sends her kind regards. Up to this time, our winter is rather mild, have not felt its severity yet. May God give you fortitude and resignation to bear your Cross a little longer! Now (like all sublunary things in this Life) I must come to a close.

Yours sincerely,
David Coffey. —

D... Inclose you ... remember Con ...

## Transcription of David Coffey's letter.

*No. 46, Dunbar St.,*
*Cork.*
*Dec 9th, 1870*

*My dear Friend,*

*You will, I'm convinced, think it a most unusual and strange thing to be addressed by a person whom you never saw. But I was well acquainted with your parents from a very early age and the different members of your once numerous family, you, Denny and Mrs Barry excepted. Your brother, Dick, lately visited you at the Broadmoor Asylum, he was giving me some particulars about you – I was glad to know from him the officials of that Estab. were lenient and kind toward you. Rumours are prevalent in our city for the past month that the Political prisoners will get their discharge. Petitions to that effect have been drawn up by the Corporations of Ireland to the Government including persons of all shades of opinion.*

*Our prime Minister, Gladstone, and those serving under him are well intentioned towards the Country and I have the strongest hopes that before the great Festival of Christmas comes around that the prison doors will be thrown open and that sons and parents, brother, sister, friends and acquaintances will meet in harmony together!*

*Your brother, Dick, requested of me to write to you, which I gladly do. He said it would be courteously received at the B-M and handed to you.*

*When you return, with God's assistance, you will find the members of your family thus circumstanced. Your brother, Dick, in Coachford doing an excellent Business in a miscellaneous way, respected and loved by all around him, as long as I know him – the qualities of his mind are good, kind and charitable – he is blessed with a wife who is certainly "a crown to her Husband" and an interesting progeny. Your mother, who is now old and feeble, lives with Dick and is well and tenderly cared for.*

*Your brother, Con, is now established in his peculiar Business near the South Terrace in our city. He is the first person that Manufactured Wax Paraffin Candles in the city of Cork. He is very clever in his Business and he has taken out Patents for same. Con's wife often speaks of you, they have an interesting nice young woman – a daughter who recollects you.*

*"The South Terrace Wax, Paraffin Estab." is now attracting the attention of the Citizens and I am most happy to announce to you your brother, Con, holds well with our Citizens. Your brother, Morgan, since he left Dublin for America we never heard from. Your sister, Bridget, (Mrs. Baldwin) is well and fulfils the Duties of her Station in Life. You may recollect some years ago when your brother,*

*Con, was living in Glasgow you spent some time with him there, I used to correspond with him – on one of these occasions you acted as amanuensis for Con and replied to me. This circumstance most likely you don't remember.*

*The Model S in Dunmanway must come to you now and again. There you winced some precocious talent in "Sketching" – Mrs. Hall of Dunmanway has, I'm informed, some of your early attempts. when you were in the habit formerly of writing those interesting and humorous letters in the Dublin Telegraph – I alway read them with much pleasure.*

*Your Uncle Con at Shanacashel is in capital condition – he is secondly married and has 3 children. Your Uncle Jerry of Slievowen is dead over three years.*

*You must be aware before this of the death of your Aunt Wall of Crookstown and Aunt Leary.*

*Great changes in Dunmanway since you left it. You recollect the LONG BRIDGE near where you lived in your youthful days – your poor father and I spent some happy hours together. I take it for granted you must have heard long since of the terrible war going on between France and Prussia for the last five or six months. Paris is for the last two months invested by the Prussians. What the result will be cannot be determined. Some think Paris will be Bombarded, others that it will be starved out. The remarkable event of the Emperor's surrender at Sedan must have reached your ears. He is the last few months imprisoned in his Palatial rsidence at WILHOLME in the Duchy of Hesse Cassel – near the sublime waters of the Elbe. Six months ago his voice could command the attention of Europe. "Sic transit gloria Mundi."*

*It would be entirely out of place here to go into all the details of this terrible and destructive war. Our past Summer and Autumn were highly favourable, not a single day to interrupt the work of Harvest.*

*Con, his wife and daughter desire me to convey their remembrance and warm affection – how I should like to see you this winter's evening at their ruddy fireside and hospitable board. But brighter times will shortly come. Hope on – Hope ever!! Your sister, Bridget, Mrs. Baldwin, sends you her love, Dick will speak for himself. – O'Sullivan, a cousin of your mothers with whom I lodge for the last twenty years sends her kind regards. Up to this time our winter is rather mild and have not felt its severity yet. May God give you fortitude and resignation to bear your cross a little longer. Now, like all sublimary things in this life, I must come to a close.*

*Yours sincerely,*
*David Coffey.*

*P.S. I enclose you this day's Examiner – a sensible aritcle respecting Con's Estb.*

revolted at the idea of dependence, even on a friend, and cast about for means of earning my bread by my own labour. I was lucky and succeeded in getting an appointment as a teacher in a school at Castletown not far from my birth-place. The salary was small it is true; but then the money I handled was my own, which was a great satisfaction."

Ricard for some reason of his own says he was a paid monitor in Castletown school. On the examination of the records of that school there is no mention of Ricard having taught there. However, when examining the records of Dunmanway Model Schools, it was discovered that he was appointed monitor there on May 1st 1853. As a paid monitor he would have earned the princely sum of £4 that first year.

## DUNMANWAY MODEL SCHOOLS

Dunmanway Model Schools, which cost £4,489 to build, was opened in 1849 on a site at the western end of the town which had been offered to the Commissioners by Mr. Thomas Bryan.

***An interesting extract from the report of James Patten, Esq, Head-Inspector, on the opening of Dunmanway District Model Schools.***

"The school-house, a light ornamental building in the Tudor style, is situated at the west end of the town of Dunmanway, and consists of male and female school-rooms, with an agricultural department attached, and a model farm of about 16 English acres, no provision having yet been made for an infant school. In addition to the school-rooms the premises comprises a parlour and sleeping apartment for the master and mistress, a class-room with gallery for religious instruction, and for separate class-teaching, pupil teacher's dining room and study room, fitted up with every necessary apparatus, including books etc; to these may be added a very commodious kitchen, store-room, larder, and scullery, with wash-house and laundry; up stairs convenient and airy dormitories have been provided, sufficient for eight pupil-teachers. The dormitory is divided by partitions, six feet high, into separate compartments, each containing one bed, and affording the master easy and ready access from his own apartment; there is

*Dunmanway Model Schools*

also an hospital-room, with sleeping apartment for two maid servants.

"On the 7th of August, 1849, I arrived at Dunmanway, accompanied by one of my colleagues, to make arrangements preparatory to the opening on the 13th; the prospectus was issued on the 8th, and Friday and Saturday, the 10th and 11th, were named therein as the days on which application for admission would be received.

"We invited the clergy, Protestant and Roman Catholic, to attend a meeting to be held at the school-house for the purpose of arranging the time for the religious instruction, and of submitting to them several details connected with the management of the schools.

"This meeting was attended by the clergy of the different denominations residing in the town and neighbourhood, and by several beneficed clergymen from the adjoining parishes, when the following arrangements for religious instruction were agreed to, namely - from 2.30 to 3 o'clock on Monday, Tuesday, Wednesday, and Thursday, and from 2 to 3 o'clock on Friday.

"Although only three days intervened between the issuing of the prospectus and the opening of the schools, we were able to commence on Monday, the 13th August, with 133 pupils; of these 77 were males and 56 were females. Up to the close of the first week the attendance was 75 boys and 73 girls, total 148; up to the end of the second week nearly the same number; at the close of the third week there were 82 boys and 77 girls, total 159; and at the end of the fourth week the attendance was 86 boys and 78 girls, total 164, exhibiting a steady progressive increase, and completing the number which the rooms were capable of conveniently accommodating.

"Of the 164 pupils in attendance at the close of the fourth week, 157 were Roman Catholics, and 7 were Protestant - scarcely 1 in 22. The remarkably small attendance of the Protestant children may be accounted for in this way;- The clergy of the Established Church, although at first apparently favourable, or at least not opposed to the attendance of the Protestant children, subsequently, however, thought proper to change their opinions, and, through their influence, the natural attendance of the children was interfered with; this influence was also extended to the Protestant operatives, artisans, and even shop-keepers, and has had the effect of inducing some to withdraw their children, and of preventing the attendance of those of the remainder. Another cause may be assigned, and perhaps, the principal one, namely - the existence of a large and commodious school-house in the town in connexion with the Church Education Society. The house consists of two rooms, one for boys, the other for girls; the average attendance about 80, and

as might be expected, these are all, with scarcely an exception, the children of Protestants."

As a monitor Ricard would be expected at the end of his first year to have reached the following standard of education:

(a) Able to read the 4th Lesson Book with ease.
(b) Be familiar with prefixes and suffixes.
(c) Spell correctly from Dictation.
(d) Solve questions on Compound Proportion and Fractions.
(e) Have a knowledge of the Elementary Principles of Parsing.
(f) Know the Geography of Ireland.
(g) Be able to teach and examine 2nd Class.

For a description of the young teacher let him tell us in his own words. "At that epoch I was only fourteen years of age, a tall, rawboned boy, rude in health, hardy and accustomed to feats of activity and strength. Owing to my country rearing I could back the wildest horse, almost keep pace with the grey-hounds in a coursing match, pick down a lark on the wing (had I the heart to shoot such a songster) with a sure eye, and was the steady enemy of the badgers, stoats and pike that teemed by the riverside and in its bed. My life as a Schoolmaster was happy enough, but too tranquil. I spent my leisure hours roaming through the woods or reading books of any and every description I came across. Recitals of daring deeds by land and sea, accounts of voyages and adventures, the novels of Cooper and Scott were my special favourites. But there was literature of another and a better, higher kind that captivated my taste still more - the national literature of my country, that which told of its glories in the past, its learning, civilization and military renown. I fed on this literature until an instinct of patriotism, an enthusiasm rather, entered into me and became part and parcel of my being. Coming down to the period of our decadence my young blood warmed as I read of the treachery of Irishmen in an Irish Parliament at the passing of the Treaty of Union; I felt that Ireland by the hand of the creator, as testified in its unchangeable geographical insularity, was marked out for independence not provincialism. On that point the young National Schoolmaster was inexorable and looked back to Wolfe Tone, the gallant Lord Edward and that pearl of purity, Robert Emmet, with as firm and fervent faith as the Christians of the catacombs to their martyrs. But man's actions do not always fashion with his desires or convictions. A change I shall ever regret was at hand!"

*Militia Barracks, Bandon.*

## CHAPTER 3
# RICARD JOINS THE MILITIA

The change which Ricard says was at hand was his first false step. This youngster, who had through his discovery of Irish literature, become a convinced nationalist, took the shilling - he joined the militia. In his autobiography he describes how this happened.

"When I look back at this episode in my career, my first false step, it seems to me like a dream. I know not how to account for it; but I was always the creature of impulse and therein, perhaps, lies the key to this and many other problems in my life.

"It was in 1853. I was standing in the porch of the school. It was a dusty sultry day. The boys, out for their usual half-hour's play, were hurling in a neighbouring field or deep in the mysteries of 'pitch and toss' in a remote corner at the back of the white-walled, slate-roofed one-roomed house. I leant listlessly against the threshold, a volume of Shenstone's Pastorals in my hand, sometimes reading, sometimes taking a look at the sweet-scented hawthorn hedge that bounded the other side of the way. Suddenly two cheery voices in eager conversation saluted my ears, and looking down to a bend of the road I recognised two of my acquaintances, farmers' sons, from the next barony. They were red with the fast walking.

" 'Morrow Rick,' cried Tom Haslam, he with whom I was more familiar, 'how goes it?'

" 'Well, as usual; but where are you off to in such a hurry?'

" 'To Bandon to join the militia. Throw down your musty books and come with us.' " (The Crimean War had broken out and recruiting for the Militia was revived once more.)

"I shook my head.

" 'Tut, man. You'll never be axed to leave Ireland - fine times - promotion off-hand for a smart, knowledgeable young fellow like you.'

"Tom was running on at this rate when I pulled him up with the remark that if I were tempted to become a soldier I should be a real and not a holiday soldier.

" 'Oh! as for matter of that, if you 'take on' you'll have fighting enough in the militia. Sure the Russians are expected every day to make an invasion of the country.'

"I objected still, not seeing what extraordinary interest Irishmen, who had nothing to protect, had to fight against a Russian invasion - if it succeeded it would be a change of rulers at most, and would have the charm of novelty - but in the end, Tom, for whom I had a strong liking, prevailed on me to accompany them to the recruiting office 'if only for gradh.'

"Before we started we had a drop of porter (drop, in this instance meaning any indeterminate quantity up to a gallon) to 'shorten the road' as I suggested; to 'wet our whistles' as Tom said; to 'clear the dust out of our throats' as Tom's companion remarked; I leave you the choice of phrases. Be that as it may, what with the quick walking and the slant rays of the hot sun pouring on our naked foreheads, the porter had begun to work in us a little as we neared Bandon.

"You know that famous old town of orthodox, hard-drinking, hard-hitting, copper-nosed and copper-fastened Episcopalianism - Bandon, pettiest of pocket-boroughs where political pot-walloping ran side by side with ecstatic Puritanism - Bandon, on whose gates once was written the warning -

*Turk, Jew or Atheist*
*May enter here: but not a Papist.*

I don't go in strong on points of theology, but I confess I can never think of the couplet the malicious Poor Scholar from Clare added to the inscription without a grin -

*Whoever wrote it wrote it well*
*For the same is written on the gates of Hell.*

However we passed the gates without challenge, and a quarter of an hour after, my friend, Tom, might be seen posing under the standard for recruits of the 87th or South Cork Light Infantry Militia regiment.

" 'Why, man, you're fit to be right file in the grenading company,' said the wary old sergeant who had stood sponsor for Tom; 'before twelve months you'll be a sergeant-major!'

" 'Or a drum-major,' dryly added another of the recruiting staff.

" 'Or gineral!' said a waggish bystander, with a wink.

" 'More likely corpo(ral)!' ventured I with a faint attempt at wit.

"Alas! poor Tom. Before twelve months the brave young Munster peasant with cheeks ruddy as the sunny side of apples in the orchards in the valleys, and voice strong as the breath of the breeze of the mountains was trundled into a burial-pit by the Bosphorus - dead from an inglorious Scutari diarrhoea. He had been led by the specious promises of a smart young gentleman (who had got a commission in the Line without the pother of previous examination on presenting a certain number of volunteers) to exchange amateur for actual soldiership and port his Enfield for the Eastern war. Dead of Diarrhoea! Not even reserved for the comparative honour of becoming 'chair a canon! food for gun-powder, in a cause he did not understand one syllable about. 'Tis too sad to think upon.

"But I anticipate.

"Hardly had the feeble attempt at a pun I have mentioned above escaped my lips when the old recruiting-sergeant fastened his regards upon me and motioned me under the standard. I refused to budge. 'At all events you'll help us to moisten your friend's good luck!' We went into a public-house, and what with sundry drops of porter and ingenious praises of Tom, ' a spirited young fellow,' and slyly introducing tales of glory and adventure, when the hour came to bid good-bye I had not the strength of mind to part with him, and I too stretched out my palm for the piece of silver. Oh! those sunny drops of porter! How many mother's pride have they not robbed from the fireside, how many a foolish Paddy Carey have they not led into the toils of Sergeant Snap!

"The third of us youngsters (recollect always before condemning me at this epoch I was but fifteen) - I mean the individual who had 'cleared the dust out of his throat' - happened to meet some friends in the town, it being fair-day, and changed his mind under the influence of their persuasions. In all likelihood he is alive and hearty today by the open wood of West Carbery rejoicing in his fortunate 'funk'; while poor Tom is a clod of Turkish clay, and I am inditing these lines within a few short paces of the graves of the ruffian murderer of Mr. Briggs and the ruffian pirates of the Flowery Land, in the shadow of the prison, deeper shadows brooding - but no matter. Let us pass that, 'as you love me Hal.' "

*Entrance to Militia Barracks*

Ricard did not like life in the militia and found it very irksome. It was tolerable while his friend, Tom, was with him. But when he went off there was no relief. To add to his misery he discovered that his colonel was none other than the son of Lord Bandon, the man who had evicted the family.

For three years he stuck the monotonous routine of garrison life. From Bandon the unit went to Kinsale and from there to Limerick, "with high hearts and rattling drums we entered the city of the Violated Treaty. A queer quaint old town it is, with its broad river flowing majestically by idle quays, and its half-deserted blocks of streets offering a strange medley of city and country costumes, the picturesque blue mantle of the snug dairy-farmer's good woman from Newcastle, side by side with the dainty lace shawl and detestable pork-pie hat (latest Cockney built) sported by the cara sposa of some heavy military swell of the garrison. For Limerick is a considerable military post; it has its horse, its foot, its horse-police, its rifles, and royal artillery." Here in Limerick he was promoted to corporal. He found life in Limerick tolerable and the ladies pleasant. "Sweet Limerick, I shall not soon forget thee, nor the glories of Garryowen, Newtown Perry and Boherbuoy. At the close of a happy stay at the banks of the Shannon we executed a brilliant flank march (in the railway cars) on the Capital, delicious Dublin."

In Dublin he was assigned to duty in the regimental office. His duties here were light and he had time enough to do some reading (a pastime he loved.) He became very friendly with a clerk in a lawyer's office down town and he got some copying work to do which supplemented his corporal's wages. In his company he spent many happy evenings, one of them in particular, which was a turning point in his career.

"We were going to the Queen's Theatre to see Mr. T. C. King in 'Ingomar, or the Barbarian,' but we met yet another barbarian on the way. It was an officer of my regiment en mufti. I did not give him the salute, not having recognised him. He turned back sharply and abused me for my disrespect. I made an ample apology (as I considered) that I did not know him on account of his being dressed in plain clothes. ... Soon after, while I was sitting in the orderly room alone, this same officer entered and handed me an envelope saying 'address that to Lord Panmure.' I did so. He took a glance at it, tore it up.

" 'That way you write it, eh?' and he handed me another.

"I addressed that too, and it was also torn up. I addressed a third and the fellow threw that in the grate and struck me in the face.

"I cannot describe to you the black feelings that arose in my breast then, the thoughts that set my nerves tingling and my brain on fire. The coward! To strike a poor friendless boy in a regiment of men where every face was strange, to insult and humiliate one whose hands were tied, one too who had always tried to perform the hateful duty he had imposed on himself in a rash moment. Shame on the dastard! Looking back on his action at this distance of time I do not hate but I despise him. And this was 'an officer and a gentleman.' ... The discipline of the service was strong in me, he was still my officer though he did disgrace his uniform. I did not strike him in return; but the iron had entered my soul. ...

To come to the issue at once and not to put too fine a point on it, I resolved to desert.

"I sought a comrade corporal in the regiment and told him of my intention. He had suffered too. I had saved up enough money from my earnings to provide for the expense of both, would he accompany me? He agreed. He left the barrack on some business, I returned to the orderly room to efface all traces of myself on the record. By some chance I had neglected to get his regimental number and could not do the same for him as I intended. I left, rigged myself out in civilian's attire in a slop-shop in Mary's Lane, and was at the appointed rendezvous in Capel Street at the hour we had arranged on. He was not there, but in his place was a note saying he had changed his mind and wished me God-speed.

"I trudged down towards the North Wall; a plume of black smoke was rising out of the funnel of a steamer for Liverpool; I jumped on board, and ere the sun had gone down on my humiliation in the orderly-room I had cleared my way from the Fag-an-Bealacs for ever."

## CHAPTER 4

# IN LONDON

As some members of his family were living in London it was there Ricard headed for. It was many years since he had seen them and a whimsical idea seized him. He wrote a letter in his own name, to his brother, and introduced himself as a young man, a friend and fellow-Corkman in search of employment. (He does not mention his brother's name.) The brother looked at him keenly but the change from the Rick he had known was too great to penetrate the ruse. When he had last seen him he was a gawky growing boy; now he had ripened into a well set, straight athletic young man, little short of six feet high and broadly built across the chest. "My military training, too, had given me a firmness of gait and neatness of appearance which little recalled the loose stripling of four years ago."

He was received "with that ready hospitality the Irish in London are proverbial for showing to a 'Grecian' as they call a new arrival from home. The best fare the house afforded was set before me, and many and anxious were the enquiries after that scapegrace, Rick, and the neighbours in Cork. You may be sure I gave them a flattering account of myself, and with the help of an odd draw on imagination and the gossip that went in the regiment, I was enabled satisfactorily to answer other inquiries." He stayed a month in London, never betraying his true identity, and all the time looking for a situation. But it was not easy for an Irish stranger to obtain employment in the world's capital. However he did not waste his time. "I roamed about, taking notes of men and things, visiting the picture-galleries and British Museum. I distinctly remember with what delight I lingered over a characteristic punning letter in Jonathan Swift's handwriting exhibited under a glass shade in the latter institution. Returning to London ten years later I sought it out and felt as if I were meeting an old friend at seeing again the well-known lines. At night I used to stroll into one or other of the theatres (of which I was very fond), or occasionally into Coger's Hall, a sort of semi-convivial debating society off Fleet Street.

"Experience is to be gathered walking about the streets of London, but at some expense. I was learning much; I had seen how a busy capital may be, large though it is, when its government is in the hands of its own people; but all this time the soles were wearing off my shoes and the silver rapidly getting down to zero in my pocket. Irish fun, the sense of freedom - that I was again my own master - and the humour of the intrigue in which I had embarked with my family, kept me in a continuous exhilaration. How I used to love to insinuate myself into a group of Irishmen to listen to them holding wildest but most polemical arguments in Paddington-Green, crooning weird melodies in the close courts off Drury-Lane, or footing it vigorously in a three-hand-reel after a hard day's work and sometimes breaking the head of some 'thundering thief of an Englishman who had dared say boo to the ould country.' It may be prejudice; but I used to fancy that in those tussles, whether of wit or muscle, Pat always contrived to have the uppermost. I shall never forget the dry humour of a response I heard one evening I was strolling down Holborn Hill, from a large, brawny Irishman who was engaged embedding paving-stones in the road with a ponderous 'rammer' something like an exaggerated Indian club. It was a close evening and my gigantic countryman was working leisurely.

" 'Lazy bloke, that,' remarked in an undertone a dapper looking Cockney of the Tittlebat, titmouse order, taking a position by my side and regarding the easy-going paviour.

" 'You'd better tell him so,' I quietly observed.

" 'S'help me, I shall!' said the perky little gentleman.

" 'Say, Pat, old man, you don't seem to be putting much strength into that ere job. The rammer don't look as if it fell heavy!'

"The giant turned round and with a glance of pitying contempt indolently remarked, 'D'ye tell me so? Would you be after puttin' yer fut undher it, if you plaze!?'

"The Cockney made tracks with a parting exclamation that 'these Hirish were dimmed witty!'

"The re-union of the temperance societies were also favourite resorts of mine. There was an excellent opportunity for studying character there - a weakness of mine even at that early age - and occasionally, I must admit in justice to the teetotallers, I have heard as good a comic song rattled off under the influence of a cup of tea as ever convulsed the beer-bibbing president of a free-and-easy, and as rousing a piece of eloquence on the wholesomeness of spring water as ever woke the echoes of Conciliation Hall. Dr. McBleutherum and Dionysius Buckley were the two great London-Irish temperance propagandists of this time. They hated each other most cordially, for each recognised the other as his rival."

Ricard had at this time some vague ideas that he should jot down reminiscences of men and manners. Little did he think then that these reminiscences would be jotted down on sheets of foolscap lent by a lawyer in an English prison while he awaited trial on a penal charge. However, he continued his education by visiting many places in London. "As I had witty Irishmen living to commune with, so also had I great Irishmen dead, and many a devout pilgrimage did I pay to the places sanctified by their memories or their tombs. I sought out the lodgings of Curran, Banim and Griffin; I knelt by poor Noll's (Oliver Goldsmith) tomb in Temple Garden, and visited the chamber in which Wolfe Tone had once resided in the Temple itself; I paused admiringly before the statues of Burke and Grattan in the vestibule of the House of Commons, and turning into the famous tabernacle of 'People who never leave town' close by, Westminster Abbey, I can recollect revelling in the exquisite satire of the 'School for Scandal' over the grave of Richard Brinsley Sheridan."

However, this aimless existence could not last for ever. He came back one evening wearied after a fruitless trudge all day on the pavements and had decided to make a clean breast of it to his brother. When his brother asked him had he any luck, Ricard said he had a confession to make. He said he had been trespassing on his hospitality under false pretences and that the letter was a fraud. His brother was literally struck dumb with angry amazement. Then Ricard made his confession. Needless to relate, the fatted calf was killed that night and there was a scene of thoroughly Irish festivity in one little nook of that strange city. When he told him of his desertion, a family council was held and it was ultimately resolved that he should leave England on the first opportunity as he was liable to be arrested.

"Accordingly, the following week saw me again on the wing; but on this occasion for a longer flight. I was a steerage passenger on board a dusky sailing ship that dropped down the Thames one night, bound on a voyage to New York. I was leaving friends, yet will I avow it, my heart was light, for I was exchanging a land that could never be other than hateful to one of my feelings and antecedents for the country that I had read, and heard, and talked, and thought, and dreamt of, until I loved it - my ideal of free government - the refuge of my race - the great Republic of the West! Since then I have fought and suffered in its cause, and I love it still - shall love it ever."

Ricard found the journey to America, which took five weeks, very irksome. The vessel was old and overcrowded and he did not find the passengers very sympathetic. He had collected some books to read during the journey. However, the heat below was suffocating and on deck the constant breeze pained his eyes. So he found himself counting the minutes until he arrived in America. "There is a stir on deck; for an instant the point of attention is changed, as the United States flag, the Stars and Stripes of my love, flutters aloft and is rapidly run up the foremast announcing our arrival.

"Gradually breaks upon our view a scene well calculated to give an idea of the go-ahead nation. We are in the centre of a majestic river. To the right lies Jersey City fringed with docks, piers and shipping. On our left is New York, half hidden by a forest of masts, above which rise innumerable church spires which tower over the surrounding buildings. Tug-boats and tenders of every imaginable species and dimension dart about among the shipping avoiding one another with wonderful dexterity. Enormous steam ferry-boats unceasingly cross our course bearing on their decks foot-passengers, horses and carts. Barges laden to the water's edge with coals, corn or stone, swing lazily around the piers to which they are moored, and seemed to be the only thing allowed to repose."

Eventually he lands on American soil for the first time. "When one has been confined for weeks to the narrow promenade of a ship's deck, the first sensation which possesses him on touching firm earth is to take a wild run. At least that is how I always feel. Before I gratified the desire on this occasion I acquitted myself of what I regarded my duty, what you may be disposed to laugh at as an ebullition of sentiment. I knelt down and kissed American earth!. Why should I not? The Spaniard kisses the relic of his saint, the Englishman the portrait of her he cherishes, and here, I, an Irish wanderer, stood on the threshold of a land I had learned to reverence and to love for its traditions and its glories, the heirloom of its Washington's name to struggling nations, the embrace of welcome it offers to sufferers of the universe. Therefore, I repeat, I knelt and kissed its soil, to my young soul sacred as the bones of the canonized, beautiful as the smile of a mistress.

"But sentiment, even in the newer continent, is elbowed rudely aside on the march of life, I was recalled to the formalities of registering myself at the castle Gardens; as soon as that dull business was over I sallied out of the station and found myself in a kind of waste ground. I must confess that I was slightly astonished at the first aspect of New York. The houses in sight were dirty, ricketty, and irregular, and altogether produced the impression of belonging to an old city."

# CHAPTER 5

# LIFE IN NEW YORK

In his autobiography Ricard is not very strong on dates. "You must be prepared, accordingly, to find me rather loose about dates. I never was a dab at dates, counting rather by the nature of events than the time they transpired. This is a peculiar quality - failing if you will; a word 'here or there' does not affect me. Ask in Ireland when did McCarthy die? 'About the time my boy, Jack, was born, your honour. 'When was that?' 'Faix it was when the bridge was built near Cullihan's house.' 'But, when was that?' 'When the young master went abroad, your honour.' What year, my good woman?' 'About the time McCarthy died.' And so on ad infinitum." He does not tell when he arrived in America but it must have been in 1856 or 1857. When he reached New York he had a contact in Eleventh Street. However, he never got there. On the quay he met a Quaker who took pity on him and invited him to have a drink. As they walked to the bar Ricard got his first glimpse of busy New York.

"Crossing an ill-kept park and treading some streets which were muddy under a broiling sun, we suddenly emerged into a scene of din and bustle perfectly unique. Omnibuses, carts, carriages, and waggons of every size and species careering through an immense thoroughfare of bright red-brick houses. Men of every complexion moving to and fro, in every variety of dress, a free nigger beside a Southern planter, a sailor returned from his voyage beside an Irishmen with the worn garb in which he made his first sad voyage across the ocean clinging in tatters to his shoulders. I gazed at it as if it were a fairy scene."

The bar also took the breath from Ricard. "On a long slip of mahogany beside the bar-tender I noticed in gilt letters a list of the liquors to be had in the establishment, amongst which occurred such tempting titles as Locomotives (for fast-moving people, I ween), Lady's Blush (for naughty fellows), Whispers, Nods and something nice (for the fair sex), Corpus Reviver (for tired-out day labourers), and Beautiful Lap (for the young generation bent on repose.)"

While in the bar the stranger "gradually drew me out over a glass of liquid of port wine flavour. I gave him a candid history of my life; he seemed to take an interest in it, struck the table as I told him of the assaulting blow of the militia officer, rolled with laughter as I related how I introduced myself to my brother, cast me a sympathetic look as I ended by the avowal that I was friendless in the strange city, provided with a letter of recommendation only to a countryman in Eleventh-street." Obviously the Quaker, Mr. Madigan, liked what he saw and got Ricard a job in Messrs Todgers, Bludge and Tatum of uptown near Haarlem, the "world-renowned portrait painters."

The three principals in the firm had their own distinguished speciality and each hailed from a different part of the Union. Ricard did any odd jobs that came his way. One day a tall bronzed, sailor like man entered the shop and wanted a life size portrait taken from a photograph he had in his possession. In the ensuing conversation the stranger announced his mother was Irish and Ricard was given the assignment with the instructions that "when finished, send him down with it to the shipping agents (handing a card) for the Captain of the Georgette, fix your own price, if the job is done to my satisfaction we'll not quarrel over a hundred-dollar bill.

"This was the first distinct commission I got on my own hook and that it was which led to an acquaintanceship which turned once more the destinies of my life into a new channel."

He worked hard at the portrait. He says himself; "I have the knack of catching the salient points in a face, and this before me now was one that was easy to be transferred to canvas - distinctly marked, decisive in its lines, a face with character in it. A woman and that woman was young." However, there was a difficulty at the outset and one "I was amazed I had not anticipated. I had a photograph before me, giving with the unflattering perfection of the sun the presentment of the original, the oval countenance, the Grecian nose, the configuration of the head, the crisp curly coronet

*Self Portrait*
*Ricard*

of hair over the brow, the swelling bust; but where was I to get the complexion on those cheeks, the colour of those eyes, and of those locks, the tone of my picture in fact?" After consulting with Mr. Bludge he decided to paint the hair blonde and the eyes blue - "salt-water blue."

Ricard was pleased with the final outcome and "on the appointed day I went down to the shipping agent's with my picture under my arm and found a note directing me to a hotel adjacent, where I was to enquire for Captain Lasso. It was a respectable, quiet establishment and I was shown up to a luxuriously furnished apartment with a folding door of buffed glass intersticed with foliage in transparent tracery at one end. After waiting for some time I heard a cough, and approaching my eyes to the tracery I looked in. In the inner room reclining on a light blue ottoman was a woman whom it struck me at once vaguely I had seen somewhere before. She appeared to have numbered about thirty-three years - an excellent age, the right age for those of the opposite sex who have had the gift of self-preservation and the thoughtfulness not to neglect it. Where had I seen this apparition before, in what vision of the night or the reverie of the day? At last it flashed on me like sunlight. She was the original of my portrait. And her hair, which Mr. Bludge had instructed me to paint 'a high gamboge, a yaller red,' was black as bog-oak."

Convinced that all his work was gone for nothing he put the picture under his arm and raced out of the hotel only to run slap bang into Captain Lasso. Back they went, Lasso inspected the portrait and was so well satisfied that he offered Ricard the commission of painting the original herself. Lasso enjoined Ricard to silence for the next fifteen minutes, going to the door he threw the folding doors wide open. "The moment she heard his step on the threshold the mysterious lady turned round, a smile lit up her face, and springing from the ottoman she flung herself on his neck in a long embrace without uttering a sound. He kissed her on both cheeks, gently disengaged himself from her arms and conducted her into the apartment where I sat a bewildered spectator. When she saw me she did not blush or start, but looking for a moment at her companion as if for token that I was present by his permission, she gravely bestowed me a slight courtesy. I rose and made an inclination in return." The captain then showed the mysterious lady the portrait who then broke into a low quick peal of strange laughter as she passed her hand over the golden yellow hair.

"The Captain next conducted her to a music stool, which lay before what I had hitherto considered a rose-wood table in one corner, but which was in reality a piano. He sat himself beside her and nodded as if requesting her to play. The melody she played, dear angels, was the Last Rose of Summer." Ricard was really entranced and, even if he wanted to say a word, he was so bewitched by the mysterious lady, he could not. When she finished playing she handed Ricard a white rose, then got a scissors and cut off a lock of her hair which she placed on the table in front of Ricard. He was so overcome that he fell head over heels in love "with a woman seen once and with whom I never exchanged a word!"

There is no doubt about it but Ricard was a ladies man!

The lady, Georgette was her name, having returned to the inner room, Captain Lasso, who was very impressed by the manner with which Ricard had kept silent as requested and also with his talent as a painter, asked Ricard to tell him his life story which he did, "and I did it very well, dramatically, acting the scenes as I described them." When asked if he had any money, Ricard answered; "None; I don't know what I am to receive from Todgers, Bludge and Tatum, I have no engagement with them, I was glad to get in there as it was the first place that offered, to have my meals and a shake-down in the corner of the studio." The Captain did not have a very high opinion of the art establishment and asked Ricard "will you make a cruise with me, boy?" Ricard thought of the lady inside, involuntarily looked down at the white rose and answered, "Willingly, sir."

"He rung for his black servant, told him to send up Mr. Smith, then pointing to the inner door in a significant manner, he put his hands to his lips, charging me not to breathe a syllable of what I had seen of poor Georgette." Mr Smith arrived - Bill -. "He was a brown-faced, hairy son of Neptune, broad-chested, short bow-legged, long armed, an ocean Hercules with a voice rough as a blast of wind and a face frank as a sailor's should be and ought always be. I took to Bill on the spot." Captain Lasso instructed Bill to "take him to your lodgings and give him a berth to-night. Treat him as one of us. Remember we hoist anchor by mid-day to-morrow and I expect to be scudding off the Hook before sunset."

"When I woke next morning and found myself with clear head in the boarding house with Bill Smith, it would be absurd to deny that I did not feel a little ashamed of myself. I could not avoid the admission that I had treated my kindly Quaker friend badly, and indeed, the artistic trio, also. In New York, as in Borrisokane, the rule is 'nothing for nothing.' And when I reflected that no service had been rendered to me by Todgers, Bludge and Tatum for which I had not given ample repayment in work, and when I had registered a vow to thank Mr. Madigan substantially at the first opportunity, I reconciled myself to the change. Then looking at my proposed expedition from a material point of view, I had a chance of making my fortune and there was the world to be seen, and I was young and - on the whole, I was happy."

## CHAPTER 6

# A CYCLONE

The Georgette was small, light and clean in the build, a picture of beauty like her after whom it had been called. Bill Smith helped Ricard to knock up a snug berth in the forecastle and for the second time he was on the broad Atlantic. He filled every position on board except, of course, the controlling one - "green hand", now "ordinary" or able seaman, clerk, "leader of the orchestra" consisting of a trombone, a violin and a wheezy fife, dispenser of medicines (principally ship's brandy) and general man of all work. He does not set down the log of his wanderings on board the Georgette as he is not free to do so. "Suffice to say that in my first voyage I swept down the east coast of America, right as far as Honduras, where I found that our Captain was a relative of the President of that Republic, who, by the way, was married to an Irish lady named Jessop from the English colony of Belleisle."

"I grew to love that little bark. When I trod its decks in the morning watch, as the rosy sunlight glided up one side of the horizon, spreading a broad flood of golden colour over the waves I used fall into most foolish fits of poetry. My mind, carried away on wings of fancy, wandered into the remote past betimes." He fancied he was Ulysses, or one of the navigators who sought the Golden Fleece, or with the flotilla of the Crusaders steering straight for Palestine, or with Cook or with Nelson.

At length, a morning came which broke the spell of this foolish but most pleasurable communing. The wind rose from the east in little puffs, filled the sails and the Georgette "sprang lightly to these provocations, like a graceful acrobat, never losing her balance." However, everything was not as it seemed. The Captain came on deck, grabbed the glass and "swept the sky with an anxious eye in every quarter. 'Hum,' he ejaculated as he lowered the instrument and commenced pacing the space between the wheel and the main-mast with an air of disgust. His step was quick, short, perturbed, and contrasted strangely with the aspect of nature around. The light breaths of wind that had given promise of change in the elements earlier had become rarer, and now the calm was deader than ever - made only more palpable by the odd lazy flap of the canvas. It seemed as if the world was enjoying an interval of lassitude, the motion of the waters was sleepy, the advance of the great tranquil sun in the heavens was slow, there was a dull heat in the atmosphere that compelled to repose, and far away on the horizon the dusky silhouette of a West Indiaman, outlined against the sky looked as if it were a fixture on the waters."

A sudden puff of wind drove out the topsail with a jerk and the Captain muttered, "I was thinking as much." He summoned all hands on deck and told Ricard that the sea "will be in the hell of a temper by-and-bye." Bill Smith lashed himself to the wheel knowing what was coming. "Turning round, what was my astonishment to see my friend, Bill, a huge comforter round his neck, huge jack-boots on his feet, a waterproof wrapper enveloping his pea-jacket, and waterproof leggings drawn over his trousers. The experienced old tar had scented the crisis; he knew we had a spell of rough weather at hand and had taken his precautions accordingly. Bill took off his sou-wester, made the sign of the Cross on his forehead reverently and cried in his stentorian voice, 'now, then, my hearties, Bill Smith's fit for any fate.'

"There may be those who will sneer at this recital, and call the sailor's act superstition. Ah! I pity them. No braver seaman ever trod planking than the same Smith, and if he blessed himself it was because he had been reared a Catholic, had been taught to do so by his mother in his youth. It was not piety, perhaps; but at least, it was a souvenir of the beautiful tradition of childhood, an involuntary testimony to the power of a higher Being in the supreme hour of danger. When death stares him in the face, even the fiercest materialist forgets his sceptism and murmurs a prayer to God. I can recall an instance of a man so demonstrative in his unbelief in Christianity, that he insisted on calling himself Pagan, and yet, in the bottom of that man's box, carefully treasured up, was - a worn scapular! But Smith had blessed himself, and amongst the crowd of hard-handed sailors that watched him there was not one who did not respect him for the act."

The captain ordered that every bit of canvas be taken down. "The sails had scarce been furled down when a sudden blast from the south-west, leaping as it were from the womb of a canopy of storm cloud, caught the Georgette and almost lifted her from the waters. At the same instant the sky darkened as if a curtain had been placed before the sun. A noise, like the distant roll of many drums, was heard in the distance, and away, some three miles to larboard, I could see the glistening crest of a mountain wave. It was the cyclone! In the fearful moment of suspense before the wave that threatened struck us, before the coming wrath of God as I had pictured it in my excited and terrified imagination had crushed, annihilated, engulfed us, I caught the voice of the Captain over the fury of the elements as he roared through his speaking trumpet, 'Steady, men, wear her round, God protect us.'

"There was a sense of choking in my throat; my temples were furnace hot; the blood trickled from eyes, nostrils and ears; I felt as if taken up bodily by some invisible power and flung upon the ground and then there was a whirl, I was spun round like a humming-top, and the moment after I was sinking down through illimitable regions of night, down, down to inexorable chaos."

When Ricard came to he had no idea of where he was. When he opened his eyes and looked round he found to his intense relief that the Georgette still floated, that he was on board, lashed to the foot of the main-mast. The mountainous wave had passed and now the boat was surrounded by a wild, angry surging sea. "To my straining vision presented itself something scarlet, like the wing of a parrot, on the summit of a wave flecked with foam, and a familiar, mournful cry struck my ears over the noise of the tempest." Ricard had no idea of what had happened and it was only when Bill Smith recounted the whole incident that he realised how lucky they were. "Wall, you see, my lad, when the sike-alone came a-top of us I was at the wheel in course, and I says to myself says I. 'Bill Smith, look out for squalls.' And didn't they come, maybe not? Wall, when the wind caught her, the Georgette plunged bows down, but I stuck to my post, and when the biller came up in all its unnatural might it struck her on the quarter while the stern was well out of the water - it gave us a shaking, it did; but we got off with the loss of the stanchions, bow sprit, and cut-water. Afterwards, you see, in course, as always happens in these sike-alones, there was a running fire of burts of enormous pressure, and then there was rainfall, and now again the weather aint so thick. With regards the West Indiaman, she won't cost its owners no more insurance money. It's gone down to Davy Jones's locker! You see, my lad, the Cap'n of the Georgette is a sailor; and the Cap'n of the West Indiaman wasn't."

Ricard was surprised that Charley Jackson, another crew member and a friend, had not come to visit him. When he inquired, Bill Smith was very reluctant to tell him about Charley. Eventually he told him that Charley had died at his post and that he died for his friend. "When the first agony of grief and surprise had passed I learned how my Newhaven friend had come by his death. The immense wave was almost upon us when he perceived that I stood heedless on the deck, taking no precaution against the imminent risk of being washed overboard. He was already lashing himself to the mainmast when he noticed my dangerous position, he stretched over to me and snatched me up in his strong arms (at the time I fancied myself caught up bodily by some invisible power, I suppose) with a rope tied me securely by his side. In the strain of the exertion to save me he undid the fastenings on which he himself depended for safety, the great rush of water lifted him off his legs and swept him to destruction. What I had taken for the wing of a bird on the crest of the wave was the scarlet handkerchief round his head - the familiar mournful cry I heard was the drowning farewell of generous Charley Jackson.

"I was moved to the depths by this story told in his own blunt, honest, sailorly way by William Smith. He was sorry as I was, but I conceived an invincible repugnance for him when he said at parting, after all this moving episode of real Christian heroism, the characteristic words; 'Hurry up and get well, Rick, for we're short of hands, and Bill Smith is all-fired lonesome since he don't hear a squeal of the fife.' Orators have repeated to applauding thousands the couplet:

*'Whether on the gallows high, or in the battle's van*
*The fittest place for man to die is where he dies for man.'*

"And this is how my brave sailor had died. If I had went off instead of Charlie Jackson, I had here a fine earnest of my requiem. The ship's company would be all-fired lonesome at the absence of the squeaking fife.

"How big we are in our own estimation, you and I and all of us, and yet how small a gap would the death of any of us make in the world. The round globe will still turn on its axis, the bright stars glint overhead, men live and move and war and intrigue though the mutes be at our door, and the coffin made."

Ricard lamented his friend, and resolved to convey his condolence to his girl-friend at Newhaven, the gentle Susan, of whom he used speak and whose address he found in the sea chest. On his return he sought her out; she was not at home, but he had no difficulty in finding her. She was in Church, before the Altar, getting married to a rich rival of her faithful sailor-laddie!

Six months had elapsed before Ricard paced up Broadway once more and he did not come back with a fortune. The Captain advanced him and the other members of the crew a portion of their wages knowing well that if Jack had his money going ashore among the sharks of the city he would come back penniless. They all had signed up for another voyage on the Georgette. But this never came off as fate took a hand.

One morning, while on leave, the clanging of the fire bell woke him and on looking out the window he saw a pyramid of flame curling up from the river. Anxious to know what it was he rushed out and raced down to the quay where he met Bill Smith, with a can of liquor in his hand and a tear in his eye. "The moment he saw me he rushed over to me, shook my hand, and in a maudlin voice he besought me to drink. 'Messmate,' he sobbed, 'I know'd her from keel to truck, every timber in her, and now there ain't a spar of her left, oh, oh!' and the big fellow began to blubber like a baby.

"I drew away, but it was not long until I learned the cause of honest Bill's emotions. A boy handed me the damp morning edition of the Herald, and the first piece of news I lit on, in preternaturally large print, was the account of the total destruction by fire off No. 16 pier, East River, of the corvette, Georgette, Lasso master!

"I rushed to the house where Captain Lasso was staying to offer him some consolation. He had disappeared, leaving no trace behind. What was I to do? I met Smith later in the evening; he was boozy - a sheet in the wind, as we say, not quite half-seas over - which was excusable, under the circumstances. He introduced me to a friend, another sailor, and the next morning saw me again in a pea-jacket, bound to make my fortune in blue water."

***Note by the Editor of the Autobiography, John O'Shea. The mystery of Georgette solved?***

The editor inserts a note which explains much as to the mystery of Georgette, and may aptly close this, the only sentimental episode in the Autobiography of a Fenian. The incidents concerning Captain Lasso, the Georgette and the mysterious lady have all the elements of a mystery story. However, this explanation by the editor seems to solve the mystery and gives credence to what Ricard wrote. As well as appearing in the Irishman, Dublin, this autobiography also appeared in the Irish People newspaper of New York in 1868. On August 29th of that year the editor received a letter at his Paris address with the New Orleans post-mark. This letter contained the following passage: "Apropos of those men and their doings in the Empire City I receive sometimes a number of O'Sullivan's paper in which I fancy I can trace the 'fine Roman hand' of honest John O'Mahony. I follow the adventures of that fine dashing fellow, Rick Burke, with liveliest of interest. What a pity that such a spirit should be pent within a prison, such a brimming life condemned to fret itself out prematurely against bolts and bars and the blank enclosure of granite walls! Something strikes me in his picture of that silent Georgette which corresponds singularly with the portrait of a lady I knew. The traits of feature were the same, the form and shape; the talent for music and the inclining airs of our country were similar; and strangest of all, that peculiarity of silence. I knew her here; she lived in Carondelet-street and supported a bed ridden man, who appeared to stand in some relationship, by lessons in the piano-forte. My Minnie was one of her pupils. It was from her she learned the Coolin, which I asked her to play so often of an evening when I returned wearied from my occupation in the shipping-office. It is like a vision of home; I can see the soft green of the meadows, smell the fragrance of primrose and violet in the lane before my father's cottage, in its tones.

"Well, the music-mistress sent me a note asking my presence by the dying couch of her uncle. I went. It was the bed-ridden. He was already dead when I arrived. I saw the rites of decent burial paid to his remains; and the niece, who was overwhelmed with grief, gave me reward ten-fold in her look of gratitude. Some two weeks afterwards she disappeared from her lodgings, leaving a note for me explaining that she could not express her feelings with living voice, as voice had long been dead to her.

"She had been born in Belize, from which her uncle also came; but his name was not Lasso, but S ... Her mother, his sister, was Irish. She had wed clandestinely a young countryman of her mother, and had to leave home. Uncle was the only relative who would recognize her after the marriage. He was a seafaring man and took the couple with him in his vessel to New York. Arrived there, her husband got an offer to go with a surveying expedition to the Pacific Coast. On the way across the party was attacked by Indians, her husband killed before her eyes; she slew his murderer with her own feeble hands, shooting him dead as he was in the act of scalping him to whom her troth had been plighted. A companion red-skin, his brother, perhaps, for he was like him in outward and inward man, seized her and cut out her tongue with his tomahawk.

"She lost her senses after the outrage, and when she came to herself found that a company of U.S. soldiers had avenged the massacre of the whites and rescued herself and the other survivors from the further cruelties which menaced them. She was carried back to New York. Her uncle received her and tenderly cared her - with a tenderness that was maternal, for she was subject to attacks of hysterical madness each anniversary of that terrible scene on the plains, which left her in low spirits for months afterwards. While in New York her uncle's vessel was burned after a return from a voyage and they were obliged to leave the city abruptly, as he had some engagements to meet, and as he could not brook the prospect of meeting a creditor without money to pay him. His efforts since had been devoted to the one object of gathering together a sum sufficient to clear off his debts. But his speculations were unfortunate. He was too honest for those among whom he lived. And then came paralysis, he was bed-ridden; on her devolved the duty of supporting her second father. She thanked me for my kindness in the final act, bade me farewell, she was going north, and had consecrated the remainder of her life to the task of paying off the debt he had left. Such was her letter. With it was a little purse containing more than double the amount I had the privilege of spending on the funeral.

"A moving story! But attend to the sequel. The war broke out shortly after. When Butler, with the Federal soldiers, took possession of our city I contrived to smother my Southern prejudices so far (you know I have always been a conscientious Secessionist, and was only prevented from fighting under the Stars and Bars by those cursed spectacles I am forced to wear); I stifled and crushed down my Southern prejudice so far as to welcome some officers of a Connecticut regiment by my hearth. Why? Because they were Irish. From one of them I heard the story of a lady, quite a musical prodigy, who had been giving concerts in the New England States under the auspices of one of those smart Yankee Barnums. This lady never spoke; and Barnum secundus used to explain this by a statement that she had been a divinity among the Aztecs, who had the habit of depriving their gods of the power of speech. 'It is a pity, ladies and gentlemen,' the Yankee was wont to add, 'for her voice, I can assure you, was something rarely heard, something angelic.' The poor creature had come by her death by the burning down of an hotel in the town of Maine, near the Canadian frontier. Could this lady have been the Georgette of Rick Burke's autobiography?"

I leave the query to the reader. I should be inclined to answer in the affirmative myself; in any case it is my duty to give the fact as it was given to me, and here my note ends.

# CHAPTER 7

# AT SEA ONCE MORE

Ricard spent the next two years on his second cruise in search "of the country where the streets are paved with gold, the roofs tiled with pancakes, and the rivers run red-wine," the land flowing with milk and honey always seemed to be just out of reach. "And in the end, as I slapped my hand on an empty pocket, I laughed an Irish laugh, congratulating myself that I had what Golconda could not buy - contentment; and made up my mind that the gold-paced, cake-tiled, wine-rivered city was not here below, but somewhere aloft above the violet clouds."

At this stage of his autobiography Ricard interpolates, to offer as is his wont, "sundry maxims of hackneyed philosophy for the rising generation of my countrymen who may trace these lines when I shall be breaking stones in Portland. Never read of the success of some digger who has turned up a nugget without asking after the thousand of his comrades who sunk into the clay under the heat and toil of the day and the heart-weariness of hope deferred. More prudent to stay at home, my boys, and stick your nose to the grindstone than tempt the fates afar. As we used to say at the fireside long ago, it is better to fall into the hands of the devils you know than the devils you don't know. Irish typhus is an ugly disease, no doubt; but I would sooner die of Irish typhus, with a priest by my side, than with the black vomit of Mexico with a company of dicers in the next room. There is no royal road to fortune - at least, it is known to very few, and they care to keep the secret to themselves. Hard work, perseverance, economy, temperance - these are the finger-posts, and they all point the shortest route. One pound earned by honest sweat is sweeter than a thousand gained in a lottery. Oatmeal-stirabout, if you get up an appetite for it with a spade, makes a more wholesome and sweeter meal than lobster-sandwich and pale ale without."

At this time Ricard was young and carefree and life at sea suited him. "I was young, in my romantic hey-day, and you may guess with what relish as the Kentucians say, I enjoyed those two years. They were to me but as series after series of dissolving views. Adventure and peril - striking contrasts - pathos and fun, tragedy and comedy - such was their burden. It was not a very heavy one, you can perceive; still it had its intervals when the load chafed my shoulders. There were days when I had to live on short commons, and nights when I had to go out on a yard-arm in a tempest; but this was in the line of duty and the lot of every sailor, and I didn't mind it. But no salad is perfect without the vinegar; I grinned and got through the acids while waiting for the oil."

His experiences during those two years were quite extensive as he was engaged in war-vessels, surveying vessels, coasters and whaling vessels. From the fall of the leaves in 1856 to the fall of the snows in 1858 he travelled extensively. "As I roam through the aisles of memory I find myself at one tick of the pendulum at home with the natives of the South Pacific Islands, spending a few months with the dashing fine fellows of the Marquesas or hanging up my hat in the cabin - palace I mean - of the Prince of Nouka-Hiva; at another time I am shivering with blue cold nose and wrinkled brow up in the white region of the Arctic Circle with the Kamschatkians, or further north with the Esquimaux, learning to tool a wicker trap drawn by a team of hungry dogs, or to stalk a cunning seal over the ice plains, Now I am in the company of double-sworded notabilities of Japan, anon hob-nobbing with some brother-Paddy in the English garrison at Hong Kong; this minute I am in the territory of that fierce French advocate, Orelie, King of Aracuania, the next under the protection of his Majesty Theodoros, King of the Kings of Ethiopia, and before the hand of the clock has traversed a quarter of the circumference of the dial I have well nigh circumnavigated the globe. I was seeing the world and I was acquiring some useful knowledge - a mastery of seamanship, in the first place, an idea of astronomy, and a fluency in the Spanish language, which is almost universally spoken in the mercantile cities of the Central and South American coast."

He eventually grew tired of this nomadic life and decided to chance his luck in the gold mines of Senora, California. As his noble craft was lying off the shores of Lower California and as he approached his captain with a request to go ashore he gives a description of himself at that point in time; "a tall, brown young fellow with curly locks, open face with the weather-beaten cheeks lit up by a smile. The movements were lithe and agile - the movements of a person who combined strength with activity. He was dressed in a tidy pair of ducks, had a red sash round his waist, a straw hat with blue ribbons on his head, and a neat, well-made jacket of blue cloth with brass buttons fitting to the upper portion of his figure, so as to show it off to greatest advantage. Evidently he was a dandy, this young man - thought no table beer of himself." The captain refused his request and drew a pistol when Ricard made an attempt to lower a small boat, fired and carried "away a tress of the hair ornamenting the front of my forehead." Ricard struggled with the captain and wrenched the pistol out of his hand and left "a visible indentation from its butt-end on his forehead was but the work of an instant." The other members of the crew overpowered Ricard and as he was led down to the bowels the ship "valedictory words of the captain, as the light of day receded from the prisoner's gaze were hardly reassuring: 'The confounded deck-swabber. I'll keep him on bilge-water and hard tack till we get into the port of New York. I will. I'll see if I can put his neck into the halter on a charge of attempted murder on the high seas. Hoist anchor, all hands, d—n you, look alive.' "

However, all was not lost. On board the vessel was Ricard's old friend, Bill Smith. Some hours later Bill approached and said the crew was planning to jump ship and would Ricard join them. Despite it looking like mutiny he joined Bill and the other nine crew members in the long boat which was well-provisioned. As the boat pulled away the captain's parting words were: "Burke, d—n you, you'll swing from a yard-arm yet." Then he tried once more to shoot Ricard but Bill Smith had taken the precaution to draw the charges when taking possession of the long-boat, during the captain's absence from the cabin.

"We spread sail to a propitious breeze, bade good-bye to the ship where we had been so unhappy, and as the moon was rising on the following evening we beached our ark of refuge in the Bay of St Lucas, not far from Cape St. Lucas, the south-western point of Lower California."

They were lucky that it was the month of October when they made entry into the Bay of St. Lucas, as during July, August and September, the hurricane months, entry is next nigh impossible. They made their way inland as quickly as possible to avoid capture. On waking the second morning Ricard found an angry discussion going on between Bill Smith and another old hand as to who should lead the party. Having concluded their deliberations, Bill approached Ricard, took off his cap with an air of respect and said: "Mr. Burke, we've had a palaver, and we're agreed on it; we've named you Captain and ax you to take charge of this party because you are the most eddycated amongst us." Ricard accepted and at the age of twenty became leader of this band of sailors.

They headed northwards on foot for the gold workings which were hundreds of miles away. However with the passing of each day their numbers dwindled for one reason or another until finally there were only three members of the party left - Ricard, Bill Smith and Pete Holmes. Ricard heads this chapter in his autobiography - "Narrative of how a Sum in Reduction was Performed." Pete was a thorough American and hated having to walk. As he said himself, "A crab carries his own house, I like my house to carry me." He went into the town of La Paz with the intention of signing on. He was back in double quick time to report that the ship they had abandoned was in the bay. It was agreed between them that Ricard would watch the ship all day and at night he would slip into town to reconnoitre. "I cautiously approached the town and lying under a bank took a sight of the ship. It was indeed the one they had left a week ago. But what meant the agitation on board? He noticed a coffin being lowered into a long-boat and he came to the conclusion that the captain had murdered the cabin-boy. However, behind the coffin, walking as mourner-in-chief, was the cabin-boy.

"I was rooted to the spot with astonishment. His eye caught mine, we exchanged looks of confidence. I followed to the graveyard, and there the youth took the opportunity of telling me they had been picked up at sea by an American schooner which had towed them into La Paz. The captain of the schooner, he thought, had laid a claim on the ship for salvage and was going to sell it off." The unfortunate wretch of a captain had taken to drink after our departure and in the excess of delirium tremens had managed to snap up a pistol on the schooner which had rescued his ship and had blown his brains out.

Pete Holmes remained in La Paz and Bill and Burke headed for Loretta. On their journey they heard the tinkling of a cow bell and knew they were near an encampment. Ricard called out at the top of his voice and was answered in the unmistakable accents of a genuine American of the woods. This American who went by the name of Uncle Sam was accompanied by an Indian called Saturday and they brought Ricard and his friend safely to the camp.

"The camp was situated at a small opening in the timber about half-a-mile distant. A fine old man of pleasing and refined cast of countenance greeted us with forest hospitality. We had a bowl of aquardente, plenty of stewed jerk-beef and tortillas (thin cakes baked on a griddle), and after a hearty meal Bill lit his pipe, got into a yarn with Uncle Sam, the Indian stretched his feet to the ashes of the camp-fire and fell asleep, and the old gentleman, rising, remarked that as it was moonlight he had a fancy to take a walk and courteously awaited me to accompany him. Nothing loath, I rose and thence sprung to conversation of such a nature that I deem it worthy of a separate chapter."

## CHAPTER 8

# AN ATTACK OF RHEUMATIC FEVER

There now followed for Ricard a series of adventures which seem incredible as he roamed through Mexico, Central America and South America over the next three or four years. It is hard to imagine that anyone could have packed so much adventure into a few years. He does not recall all that befell him as the manuscript would tire the reader and "not attain its close, perhaps, sooner than I shall my freedom. For the future I propose to relate only such episodes as vividly impressed me or altered my condition, getting as rapidly as may be over the less stirring incidents that come between, and connect them. Excitement, itself, becomes monotonous, and that now after the lapse of years, no diary at hand, it is hard to recall sensations, strong at the moment, but which time, the great anodyne, has subdued."

This fine old gentleman who greeted Ricard with forest hospitality was named Icarus Taunton. His father had been a wealthy brewer in Warwickshire and had seen to it that his son was well educated. When his father died, Icarus sold the brewery and moved to London. There he founded a newspaper which lasted only three weeks and deprived Icarus of a large part of his fortune. He had learned his lesson and had the good sense to invest the rest in Govenment Funds. He then set out on his travel which took him across Europe and Siberia. Crossing the Behring Straits into North America he travelled southward by the Pacific coast until he met Ricard. From there "he proposed continuing his wanderings by Mexico and down the Rocky Mountains, even on through the Republics of South America until he had penetrated to the far Terra-Del-Fuegians when he proposed to turn and come northwards by the Atlantic shores."

The first welcoming salutation startled Ricard when he reached the camp because Icarus greeted him with, "You're from Cork, young man, by your accent." Ricard at first thought he was in the presence of a fellow countryman. But Mr. Taunton explained that he had made a study of languages, that he was English by birth and cosmopolite by temperament and theory. Ricard then asked him to favour him with his theories and philosophy and as they walked under the trees Icarus explained some of his theories to him.

First of all he stated that he was a Cosmopolite Utilitarian - he favoured no theory which was not for all mankind and which was not practicable. When Ricard enquired if he believed in God, Icarus, pointing to the moon which was shining down silently upon them through the over-arching foliage, replied; "Can I look on that and deny his existence? No, my friend, the astronomer can never be an atheist. I believe in God and I worship Him, here in the temple built by his own hands, not in the temples built by man, where there are those who clasp their fingers so tightly in prayer that they cannot open them when the poor-box goes round.

" 'You have studied astronomy then, sir,' I resumed, 'so have I, a little, and I agree with you, I fancy, and also with what Young has said in his *Night Thoughts*.'

" 'Ah! precisely, beautiful lines - 'the undevout astronomer is mad.' Yes, sir, Icarus Taunton has studied astronomy.' "

Their conversation that evening ranged over a wide range of subjects including balloon-navigation and aerostation and decimal measurement. On this latter subject he said none but the decimal system should exist in coinage, weights and measures and he hoped to live to see the day when a uniform table will universally exist. He believed "gymnastics ought be a part of education. I am old, but I can clear any wall I can touch with the tip of my hand. I can master the wildest untrained colt, I can - - What's the matter, young friend, why do you shrink?"

"I had started back, smitten with sudden horror at a something with which my face had come in contact. So much had I been engrossed by Mr. Taunton's conversation that I had not perceived it until I bumped against it, and drawing back I recognised to my horror the limp body of a human being hanging from a tree, the ghostly moonlight falling straight on the blackened, swollen face and the protruding tongue.

" 'Why do you shrink? It's only the corpse of a horse-thief I shot and strung up this morning.' "

At Ricard's suggestion they returned to camp. Ricard was trembling and Icarus had the same gentle smile on his lips, the same mild benevolence in his clear eye, the same quiet steadiness in his mien and walk. When Ricard suggested to him that the abolition of capital punishment wasn not one of his theories, Icarus replied; "On the contrary it is, where society is strong enough for its own protection. But here where the individual is obliged very much to trust to his own right arm for protection, the most merciful code, indeed the only possible one, is that of Lynch. Short shrift and the dog's death for the thief: that is the only guarantee for the security of property."

When they returned to camp Mr. Taunton expounded on another of his theories - incremation and "he lulled me to sleep with a description of the facility with which it could be performed with an oxy-hydrogen blow-pipe, whereas it had taken Byron and Leigh Hunt the length of a summer's day to cinerise the body and brain of the author of Queen Mab. He was about methodizing his theory when I dropped off into dreamland and found myself busy with a comment over that line in Byron, of all others, 'as mild a mannered man as ever cut a throat.' "

However, that night Ricard had a bad night's rest, "tossing about like a porpoise in the blankets, dreaming at one time I was sea-sick from smoking too much opium with Jonas in the whale's belly, at another, that I was descending into the place that is paved with good intentions on a non-stop, double-action, flying-machine, and it was not till the morning breeze was springing up and the early birds chirping over their toilette of the dawn that I fell into a sound dreamless sleep.

"When I woke I was raving tight in the clutches of a violent rheumatic fever. For what happened to me during its continuance I am indebted to hearsay. Bill Smith remained by me and tended me like a brother; the old philosopher, who, among his other theories, had some on medical treatment, watched over me like a father. He nearly killed me outright with kindness. Perspiration,

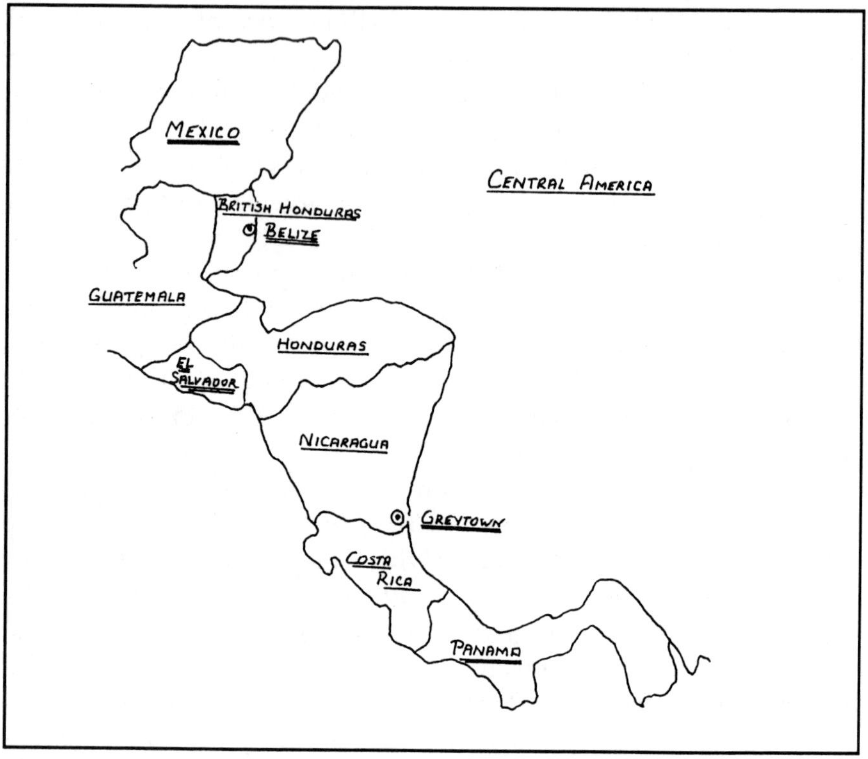


*Ricard's travels in Central America*

in his notions, was the only remedy for the ills that flesh is heir to - the pores acted as so many channels for carrying off the evil humours of the body. Acting on this idea, one hot day in the absence of the others on a hunting expedition he wrapped me in a sheep-skin, Bryan O'Lynn fashion. *'The fleshy side out and the woolly side in,'* and covered me all over, head excepted, with shovelfuls of sand. I was not in my clearest senses, but a vague apprehension rose in my disturbed brain that Mr. Icarus Taunton had hit on some theory of annihilation of corpses newer than incremation. He was trying it practically first on me, on the principle, *fiat experimentum vili corpore.* Before I had succumbed to the rough treatment of the philosopher, the remainder of the party returned. Bill Smith dug me out of my sandpit and rehoisted me into the hammock I occupied in the common tent, and proceeded to give Mr. Taunton such a rebuke as must well have astonished the well-meaning gentleman. It was a most Christian rebuke, but plentifully interlarded with strange oaths. Nevertheless, to that very vagary on his part do I attribute my recovery. My burial in a shroud of sheep-skin had acted like a veritable Turkish bath: when I was taken out I was teaming with sweat; streamlets of liquid streaming down my sides; I sank into a slumber from fair exhaustion, and when I woke the pains had left me and my brow was cool; I was weak but refreshed and hungry.

"During the period of my convalescence I drank copiously of a sulphur spring which ran near our camp, and this so radically confirmed my cure that I am not conscious of having the slightest symptom of a visit from rheumatic fever since, though frequently have given it invitation sufficient. Mr. Taunton paid me every possible attention; would not hear of my joining in their trapping excursions until I had fully recovered. He used to sit for hours beside my couch of dry grass, enlarging on his theories, recounting his experiences, talking on the duties of the individual man to the human family, and the duty of man in governing station to his individual brother. In the end I was involuntarily compelled to believe that my entertainer had in him more than the usual share of the milk of human kindness, inexorable though he was on the matter of horse-thieves., He was a very sincere man, and herein I feel that I owe a tribute of praise to the English character. It is cold, has not the demonstrative warmth of other climates, but, as a rule, it is not hypocritical, you can trust it. I do not like the English nation, cannot, never did; but for individual Englishmen I have much respect.

"I reckon some such among my friends, they were slow to stretch me their hands, but once having admitted me to the circle of their intimacy I have the confidence that they would listen to no dispraise of me behind my back, no defiance of me without challenge in return. Of such was Icarus Taunton, and if by any turn of fate, these lines should happen to reach his eyes, I beg of him to accept again the thanks of the sick Irish youth whom he nursed in Lower California, and to rest assured that Ricard Burke, though he may smile at the visionary theories of the philosopher, will always be grateful for the genuine hospitality of the man."

During Ricard's recuperation Icarus had plenty of time to air his views on politics. He believed that within one hundred years Europe would be divided into five Confederations, "the Panslavic consisting of Russia and the people attached to Russian interests; the Teutonic; the Scandinavian; the Ibero - Guelo - Italian as Alphonse de Lamartine calls it, but the Latin, as I would call it, consisting of France, Spain and Italy; and the British, embracing England, Scotland and Ireland." Ireland would have a distinct native legislative assembly subject to the general assembly at London. Icarus was puzzled when Ricard didn not agree with this theory and asked him why.

"I tell you what I mean, Mr. Taunton; I mean just this, that in a council of twelve men, where eight are blue and only four are green, the green stands a poor chance of fair play. The blue are the English, the green are the Irish, and the council of twelve is your general assembly." Icarus told him to put his trust in the English sense of justice and to appeal to their better feelings with trust. However, Ricard felt that "a touch of Brian Boru" would get far better results. The simple man did not understand!

## CHAPTER 9

# A DUEL IN MEXICO

As soon as Rick had recovered strength after his attack, his generous host stood by the camp-fire in the manner of an Indian chief and summoned his followers to attention and announced the time had arrived to move on. His mission, like the purgatory of the Wandering Jew, was to keep ever moving on. He never ceased moving only when the interests of science preferred a demand, or those of humanity a claim, such as in the case of Rick's illness. His companions were bound by no such obligations of the spirit and were free to accompany him or stay behind.

Uncle Sam, "the gruff hunter who had bidden us to the camp on the night we first fell across this strange trio, took his age-blackened pipe from his mouth as Mr. Taunton sat down on a mound of turf, and, raising himself to the full height of his muscular person, ejected a stream of tobacco-spittle from his mouth on the red embers and began - 'Uncle Sam,' he said, speaking of himself in the third person, 'is known in these diggins this forty year. He likes a small hunt still, though his eye is not so bright nor his hand so steady as it was forty year a-gone. He has chased in the Missouri Valley with the Crows, fought with them, lived with them, married with one of their tribe, made himself as much Injun as it is the gifts of a white's nature to be. The emigrators came and pushed back the Crows into the wilderness. The emigrators love iron, but it is the iron of the spade and not the rifle. The emigrators will push back the redskin, back, back, until the sea roars behind him. Its roar is his funeral-song. It is written. Uncle Sam saw these things and came to Calleforrny up above (pointing to the interior) afore any white man knowed it; but the goold was found and the emigrators came - they love goold more than they love iron - and they pushed him before them. He came down here, and now it's getting too much folk here, but the game will last as long as Uncle Sam has a clear eye to bring it down.

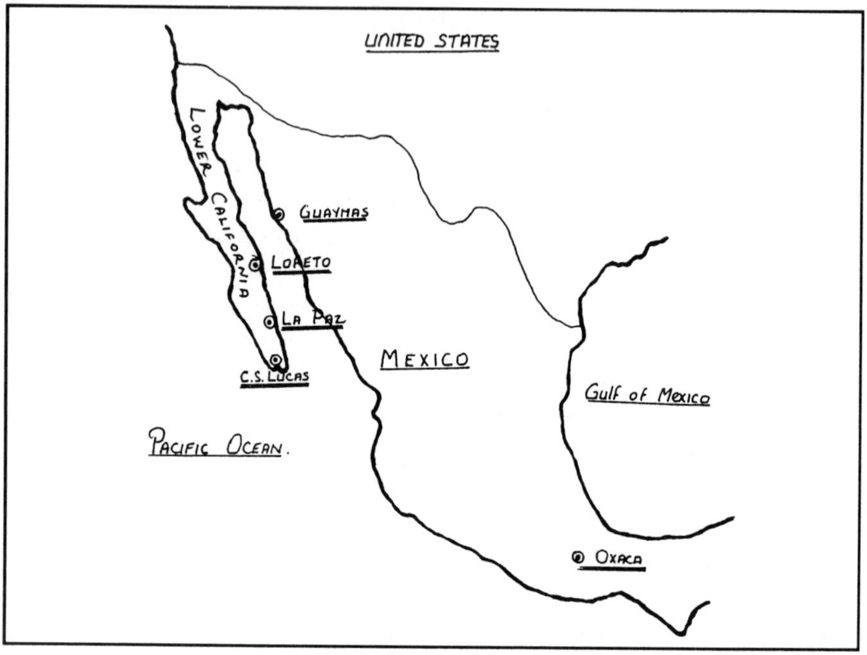


*Ricard's travels in Mexico*

Uncle Sam loves the forest and in it Uncle Sam will stay. And Saturday sticks by me. Isn't it so, Saturday?'

"The Indian, who had been listening intently, a blanket wrapped round his shoulders, and his toes shoved far into the embers of the fire, grunted approval."

Then the philosopher turned to Rick with an inquisitive glance. "I took up a small stone that lay at my feet, spat on one side of it and threw it in the air. The wet side came uppermost. I had resolved that as a token that I should cross the water. 'I go.' "

Bill Smith was unhappy at Rick's decision and when asked for his own announced that he was going back sailing as the sea was his life. There was a ship in Loretto which he was going to join immediately. "And Bill stretched out a brown hand in which he grasped mine as in the pressure of a bear's paw, murmurs an affectionate good-bye, hitched his trousers, put a quid in his mouth, and bore away sea-wards with all sail on." Rick was astonished at Bill's sudden departure that night and it wasn't until a few hours later that the reason dawned on him. The next day was Friday and in Bill's book no sailor commenced a journey on a Friday as it was unlucky.

Next day the philosopher and Rick crossed the Gulf in a small schooner and arrived in Guaymas, a town in north west Mexico, and from there they journeyed on to Guatemala. You may wonder where the money came from for all this travelling but Rick explains this in his autobiography. "Mr. Taunton was generous to a fault, yet he had enough of the English virtue of providence about him never to leave himself without money. The interest on his investment in the funds was received by a friend in London who faithfully remitted it to him at intervals as regular as his irregular mode of life, his frequent change from place to place, permitted. With money you can do almost anything here below, build conspiracies or churches, furnish a house with a wife, or an orchestra with a Cremona (a violin), or a snug corner in perpetuity in St. Paul's Cathedral. A grand thing is money, precious by whatsoever name 'tis called, brads, blunt or rhino, currency, bullion, or specie, spondulicks or sinews of war.

"The terms on which I stood with the philosopher were of a mutual accommodation kind. My pay was small, my personal liberty ample. I was both Purveyor and Historian to the expedition, holding the key of the money chest and responsible for the entertainment of both man and horse, and holding the pen and responsibility for the due noting down of the chronicle of each day. But the events to be noted down were peculiar; a battle in our vicinity, the burning down of a city - that would be of no importance; but the discovery of a strange flower; the occurrence of a peculiar vein in a stone, that in the eyes of Mr. Taunton would be of transcendent magnitude, to neglect its faithful record a crime of the deepest dye. For of such were the good man's researches - he botanized, geologized and mineralized; and I - I poetized and killed time."

At that time in Mexico a war was raging between Church and State, and the country, accordingly, was dangerous to traverse. However, Ricard and his companion were not molested by either side. On the contrary, in many instances they were treated with the hospitality of old attributed to the outlaw. "There is a dash of Spanish chivalry in the Mexican character; it is hot as their clime, but under its influence many generous qualities flourish. A Mexican will pray to the Madonna and poniard you conscientiously afterwards; but he will not shake hands with you and invite you to his home and speculate how he can best cozen you under his own mahogany, like many a godly and puritanical soul in New England. Life is insecure in Mexico, for they are passionate and blood is accounted of little reck where honour, so called, or the thing recognised as such, is at stake."

One night they arrived weary after a long ride, and hungry as well, in the town of Oaxaca. They had taken their siesta under a grove of mahogany, where an unfortunate Leperos, with his head lying on a tattered blanket, had lain down to rest before them. The poor fellow was obviously very tired as the end of a cigarette, which had singed his moustache, was still in his mouth. Ricard was puzzled how the unfortunate man had fatigued himself, "for the Leperos, homeless and houseless, are the American kindred of the Lazzaroni of Naples. They do nothing, have nothing, not even feeling - and they care nothing for nobody. And yet some of these wretched, restless creatures, roaming about in their scanty costume of cloak, trousers and sombrero, the eternal cigarette between their lips, have been known to fashion gold chains that would be wondered at in Geneva, and to model statuettes that would be masterpieces in Rome. On resuming our march this Leperos attached himself to our party, and as he had been highly entertaining in his conversation, the generous Taunton invited him to share of what was going with us as we entered the hotel Oaxaca."

In Mexico the hotel is the resort of all classes, for it is generally furnished with a gaming table which seems to have an irresistible attraction for the excitable people. After a meal of maize cake and

*Ricard's travels in South America*

chocolate they went to the gaming room in which was a large table covered with piles of gold and silver. "The eyes of the Leperos glistened as he saw it, and taking three reels out of some unknown corner of his dress, he stuck a coin in each ear for good luck, made the sign of the Cross and threw down the remaining coin on a card. It won, and the banker shoved him over a pile of money. He put it all on the same card a second time, again it won. He placed the stake, which was now heavy, on a fresh card. He won again. A fourth time fortune favoured him, and now, staking his entire winnings on the turn, he stood statue-like at the table, rigid as bronze in the attitude, impassive as stone in the face, but with sparks of fire gleaming from his anxious eyes. The interest was intense, a pin could be heard drop in the room. He won again and the bank was broke."

The unlucky banker rushed from the room and as he did so he knocked off Ricard's hat. Turning around he cursed Ricard roundly and made off out of the room muttering a single word, "gacuphinos," which means thieves. Ricard was for following him and demanding an apology saying: "I think that fellow wants to be drained of a little blood as well as a little money." The philosopher, however, calmed him down saying that a gambler wasn't responsible for what he does.

The moved out into the freshness of the street, fanned by a gentle breeze. There they were accosted, once more, by the gambler as he was returning to the gaming table with a fresh supply of money. Ricard's first impulse was to rush at him, catch him by the throat and roll him in the dust. Again, Mr. Taunton restrained him. The gambler taunted them again and again and all that Mr. Taunton demanded was that he should give up gambling. This annoyed the gambler more. *"Amor de Dios!"* said the Mexican, making a cross on his lips; "the dotard has escaped out of a hospice for the insane!" He rushed at the philosopher with a knife in his hand but stopped dead when he saw a pistol in Mr. Taunton's hand. The upshot of the argument was that they arranged to fight a duel with pistols early on the following morning.

Ricard and the philosopher spent the night walking up and down the road discussing honour and duelling. "When the day-star was peeping brightly from the blue, it warned us that it was time to get to the trysting-ground. The Mexican, accompanied by a friend, strode up as we approached,

" *'Bonos dies caballeros!'* he cried as he caught sight of us, raising his hat with mock deference. His gait was that of a slightly-drunken man, his face was flushed, eyes blood-shot and hair disordered.

" 'You have lost your money?' said Mr. Taunton cooly.

" 'Caramba, I have, but I have not lost my revenge. You shall console me for the loss of my money by the loss of your life.'

"The philosopher smiled and politely inquired whether he would promise to give up the evil habit of gambling, which gave bad example to youth, made its victim overbearing to his neighbours - in fine emptied his pockets, which emptiness led to crime.

" 'Gojo, quequieres?' (Dog, what do you mean?) shouted the Mexican, his eyes flaming in their scarlet sockets; 'I came here to fight not to talk.'

" 'There are the weapons,' said Mr. Icarus Taunton, inclining his head as he laid two exquisite naval revolvers on the ground; 'both are true, and both carefully loaded. Take your choice.'

"The Mexican lifted that which was nearest to him, dug a line in the turf with his spurred heel, another at six paces from it, and regarding his adversary asked him was he willing that they should stand back to back at six other paces from these lines respectively, turn when the word should be given by his friend and deliver their fire immediately or reserve it until each reached the spurred line which marked the limit of his ground.

" 'Yes,' answered Mr. Taunton, 'on one condition; that each shot be alternate after the first discharge.'

" 'Agreed,' said the Mexican.

"The men were placed, the stranger and I got out of the line of fire.

" 'One - two — THREE!'

"Both turned simultaneously. Taunton raised his pistol as if to take aim, the Mexican pulled trigger to anticipate him. It was but a feint on the philosopher's part, but the precipitate shot of the other was near costing him his life. A bullet whizzed through his hair. With countenance undisturbed he advanced steadily to his spurred boundary, keeping his pistol in direct line with the Mexican's chest, halted, and asked quietly, 'Do you promise to give up gambling?'

"The Mexican who had crossed his arms after firing his shot, awaited him without a tremor of a muscle, shook his head defiantly as if disdaining to reply and challenged the philosopher to fire.

"Mr. Taunton did fire - in the air.

"With an exulting glow over his features, a sort of reflection of hell, the Mexican sprang to the extremity of his ground in one wild bound, and fired. The smoke cleared away, my old friend was still standing, the last bullet had not sped so truly as the first, anger is even a worse guide than impatience. Now was a critical moment. The philosopher deliberately raised his shining barrel, kept it on level with his antagonist's head for a moment, smiled and pressed his forefinger on the trigger. The unhappy Mexican gave an unmerciful yell, leaped into the air and fell dead on the broad of his back.

" 'Cabaleros,' said the stranger, 'I undertake to have my friend interred; your conduct in the affair has been perfectly honourable, everything has passed off beautifully. Never witnessed a more satisfactory duel.'

"Mr. Taunton bowed. 'I meet a disciple of the art of killing in you, cavalier.'

" 'And I in you, senor,' retorted the stranger, 'I salute my master. You will find your horses awaiting you in the shadow of the house yonder; we took them out of the hotel and paid your bill to ensure your presence and your means of escape afterwards. Adios!' and he gracefully kissed his hand as we turned from the scene and repaired to the spot where our horses were tied.

"We afterwards learned that the courteous stranger was an eminent fire-eater of the province, referee in all affairs of honour, and that his friend, on the occasion, had found the means of replenishing the purse by slitting the throat of his uncle and rifling his pockets. Before the sun had well risen on the murder done, he had met the murderer's doom."

## CHAPTER 10

# AN UNPLANNED BALLOON FLIGHT

The recollection of the mysterious lady, Georgette, his ideal love, came sometimes to torment Ricard in his dreams. He told the story of Georgette to Mr. Taunton and succeeded in turning his steps to Honduras in the hope that they might find some clue as to the whereabouts of the lady or Captain Lasso. They descended from the high ground of the interior to Belize, by the Old River, a rapid stream navigated by long canoes, which under the skilful handling of the Indians, traverse its rapids with speed and security. After a diligent search "we left without having attained the object of our visit. No person of the name Lasso was known there; no tomb with the name Georgette lay in the cemetery. I was forced to give up hope of ever solving a problem that has vexed me so much: who was Georgette, and why was she so silent?"

After leaving Belize, they headed for Panama. "We made down east by the Mosquito Territory, passed Greytown, which had been bombarded by the United States a few years before, struck the southern path along the low lying coast until we reached Panama. The Isthmus is very unhealthy, and numbers of workmen employed there on the railway and other enterprises, to meet the great traffic between the Atlantic cities of the Union and California, were dying off day after day. Fever and ague were in the air, one respired pestilence at every breath. Yet I never caught the slightest attack of malady of any kind.

"We took the Pacific coastline after passing Panama. We crossed the paramos of the Andes, desert plateaux in the heart of the mountain; the llanos, wide plains of grass over which roam vast herds of cattle and troops of wild horses, saw the Falls of Tequendama, near Bogota, where a river rushes in thunderous white volume through a cleft twelve yards wide, and tumbles full six hundred feet into a rocky chasm; we went ever on until we reached the Republic of Ecuador, where its western surface is cut into furrows by the ribs of the Andes. We ascended Pichincha, a volcano, beside which Vesuvius sinks into pale insignificance, and nestling in a cosy valley on its eastern side we lit on the homesteads of Quito. I never was so near heaven in my life - that is, in the sense of being elevated. Quito is the loftiest city in the world in situation, being nine thousand five hundred feet above the level of the sea. Eternal summer does not gild its turrets, but a pleasant, perpetual spring bathes it in mild sunshine and stimulates with a genial warmth. From its streets eleven summits of the Andes, capped with crown of snow, appeal to the eye and lead the thoughts of the observer from nature up to nature's God."

On their second day in Quito, Ricard was amazed to find his friend in a state bordering on excitement. On inquiry, Mr. Taunton told him that this was the happiest day of his life because on the morrow he was going to visit a great man. This great man was a Spaniard, one Juan Chevalier, who lived in a comfortable villa in the suburbs and had spent a fortune on aerostatics - a hobby which he held in common with Mr. Taunton. A nice kindly man was Don Chevalier who had a cellar well stocked with rich wine, and this cellar, which had been luxuriously furnished, was his favourite sitting-room after dinner. There the two worthies discussed cosmopolite utilitarianism, variegated with aerostatics now and then, while Ricard enjoyed a book from the Don's library, with a cigar from the Don's case and a glass of rich wine from the cellar.

Having spent three weeks in Don Chevalier's company, Ricard was prevailed upon without much difficulty to accompany the other two on their aerial excursion in the Don's balloon, Don Quixote. "The day appointed for the ascent came. The balloon was inflated, we three had entered the car; a company of Indian servitors hung on the cordage which retained us, when Mr. Taunton suddenly cried:-

" 'The hygrometer, the hygrometer! Have you got it, Burke?'

"I didn't know what it was then, nor do I now.

" 'No, sir.' I answered.

" 'Run down quick; it's in the cellar.'

"I descended, but as I did not have a clear idea of what the hygrometer was, I did not find it. After searching for a quarter of an hour I came up. There was confusion in the open space before the villa where I had left the balloon. The Indians were looking up and clapping their hands.

" 'Where is Don Juan?' I demanded.

"They pointed skywards.

"I could see dimly a black figure like that of a crow sailing in mid air.

"It was the Don Quixote which had escaped from their hands!

"I stopped at the house of Don Juan Chevalier for several days expecting that some tidings would arrive of my poor friend. In vain. His exit had been like that of Elias, and it seemed as if I would have to wait as long for his re-appearance on earth. The event, naturally, created a great sensation in Quito, and an inquiry was instituted by the brother of Don Juan, who arrived from a distant part of the country, as to how the premature elevation of the balloon occurred. The most natural explanation was that the burden being eased by my descent in search of the unhappy hygrometer and the Indians not understanding that I had left with the intention to return, or not being prepared to resist the additional strain on their arms arising from the augmented lightness of the balloon, slackened the strain and let the Don Quixote follow its upward path of adventures. Once in the air, the two gentlemen naturally did not care to lose the chance of a voyage for which the time was highly propitious; and as they had to ascend to a considerable height to escape the cloud-capped region of the Andes summits, the possibility was they were caught in some high current of air and drifted into the far regions of the central south. Making my calculations on the direction of the breeze in this latitude, the probable speed of the balloon and the length of time during which their provisions might be presumed to last (for two such zealous aeronauts would not think of descending while a slice of food or a spoonful of liquid remained to them), I came to the conclusion that they must land eventually somewhere in the territory of Chili. To Chili, therefore, I determined to start in search of two intrepid pioneers of air-navigation. I was the more inclined to this course as the brother of

Don Juan Chevalier (who fell into a tidy piece of property and doubloons by the accident) assumed an inhospitable look, muttered that I was the cause of his brother's precipitate farewell to earth and gave me a pretty broad hint that my room was more welcome than my company."

Ricard, taking him at his word, was off once more on his travels - this time on his own!

# CHAPTER 11

# A BRUSH WITH DEATH

Ricard trudged to Guataquil, one hundred and fifty miles away, where, luckily, he met a French Whaler driven into harbour by bad weather. He was hired partly as A.B., partly as interpreter and eighteen days later they cast anchor in the Bay of Conception right in front of the Chilean town of Talcahuana. The captain informed Ricard that they would be staying there for at least ten days to carry out various repairs and he gave Ricard permission to use the ship as his hotel while it stayed. So day after day Ricard went ashore and commenced taking notes of the manners and customs of the people.

"Never have I seen a country that I liked so much - except one; never have I met a people to whom I cottoned so thickly and so quickly - except one. What the exception is I leave you to guess. The climate is good and vegetation luxuriant; fancy an oasis twice the area of Great Britain, and set in nature's framing most majestic; to the north the vast desert of Atacama unknowing of rain, to the east the giant Cordilleras, snow-crowned and fire-hearted, and to the south and west the boundless Pacific, an oasis teeming with rank fertility and lapful of every gift from maize to melons, from gold to guano.

"The Chilian drinks aguardiente, a colourless rum extracted from the sugar cane; the mosto, or light red wine of the Bordeaux brand; egg-punch; and the national beverage, the mate, a sort of tea-ey infusion. When you visit a house in Chile the macerina is produced, a silver vase, the size of a table-glass, with a cover pierced with a single hole, for all the world like the cover of a mustard-pot. This machine is filled with boiling water, the lady of the house throws into it a pinch of pulverised mate and powdered sugar-candy, and when the process of infusion has taken place - when the mate is drawn granny would say - she sucks the first gulp of it through the bombilla, a metal tube with a bowl pricked like a pepper-caster at the end, which is inserted through the orifice of the macerina. The bombilla, as the intelligent reader will have perceived, plays the part of the long straw of the New York bar. After the lady of the house has taken her suck, she passes round the cheerful goblet. I'm not difficult, but I confess, I'd prefer fresh butter-milk, on the whole, in my own particular noggin to the macerina through everybody else's bombilla.

"They are hospitable these Chileans, and, I am afraid, ever so little ostentatious. They have a passion for horse flesh. If a Chilean wants to cross into the next street to fill his snuff-box, I verily believe he would consider himself dishonoured if he went on foot. They go to church to say their prayers on horseback (I only wonder they don't enter the sacred building itself in the saddle), they go to the town fountain to draw water, still on horseback; they go to hell, by which I mean, of course, the gaming table, to lose their money and their temper, always on horseback; and I have a crazy conviction grown on me that they will come into the world finally on horseback, a new race of Centaurs.

"It will be more interesting to one class of my countrymen (those who love the fair sex, and who with Irish heart does not?) to devote a little space to the tender subject of matrimony. The road to the altar where the mystical knot is tied is smooth in Chile, no publication of banns is required, marriage settlements are dispensed with, love signs the contract and the contract is kept as fondly and faithfully as if the quiver of Cupid were filled with notary's quills instead of the old-fashioned mythical article. Marriage in this Arcadian land is a Sacrament, not a commercial contract. It is enough to love and be loved. Then hie to the feet of some good Padre - it matters not whether the orange blossoms and white tulle be to the fore - the stole is adjusted, the willing pair kneel, the form of conjungo is pronounced, two piastres are paid, the alliance is inscribed in the Parish Register and Darby and Joan emerge 'bone of one bone and flesh of one flesh.' But if the law does not interfere at this stage, and that abomination tolerated in some Christian countries - the civil marriage - is unknown, woe to the faithless wight who repents of his bargain and imagines he can slope away after the honeymoon, leaving the better-half to the freedom of grass widowhood. The instant the spouse suspects your intention, the law steps in to her aid, the alcayde, the corregidor and the alguazils of your adopted country pounce upon you and confine you the conjugal roof, where you are doomed to rest in loyal Benedict unless you can coax the dear creature into formal permission to double Cape Horn!

"The women of Chile are beautiful as the flowers, and like the flowers fade early. Their life is the life of the rose, a brief morning of freshness and perfume, an evening withered and scentless. After thirty years of age the Chilean belle feels that her season is past, grows old as Marie Antoinette grew white, and retires to a corner of the family habitation where she tells her beads and tries to feel interested in the conquests of younger relatives in the field she has left. Human blood courses quicker in woman's veins under this glorious sunlit climate than in our mild Ireland of balmy skies and perennial rain coaxing the meadows into verdure. A vow of love is quickly made in this land of hot passion. To accept a flower from the hands of a female and to offer her one in exchange is equivalent to the plighting of a troth of Cupid for ever, and woe to the unhappy Lovelace who forgets it!"

Ricard, during his stay with Mr. Taunton, picked up a good deal of information on herbal medicine. This, added to his experience as ship's doctor on his voyages with Captain Lasso, left him fairly skilful in the science of medical care. He amused himself practising on his acquaintances, and as he charged nothing, he had an extensive clientele. "One day I went to render a visit to a certain young senorita, a friend of the lady with whom my mates messed during the ship's stay. I had brought her from the bed of sickness to the couch of convalescence through my care. I found my patient seated on an estrado beside her mother and busy with her toilette. Her thick black locks fell in luxuriance on the carpet, she was engaged parting them into two long tresses; for two such tresses brought evenly from her fair forehead, brushed back, soft and shiny, and carried down over her ivory shoulders, set her off to perfection, and she knew it. My entry into the apartment was hardly noticed. The large stag-like eyes of the convalescent never quitted her pocket-mirror, and when I inquired after her health she answered in a voice hardly audible from between half-closed lips to retain a pin, 'gratias senor.'

"The mother, astonished at the speedy recovery of her daughter, offered me a liberal fee, which I declined to accept, and I was on the point of leaving when the senorita, who wished also to testify her gratitude, suddenly stood up, her toilette finished, and amazing me by the splendour of her beauty completed by art, honoured me with a gracious courtesy and smile. As I looked at her, I trembled with visible admiration, and my fixed regard only too plainly told how worthy of worship, in my thoughts, was this glorious creature. The enchantress, reading my soul and anticipating my desires, detached a rose from her hair and offered it to me. I carried it to my lips, this rose, and afterwards placing it in the button-hole of my coat, I cried in execrable Spanish, but with the tone of a chevalier; 'It will never leave me. It will rest here until it withers and when it withers I shall wear it next to my heart. By my word!'"

Ricard left the senorita to join a group of his ship mates in a nearby restaurant. On his way he was accosted by a friend who asked him to visit a sick infant. Ricard prescribed some simple remedy and as he was leaving the sister of the sick child begged him for the rose. "I began to think that the women of Chile were a trifle free and easy. I looked at her and by degrees the conviction dawned on me that she was really very handsome. Not at all a girl to be refused. 'Give it to her,' urged my friend, 'she asked it of you because they believe here that there is some virtue in the flower once worn by a learned doctor that soothes the suffering of a sick person. Give her the rose, Burke, it's a compliment that she pays you.' There was no resisting that argument. I did give her the rose."

The following afternoon he visited the lady with the Juno-like locks of ebony. He found her playing a mournful song on her guitar, her eyes were lustrous and wild and she seemed to be in the grip of a violent agitation. Immediately she asked where was the rose. Ricard rose to the occasion. "Your rose! You ask me where your rose is. Why, darling, where should it be but aboard my ship, safe and snug in my own cabin, in a little bag of silk hanging at the head of my hammock. I keep it there the way I can look at it before I go to sleep, that you may come before me in all my dreams, and the way I can open my eyes on it when I wake, and my first daylight thoughts be yours. If I don't wear it any longer in the buttonhole of my coat, it's afraid I am the jealous wind would carry it away. Ah! senora, senora, could you have the heart to be after asking me what became of your rose?"

The senorita then asked him if he would have a drink. She poured out the cool red wine of the Cordilleras until it bubbled in froth over the rim and he emptied the glass at a gulp "prefacing its downward fall with a toast to our lasting and more intimate mutual acquaintance." She sang another mournful song and when Ricard asked her to strike up a fandango or a frisky bolero she refused saying that these tunes do not suit one who is about to die. And when he asked her who this was she shouted that it was himself. "Breaking off in her funeral psalmody she flung aside her guitar, rushed across to the toilet-table, removed the mirror and lo! behind it was a glass of water on which floated a scarlet rose crumpled and withered.

"In a voice almost inarticulate from anger she said: 'There is the rose you said was hanging at the head of your hammock, the rose that you promised you would preserve till death, through love of me, the rose,' and the syllables came hissing from her lips, 'the rose you gave to another. You did not swear a lie when you swore to preserve it till death. Look at it well for your last hour is come!' I shuddered. She came close to me and looking into my eyes with the metallic glitter of the gaze of the serpent she whispered, 'The wine, was it good?'

"The senorita fell on a chair, silent from exhaustion, but kept wildly regarding me from the orbits of her eyes distended by passion. Suddenly I experienced an atrocious sensation in my entrails, a tearing of the coats of my stomach, and then the awful truth flashed upon me. I quivered as quivered the guests of Lucretius when their host announced to them that they were all poisoned! Rising from the estrado with an effort to master my sufferings I glided over to where I had left the glass out of which I had drunk the wine. In the bottom there were discernible grains of whitish powder which was plain to be recognised as the sediment of corrosive sublimate! I felt that if I were to be saved much depended on expedition in the search of a remedy, and I ran to the door. Turning on the threshold, I cried that we should meet again, and threatening the woman with dire chastisement - a threat which she answered with a scornful smile

"I started at full speed down the street, determined to take the first boat in the harbour, row to my ship, and ransack the medicine chest. Passing along that rugged pathway a roar of mocking laughter reached me from the interior of a building opposite. It was a hotel and the laughter from the company in the billiard room, which opened on the street. A sudden idea struck me, I jumped furiously through the large window, rushed to the table, the players fell back affrighted at the suddenness of my apparition, and held their cues in attitude of defence before them - but my object was not of attack. Instead of knocking down one or other, or arming myself with the balls as missiles of bombardment, I simply snapped up all the lumps of chalk which lay about for preparing the tips of the cues and commenced ravenously eating them.

" 'The man is mad,' were the last words I heard as sinewy arms were laid on me from behind, and I fell off in a swoon. When I came to my senses I was in the strong room of the town prison, pinioned in a strait-waistcoat. A man of kindly face, who I afterwards learned to be the physician of the district, was watching over me, and on convincing him that I was a rational being, and relating my story, he had me released from my bonds and paid me every attention."

His convalescence was slow and when he was able to sit up the French ship had lifted anchor for her homeward voyage. On one of his visits the doctor asked him where did he hear that chalk was one of the antidotes for poisoning by corrosive sublimate. "Well, I read an anecdote given in the life of one of the patriots of my country as proof of his presence of mind, how, having swallowed some corrosive sublimate once by mistake, he went into his father's library, consulted a book on toxicology, found it stated there that chalk was an article to use, got the chalk, took it, cured himself, and came down to breakfast next morning as if nothing had happened. That trait was a key to Emmet's character, and he did not be-lie it on the scaffold for Ireland."

Ricard had many discussions with the doctor during his convalescence and was proud to hear that an Irishman, O'Higgins, was the first supreme director of the Republic of Chile. When the doctor asked him was Ireland a republic Ricard blushed a high, hot, red, and parried the question by asking if Chile was a Federal Republic like the United States.

" 'No," said my friend, it is one, democratic and representative.'

" 'God keep it so,' I murmured - and inwardly I breathed a prayer that He might wipe the scales from the eyes of the people in another land, that they may see that government such as this, government where man is equal to his fellow man by birthright, where the gates of power are not shut against intellect and open only to the 'gentle-born,' where each citizen has a voice in the commonwealth, and where all who are not criminals or fools are citizens; in fine, where the many do not pine in semi-starvation while the fat of the earth is monopolised by the few - I prayed that my countrymen might finally see that government of this form, Republicanism, one, democratic, and representative, is the nearest approach to the ideal of justice in this sublunar planet, and the fittest for freeman to adopt.

"Yes, here let me pause for a moment in my narrative and make this confession of faith. I believe in Republicanism with my whole heart and soul, with my tongue, and with my extensor and contractor muscles of my right arm, throughout my entire being from my innermost organ right out. This is my political creed. I have fought for its maintenance. I have endured privations innumerable in its maintenance still, and I am doomed to long prison tortures in its maintenance yet. And I do not regret it! Welcome the burden so long as there is principle to prop the weak human shoulder against it with its aid akin to the grace that comes from above. Believe me that principle will carry a man through and solace him in his deepest afflictions. It can make the brown bread of Kilmainham taste like the manna in the desert; it can gild the damp, chill cell of Portland with God's sunlight, and people it with consoling spirits. It always tells in the long run. For what is principle but truth, and truth is mighty and will prevail. Aye, prevail, even in Ireland."

## CHAPTER 12

# AN ENCOUNTER WITH INDIANS

But time was passing for Ricard. He still had to find his balloonist friends, Mr. Taunton and Don Juan Chevalier, and so he decided to travel into the interior. With the funds in his possession he arrayed himself in the garments of the country - the broad sombrero of Guyaquil straw, the baggy trousers bound around the waist with a coloured belt confined from the thigh with gaiters fitting over boots armed with monster spurs. Over this garb he wore a poncho. The physician supplied him with a horse - a spirited brown bay of Andalusian breed - in exchange for a box-sextant and a prismatic compass, which were all that remained of the store of poor Taunton. Mounted on his horse with a long white-handled knife peeping from the top of his gaiters he would defy his own mother to recognize Don Ricardo de Burgho as the yellow haired gossoon that served Father Daly's mass in Cork's own county.

At the end of the first day's journey out of Telcahuama he overtook two horsemen dressed exactly like himself. They were smoking as they jogged along. Ricard was dying for a smoke himself but did not have a light.

" *'El fulgo, senores?'* I politely requested.

" 'Mick, haven't you got a lucifer in your pocket to give that boy?'

"Could I believe my ears? No, I was not mistaken. The accent was pure Milesian, and I jumped off my horse, threw up my sombrero as high as any caubeen was kicked at a fair and gave one yell as loud as ever woke the echoes of Slievebloom!

"They were as glad to meet a countryman as I was, and delighted me by the information that there was an Irish colony, to which they belonged, on the side of the Cordilleras, two day's journey further on. The colony was much annoyed at the time by the depredations of unfriendly Indians; it had organized a band of Rangers, some eighty rifles strong, for its defence, and to this little Irish army my new found companions were making with all

*Don Ricardo De Burgho*
(Gabriel Clark Browne M.F.A)

speed, as an expedition was at hand. They had been dispatched to Talcahuana, and for what, do you think? To convey to the colony a pot of shamrocks which had arrived in a European ship, by the care of a Dungarvan sailor on board, one of their cousins.

"We arrived at the colony as the sun was setting the third day. Talk of the Peri of Eden, with the price of entrance. She was not half so happy as I when I heard the bitter 'carajo' yield place to the good natured 'begor!' - Castile elbowed aside by Munster.

"Our arrival was celebrated that evening by a fandango given at the house to which we were invited. The company, to the number of some thirty or forty persons, young and old, were assembled in the largest room in the house, the floor being hard clay. The only furniture contained in the room was a bed, and some benches upon which the couples seated themselves when not engaged in dancing. A singular custom prevails at these fandangoes. It is this: during the intervals between the waltzes, quadrilles and other dances, when the company is seated, a young lady takes the floor, solo, and after showing off her graces for general observation a few minutes, she approaches any gentleman she may select and perform a variety of pirouettes and other Terpsichorean movements before him for his special amusement and admiration, until he places on her head his hat or cap, as the case may be, when she dances away with it. The hat or cap has afterwards to be redeemed by some present, and this is usually in money. The motions of the females of all classes in the dance are highly graceful. The waltz is their favourite measure, and in this they appear to excel as much as the men do in horsemanship. During the progress of the dance the males and females improvise doggerel rhymes complimentary of the personal beauties and graces of those whom they admire as expressive of their love and devotion, which are chanted with the music of the instruments, and the whole company join in the chorus at the end of each verse. The din of voices is sometimes almost deafening. The custom, that is the money portion of it, I like as little as the sending round the plate at a wedding. It is more Spanish than Irish and more English than either. It reminded me of a pastime called 'Kiss-in-the Ring,' which I witnessed once on a Good Friday in St. James's Park, London, and I am inclined to think that some speculative Cockney must have introduced it into Chile."

One of his two companions to whom Ricard refers only as M— asked him to a shake down in his quarters which was a large stable in which were a number of men lying about in various attitudes, some smoking, a few playing cards, but the majority sleeping heavily. These, he told him, were his squad of Rifle Rangers, stout Irish lads, all, and he had given them the word to muster in the stable that night that they might be early in the saddle in the morning. M— asked him if he would join them on their expedition. Ricard was not too anxious. "Well, I don't belong to the colony and I have scruples against rushing unnecessarily into bloodshed. I raise my hand against no man without cause given. I shall go with you as a spectator and if conscience prevents me from fighting it does not hinder me from giving such assistance as lies in my power to the wounded." M— was more than satisfied with this reply.

The Rangers were on the move early next morning - fifteen of them. The main body had gone on ahead to the spot where they were to await the Indians. M—'s group was to seek out the enemy and lead them to where the main body waited in ambush.

"During the heat of the mid-day we drew saddle in the shadow of a grove of aracannia pines. Guards were set and we were prepared to take our siesta. M— lay beside me and before we sunk off into sleep an earnest conversation arose between a recumbent group a-near as to the conditions and prospects of the island from which they had come. Sundry mysterious hints were dropped in relation to a secret political association which, as far as I could gather, had for some time existed in Ireland. I listened with the greatest attention; but their allusions were altogether so vague that I was unable to arrive at any definite information on the matter. I own I was somewhat surprised to find there, so far away from home amid those wild solitudes, countrymen of my own, apparently, too, as imbued with revolutionary ideas as myself."

That night as they sat around the camp fire M— explained to Ricard what was happening in Ireland. A secret organisation - The Fenians - had been established and when the time was ripe they would rise. Though, at this time, Ricard was aware of the Phoenix Trials in Cork, he was not aware of the existence of the Fenians and as twilight deepened into the lines of night, and thoroughly convinced of the soundness of M—'s arguments and the truth of his statements - "if I did not then and there become a practical proselyte to his doctrines I can only say that I ought to have."

Just as the company was beginning to dispose themselves for sleep a sharp crack of a rifle rang through the forest followed by a savage yell. Naturally, they thought the Indians were upon them. Then into the camp burst one of their members - Thade Carroll - (the only one that Ricard names). He explained that, as he lay beside his post, he heard an approaching Indian. Thade challenged him and when the Indian went for his gun Thade shot him. As they were listening to Thade's story another shot rang out and M— fell dead. Ricard turned and fired his colt right into the centre of the little puff of smoke that lingered. A plaintive moan rose distinctly from the brushwood which told him that his shot had hit the target.

At this stage Ricard took charge and ordered the company back into the positions they held prior to Thade's appearance. "I beckoned the trooper nearest to me to my side and in a whisper, almost inaudible, instructed him to get back stealthily to the horses, lash them into fury, and let one loose - at the same time directing their guard to raise a cheer as of delivery. Implicitly my orders were obeyed, and in a minute the wild snorting of chargers and the shrill cries of men startled the forest. The ruse succeeded. A cloud of dark forms darted into the opening before us with a fiendish yell.

" 'Fire,' I shouted, and a withering volley flung them into confusion. They retreated as if appalled. Again they came with the fierce desire of vengeance for the slain braves of their band; but our cool, well directed fire repulsed them a second time and sent them reeling back.

"At that moment a loud triumphant shout rose from the rear, such a shout as the few men we had left in charge of the horse could not have raised. Hurrah! It was the main body of the Rangers come to our assistance! The enemy discovered it instinctively even before we did and fled in dismay, leaving us masters of the field.

"This, the first, is the only rencontre with the Indians I care to relate. By acclamation I was chosen Captain of the Irish lads in the room of the dead M—, whose remains we conveyed back to the colony, and buried with our best military honours."

# CHAPTER 13

# RICARD RETURNS TO NEW YORK

The time Ricard spent with the Rangers was the heartiest and jolliest he ever spent before or since. There was just enough dash in it to make it exciting. However, even the fast-changing, novelty-bearing life of the Rangers soon palled on his senses. Expenses were many and cash was running low. The life gradually became duller, no excitement but rarely; even the fandango every evening regularly became monotonous - the same dances, the same dancers, the same faces day after day. Much as he liked it Ricard found himself looking beyond it for a new occupation.

He resigned his elected position and left the colony. He will never forget that day: there were about 2,000 people in the settlement - Irish, Spanish and friendly Indians - and he had become a friend with all. Two months later he was employed as a tutor in the house of a Castilian gentleman. He performed these duties poorly. After adventures lasting four years he longed for a glance of old friends in New York and the States. As he had no further business in Chile, like the rest of the 'Gringos', he went home.

He was shipwrecked off the coast of Peru on his return journey and came ashore near Lima. His itinerary then brought him to Callao, to Tombas, to Pasti and to Aquequi. "I had made all arrangements to return to the States; and on New Year's day, 1861, after a career of over four years of adventure, rich in stirring scenes, I returned to New York city.

" 'Had I made my fortune?' Well, I'll tell. I did not devote those years to money-making, but rather to sight-seeing. Had not accidents befallen me, I would, however, have a few thousand, which, doubtless, I would spend in still 'going on'. I don't regret one of those years, though, doubtless, the wise ones of the world may say they are so many years thrown away. And yet, though barren of any pecuniary advancement, they have taught me much of love and duty; giving a breadth and depth to one's feelings, and showing me the world was not made for self, that there is a higher feeling than a money greed, though rarely cultivated.

"I gained no money during that buoyant time, but I gained much knowledge of men and countries and lost illusions, which I consider still a gain, and great gain. I shall look back on it as a clearing of brighter green than common in memory which is not quite waste, and if God ever grants it that I shall be a father, I shall pray that my son may have a similar ordeal to pass through. It purifies a man and indurates him. None amongst us knows what is in him until he is put on his own mettle. Our modern European society is over civilised; we could afford more nature, more Robinson Crusoe - more rifle and less desk, more tent and less city-basement, said the boys out 'on their own hook.'

"When I stepped again on the pavements of old Broadway, I had, as before, a light purse, but a lighter heart; and exchanging my sombrero and poncho for the latest Fifth Avenue fashions, I thought I had nothing better to do than to relapse into civilization."

***The Editor of Ricard's Autobiography, John O'Shea, inserts a note here in the narrative.***

The handwriting at this stage of the narrative loses the fine clerkly style which distinguished it in earlier chapters. It has the appearance of having been written by a wearied man, one who was beginning to lose hope and heart from the weight of terrible accusation brought against him. The reader must always bear in mind that at the time these souvenirs of free adventurous life were penned, Ricard Burke was lying in jail, treated as a felon before conviction, and darkly threatened with the gallows as punishment for a crime committed by men outside the prison walls while he was actually detained in them.

His leisure, long enough in God's good sooth, was liable to interruption at any moment; this man was shifted from cell to cell by his alarmed jailors; he was worried by anxiety of mind, and harassed by the preparations of his approaching trial, therefore, as will at once be clear he could not give the manuscript the attention that would be looked for under other circumstances. Recollecting these things, the rapidity with which the circumstances attending the latter portion of his sojourn in Chile, his experiences as tutor, and his diversified voyagings on his return to New York is passed over, is easy of explanation. Indeed, the difficulty is to conceive how any human being in his awful position - a charge of treason-felony laid against him, and the possible capital charges of high treason and wilful murder impending - could have brought his mind to bear on such a work as this Autobiography. But, as inaction is the severest of trials to an energetic spirit like his, Burke may have wisely thought it his readiest relief to write and write and keep writing, that he might kill thought and people solitude. Men who have been confined to solitude have assured the Editor of these papers that without some mental occupation which they had the prudence to set themselves - the reading of some deep book that suggested reflections, or better, the study of some problems in mathematics - they would have gone mad; are we not justified in believing that Burke devoted himself to this labour of the pen, that his active brain, too, might have some means to expand its forces? This Autobiography, in short, may be looked on as a sort of celebrated safety-valve. ***(End of Editor's Note.)***

As the Editor's note explains the rest of Ricard's autobiography is quite sketchy. He just gives us the merest outline of his services in the army of the United States. "However, on another occasion, with less gloom brooding over me than that whose long hours I have endeavoured to brighten by these scribblings, I may be tempted to retrace my own experiences in the struggle of Republicanism against Rebellion, and fight my battles o'er again." If Ricard did retrace his experiences in the American Civil War and, indeed, his experiences in the Fenian movement, they have not yet seen the light of day.

"I was in the publishing house of Sadlier and Co., of New York, in a dry region of folios and cyphers, ramparted by tall columns of foolscap - a tremendous transition from the rover's life - when the fratricidal gun boomed across Charleston Harbour. The North was thrilled to its core. What! Had Americans, Republicans, the children of those who fought the English at New Orleans, actually dared to fire on that flag? Shame! It was enough to galvanize the bones of Franklin, to make Washington quiver in his shroud. Had Niagra Falls turned in its mad course and commenced to flow upwards, the North could not have been more astonished. The nation started to its feet, and the nation had reason.

"I am a convinced and conscientious Federalist, not a fanatic one. I went in for the North for three reasons; because its cause was a Republican cause and I am a Republican; because it sought to abolish merchandize in man as a chattel - a good old relic of British connection - and I am a Christian; and because the United States had been the asylum of impoverished Ireland and I am Irish, that is to say, I am grateful. I went in for the North with hatred for Southern principles, none for Southern men.

"I am powerless to realise to you the wild excitement that reigned in New York when the first call to arms came. My scientific lectures and classes at the Cooper Institute, the sketching and studying with which I was to occupy my leisure hours were abandoned. The clarion of the Republic had sounded the alarm. Every young man who had any sentiment of pride or instinct of duty, shouldered his musket. I, trained in bitter experience, felt that my poor right arm might be of service to the Union. And when good and great 'Old Abe' demanded soldiers to protect the honour of the Stars and Stripes, as John Savage has sung it -

*To plant that flag*
*On tower and crag*
*With the people's voice of freedom.*

I found myself a high private in the 15th New York Light Infantry. That was my maiden regiment in Uncle Sam's service, but this enlistment having been made for three years, was declared illegal. The regiment got the opportunity to leave the Flag, but I did not choose to leave it. Almost immediately on my discharge from the Light Infantry I joined the ranks of the 15th New York Regiment of Engineers."

***(This ends Ricard O'Sullivan Burke's Autobiography.)***

# CHAPTER 14

# THE FENIAN RISING

The Fenian movement had its origins in the disasters which overwhelmed Ireland in the late 1840s. O'Connell's Repeal Movement foundered on the resolute action of the British Government. The Young Irelander's attempt at a rising came to naught in 1848. The calamity of the Famine shattered the spirit of the Irish people and the exodus began.

With the death of Fintan Lawlor, whatever revolutionary organization existed in Ireland up to then virtually disappeared. But there still was a powerful centre of disaffection in New York which had a large Irish population. By 1850, 133,000 - a quarter of the whole population of the city - were Irish born. In New York the revolutionary organization of 1848 survived.

In 1853 James Stephens, a Kilkenny man, returned to Ireland from Paris where he had gone after the abortive rising of 1848. While in Paris he had fought on the republican side during Louis Napoleon's coup d'etat of 1851 where he earned the reputation of being a Marxist. Whether he was or not he never tried to impose his views on his colleagues at a later date in the Fenians. He reached Dublin in 1856 to find that the secret societies of 1849 had now collapsed. His first action was to make a tour of the country on foot to find out the opinions of the people. Having completed this tour Stephens seems to have done little until a message came from John O'Mahony and Michael Dohney in America in the autumn of 1857 and asking if he would set up a revolutionary organization in Ireland with which the American exiles would co-operate. Stephens undertook to do this and a secret revolutionary organization was launched in Dublin on St. Patrick's Day, 1858, dedicated to the establishment in Ireland of an independent democratic republic. This was the society which was later to be known as the Irish Republican Brotherhood. (I.R.B.)

This was a secret oath bound society. The original oath administered to the members appears to have run along the following lines. *"I ... swear in the presence of God, to renounce all allegiance to the Queen of England, and to take arms and fight at a moment's warning, and to make Ireland an Independent Democratic Republic, and to yield implicit obedience to the commanders and superiors of this secret society ..."* As yet the organization had no name but the members referred to it as "Our Body", "Our Movement" or "Our Organization". It did not assume the title of Irish Republican Brotherhood for some years. The name Fenian was bestowed on the society by John O'Mahony who, as a Gaelic scholar, admired the Fianna and Fionn McCumhaill. The society was organized on lines quite similar to such societies on the continent - here the influence of Stephens was evident. At the head of the organization was the Head Centre - in this case, Stephens, himself - and below him came numerous Circles. Each Circle, which was commanded by a Centre, consisted of 820 men. Under each Centre were nine Bs or captains and under each B were nine Cs or sergeants and each C commanded nine Ds or privates. The idea was that no member should be known to any other member except those in his own circle. This rule was not always strictly adhered to and made the organisation very vulnerable to spies.

Stephens started on another tour of the country, this time accompanied by Thomas Clarke Luby. Before long they found a little organization called the Phoenix Society in Skibbereen. This was a literary and debating society which had been founded by Jeremiah O'Donovan Rossa. The members became enthusiastic followers of Stephens and provided an impetus for the growth of Fenianism in south-west Cork. However, arrests soon followed and Rossa and others stood trial - the Phoenix Trials. They pleaded guilty and bound themselves to be of good behaviour and Rossa was released having spent nearly eight months in jail.

The organization was well on its way to success in 1861 when Terence Bellew McManus, one of the 1848 leaders, died in California on January 15th and the nationalists there decided to send his body home for burial. The funeral, in Dublin, was an impressive demonstration. As the procession passed the spot in Thomas Street where Robert Emmett was hanged in 1803 each

*Jeremiah O'Donovan Rossa*

*Ricard O'Sullivan Burke*

*John (Pagan) O'Leary*

*John O'Mahony*

contingent stood for a moment. At every historic spot, on the way to Glasnevin, there were appropriate demonstrations. Many of those from the country who had attended the funeral were sworn into the organization and they, in turn, started it in their own home districts. From that time on the organization began to flourish. It had established a relatively strong position in the towns particularly in the south and east of the country. Its members which numbered about 80,000 were drawn mainly from the working class - labourers, small farmers and clerks. The organization had infiltrated the British Army in Dublin and boasted of thousands of recruits among the soldiers.

McManus's body did not lie-in-state in the cathedral as Archbishop Cullen would not allow this. It was a radical priest, Patrick Lavelle, who led the prayers at the graveside. This was because the Fenian movement was strongly condemned by the Catholic Church. This opposition was based on the fact that it was a secret, oath bound organization, although John Devoy was convinced that Cardinal Cullen, Archbishop of Dublin, would have opposed it anyway because of its extremism. He said that the Catholic Church excommunicated all those who were engaged in secret societies and its members were refused absolution in confession unless they promised to give up the organisation. Some of the altar denunciations seemed very unjust in their sentiments. Bishop Moriarty of Kerry said: "Hell is not hot enough nor eternity long enough to punish the Fenians." There were only two bishops in the country who did not adopt this hard line - Archbishop McHale of Tuam and Bishop Keane of Cloyne. Despite the stiff opposition the Fenian leadership withstood the hostility of the Catholic Church, creating what many historians see as a watershed in Church / State relations in Ireland.

In November, 1863, Stephens founded the paper, "The Irish People" to put the ideals of the society before the people. Joint editors were Thomas Clarke Luby, John O'Leary and Charles Kickham. O'Donovan Rossa ran the business side of the paper and John Haltigan from Kilkenny was the printer. It was not the financial success it had been hoped and never managed to compete against "The Nation." It continued to be published until it was suppressed by the Government on Sept. 15th, 1865.

The outbreak of the American Civil War in 1861 proved to be a setback for Stephens as it confined American-Irish energies for several years to the other side of the Atlantic. On the other hand it provided the Irish in America with experience of modern warfare. In 1864 Stephens visited America and toured the Union armies recruiting members for the Fenians. He states in a letter to John O'Mahony in New York that he had a hundred thousand men ready for Ireland!. It is highly probable that Ricard O'Sullivan Burke became a member of the Fenians at that time.

When Stephens returned from America, encouraged by the growth in numbers in Ireland, America and in the British Army, he announced to practically everybody that 1865 would be *"the year of action."* The Government, however, knew the broad outlines of what was going on in secret and the identities of all the important people through its system of informers. In the autumn of 1865 the Government took action. The Fenian newspaper, "The Irish People" was suppressed and the leaders, O'Leary, O'Donovan Rossa, Luby and others were arrested. Stephens managed to avoid arrest only to be captured on November 11th, 1865 along with Kickham, Hugh Brophy and Edward Duffy. Stephens' dramatic rescue from prison alarmed the authorities but was not of any practical value to the Fenian movement. The organization was hard hit by this strike. Most of its leaders were in prison and the habeas corpus suspension act gave the police wide powers in detaining suspects. The posting of the Fenian regiments abroad deprived the organization of an important source of manpower and arms. As well as that, the organization was seriously divided by internal disputes about leadership and policy. The Fenian movement from then on is full of personal quarrels and charges of cowardice levelled against some members - many of them directed towards Stephens, himself.

Stephens, having promised that 1865 was to be the year of action now announced that 1866 would be the year. But 1866 came and went, Stephens remained in America and nothing was done.

*James Stephens*

*Thomas Clark Luby*

*Terence Bellew McManus*

Police Gazette

HUE-AND-CRY.

Published for Ireland every Tuesday and Friday.

By the Lord Lieutenant-General and General Governor of Ireland.

A PROCLAMATION.

WODEHOUSE.

WHEREAS, *James Stephens* has been an active Member of a Treasonable Conspiracy against the Queen's authority in *Ireland*, and escaped from the *Richmond Prison* on the *Twenty-fourth* day of November last.

NOW WE, being determined to bring the said *James Stephens* to Justice, Do hereby offer a Reward of

ONE THOUSAND POUNDS

to any person or persons who shall give such Information as shall lead to the Arrest of the said *James Stephens*, and a further Reward of

One Thousand Pounds

to any person or persons WHO SHALL ARREST the said *James Stephens*

AND WE do hereby offer a further Reward of

*THREE HUNDRED POUNDS*

to any Person or Persons who shall give such information as shall lead to the Arrest of any one whosoever [illegible] has knowingly harboured or received, or concealed, or assisted or aided in any way whatsoever in his Escape from Arrest, the said *James Stephens*.

And We do also hereby offer a FREE PARDON, in addition to the above-mentioned REWARD, to any Person or Persons concerned in the Escape of the said JAMES STEPHENS who shall give such Information as shall lead to his Arrest as aforesaid.

Given at Her Majesty's Castle of *Dublin*, this [illegible] day of *January*, 1866.

By His Excellency's Command,

THOS. A. LARCOM.

*Description of the above-named JAMES STEPHENS.—*

*Reward offered for James Stephens*

Irishmen who had served in the American Civil War played an important role in the actual organisation of the Fenian Rising which took place in 1867. Between 1865 and 1867 many Irish American officers, including O'Sullivan Burke, visited Ireland and England. These men helped to depose Stephens from the leadership of the Fenian movement in the closing days of 1866 and Col. Thomas J. Kelly (of the Manchester rescue) became head of the organisation. Early in January, 1867, Kelly and a group of Fenian officers, including O'Sullivan Burke, reached England and, after some hurried consultations, it was decided to rise in rebellion on 11 February.

However, whatever slender hopes there may have been of a successful rising in 1867, the activities of informers such as John Joseph Corydon ensured that the authorities and the police knew a great deal about the planned rising. Part of the plan was to seize Chester Castle with its store of arms and rush them to Ireland. Hundreds of Fenians assembled in Chester that day to take part in the raid. Again, due to the activities of informers, the plan was well known in advance, the guard on the castle was strengthened, the Volunteers had been called out and a detachment of the Guards was on its way from London. So the operation had to be called off. This led to the cancellation of the February Rising. The countermanding order did not reach Kerry in time. There, Col. John O'Connor seized the coastguard station at Cahirciveen. When O'Connor captured a constabulary dispatch rider and found in his pocket a document addressed to himself telling him that the February Rising had been cancelled he disbanded his small force. Eventually he, himself, returned to America where he died a few years later.

A new date was then fixed - the night of the 4-5 March. From a military standpoint it was doomed from the start. The favourable elements which prevailed in 1865 were no longer present. The night of the Rising was bitterly cold with snow storms. The main areas of unrest were Dublin, Tipperary, Limerick and Cork and on a more limited scale in Louth, Clare and Waterford.

**Dublin**
During the evening of March 5th the Fenians began to move out of the city towards the assembly points near the Dublin mountains. One section captured two small police barracks at Glencullen and Stepaside. Another section, as they marched towards Tallaght, was confronted by a group of fourteen constabulary and, after an exchange of fire, the Fenians dispersed. This more or less quickly put an end to the Rising in Dublin.

**Tipperary**
The Rising in Tipperary, as in other parts of the country, was a failure through a lack of arms. They had not in the whole county enough arms to face fifty policemen. However, three police stations were attacked and there were some minor skirmishes with military and police patrols. The arrest of Godfrey Massey at Limerick Junction provided the Government with an invaluable source of information when he turned informer.

**Limerick**
The only serious fighting in Limerick was at Killmallock where the Fenians attacked the police barracks but were unsuccessful. Some 250 Fenians tried to take the barrack at Ardagh, again without success.

**Cork**
In Cork a party of Fenians under the command of James O'Brien and William Mackey Lomasney seized a coastguard station at Knockadoon and a police barracks was burnt. There were encounters with the police at Midleton and Castlemartyr. The insurgents were poorly armed and were soon forced to disperse.

**Last Action**
Mopping up operations continued for several weeks. The last dramatic action of the Rising took place on the last day of March. The leaders of the attack on Knockadoon coastguard station were surprised in Kilcooney Wood in Co. Cork. There, Peter O'Neill Crowley was killed and the others arrested.

The Rising was sharply condemned in the British press which demanded that severe penalties be imposed on the captured Fenians. In Ireland most journalists wrote in the same vein. Dr. Leahy, the Catholic Archbishop of Cashel, described the Rising as a source of grief and shame. Though the Fenian's fortunes could hardly have been at a lower ebb they still retained a certain amount of sympathy among the people. It could be said that the Rising marked the end of the old Fenian conspiracy. But with the foundation, in 1867, of Clan na Gael in America, Fenianism lived on for the next fifty years although, at times, had a hard struggle to survive. It was maintained almost entirely by moral and material aid from Clan na Gael and in 1916 the kind of rising Stephens had hoped to see in 1865 occurred. It was planned mainly by men who were members of the I.R.B. and led by an old Fenian, Tom Clarke.

# CHAPTER 15

# THE IRISH AND THE AMERICAN CIVIL WAR

When the American Civil War broke out the Irish joined both the Union and Confederate armies in droves. It is estimated that 150,000 Irishmen fought on the Union side. The figure for the Confederate army was between 20,000 and 40,000 - probably in the region of 30,000. The reason for the higher figure in the Union army was because most Irish emigrants settled in the North-East of the United States. However, a greater proportion of the Irish in the south joined the Confederate army - probably 80% of all able bodied Irishmen out of a total of 85,000 in the south participated in the conflict.

Really the Irish had no compelling reason to join the Union army. The Irish in the north were despised and looked upon as outsiders. In many cases employers found blacks more acceptable and noted in their ads that "Irishmen need not apply." Society's contempt could not have been more clear than it was in an ad for household help that sought applicants of "any country or colour except Irish." The Irish were Catholics in a predominantly Protestant country. Unlike Ricard O'Sullivan Burke, the Irish emigrants were 90% Democrats and it was a Republican war. They feared the emancipation of the slaves because they would be competing with each other in the same job market. So, basically, the Irish were anti black. The Confederates were doing what the Irish wanted to do - break the union. As well as that the Irish in Ireland supported the Confederate cause.

So why then did the Irish answer the country's call to arms as readily as any group in society?

(1) First of all they were grateful to the United States for allowing them into the country and giving them work. Burke in his autobiography gives that as one of the reasons he joined the army. "The United States had been the asylum of impoverished Ireland." The feeling was general that whatever hardships the Irish had met in America, they owed it a great

deal, and allegiance to the government in its hour of need was one way to repay that debt.

(2) The Irish were despised and treated as outcasts in American society. They wanted to be accepted and they wanted to prove their loyalty to their new country. They wanted to show they were good Americans though they were Irish. The Boston Pilot was well aware of the prejudice the Irish encountered in America and it had strongly rejected the party of Lincoln in the 1850s, but in 1861 it told its Irish Catholic readers that they must "Stand by the Union; fight for the Union; die by the Union." The same paper also looked forward to the day when future generations of Irish-Americans could proudly say that "we too are Americans, and our fathers bled and died to establish this country."

(3) Many of the Irish wanted to gain military experience so that they could go back home and fight for Ireland. The solid core of the Irish-American soldiers wanted to use the experience gained in the war on Ireland's behalf. When the war was over one leading Irish-American paper carried two leading articles. One was entitled "The War is Over." The other was entitled "The Next War" - a reference to the coming conflict with England. One Irish-American poem made this point very clearly:

*When concord and peace to this land are restored,*
*And the union's established for ever,*
*Brave sons of Hibernia, oh, sheathe not the sword;—*
*You will then have a union to sever.*

(4) The English supported the Confederacy so the Irish felt that they should be supporting the other side. Many believed that the break up of the Union would only enhance British power in the world and that, in fact, for this reason the British themselves earnestly desired the destruction of their young republican rival. The Irish also felt that if there was conflict in Ireland that the Americans would support the Irish. After all

they had helped to maintain the Union so the Americans should support the Irish in their disputes with England.

(5) Joining the Union army gave steady employment and money. The dislocation of the economy caused by secession hit the working classes hardest. Unemployed Irish labourers often found enlistment in the army as the only alternative to starvation. Pay was $13 per month. These economic pressures eased as the war went on, but economic incentives to enlist, as the number of recruits fell, enticed the impoverished Irish to continue volunteering. A new recruit could earn up to $700 in bounties - County Bounty-$300; State Bounty- $75; U.S. Bounty-$302.

(6) Many Irish just joined for the sheer love of combat. Irishmen have always been attracted by military service and from earliest times found employment in foreign armies. The Irish soldier was courageous, resourceful, cheerful and strong. They seemed to be able to fight everyone's battles but their own. General Richard Taylor of the Confederate army had this to say about the Irish. "Strange people these Irish. Fighting everyone's battles and cheerfully taking the hot end of the poker. They are only to be found wanting when engaged in what they believe to be their national cause."

The Irish joined the Confederate army for much the same reasons. They too were grateful for what the region had done for them. Patrick Ronayne Cleburne, the Cork born general in the Confederate army, when giving his reasons for joining the army wrote: "I am with the South in life or in death, in victory or defeat. I never owned a negro and care nothing for them, but these people have been my friends and have stood up for me on all occasions." John Mitchell, the Young Irelander, who fought on the southern side, wrote: "I die willingly for the South. But, oh! that this was for Ireland."

Up to 1860 the Irish in the Southern States were as ardent in supporting the Union as were those in the North. However, after the election of Lincoln as president, they feared the liberation of the slaves and felt the region was under threat. As adopted

*Union Headstones, Gettysburg National Cemetery*

*Confederate Headstones, Arlington National Cemetery*

Southerners they fought to oppose any imposition being placed on them. To them the dissolution of the union in America was similar to the repeal of the Union in Ireland.

While the numbers of Irish in the south were not great, they, nevertheless, volunteered in droves. They formed their own companies in many cities and towns. Companies such as True Men of the South, Sarsfield's Saracens, Davis Guards, Irish Jasper Greens of Georgia, Emerald Guards of Alabama, Louisiana Tigers and the First Virginia Irish Battalion fought on the southern side. There even was an Irish Brigade in the Confederate Army. When no Irish company was available they served everywhere even in the Polish Brigade.

Many of them were stout hearty fellows who fought bravely, particularly under pressure and they needed a strong hand to control them. Alcohol, religion and letters from home helped to relieve the boredom of army life. Alcohol was a big problem and they consumed vast amounts of bootleg whiskey. Gambling with cards and dice was also a problem. Attending mass was very important to the Irish soldiers and they were a cause of a religious revival in the Confederate army as the tide of battle went against them. They liked the calmness and serenity of mass before the battle.

The Confederate army suffered high desertion rates and this increased as the war went on. After the fall of Atlanta at any one time two thirds of the army were absent without leave. In all there were 104,000 Confederate desertions. These deserters did not join the other side but merely went home to look after things there. The Irish did not have much sympathy for turncoats. However, they did have the highest desertion rates and also the highest casualty rates in the South.

In the Northern States, while many Irish-Americans answered the call to arms, there were some who were not enamoured of the Republican war aims, especially emancipation. Many Irish-Americans were fiercely anti Negro as they were competing for the same jobs at the bottom of the social order. They had frequently rioted against the black people in northern cities and continued to do so during the war. Irish-Americans participated in anti-draft riots in the coalfields of eastern Pennsylvania, in New York and in Boston.

Most of the Irish like O'Sullivan Burke served in predominantly American units where their achievements seldom redounded to the benefit of the Irish-American community. The performance of the Irish in battle became associated with the Irish Brigade led by the Young Irelander, Thomas Francis Meagher. The members of this brigade were either Irish born or sons of Irish emigrants. They were drawn mainly from the labouring class in the North East and the vast majority of them were Catholics.

Statistics demonstrate that the brigade's fighting reputation was well deserved. It served in the northern army that sustained most casualties - the army of the Potomac. The brigade itself suffered more than 4,000 casualties, despite the fact it never put as many as 3,000 in the field at any one time. During the war, two soldiers died of disease or accident for every one who died as a consequence of battle. For the Irish Brigade, however, the ratio was reversed: two died of battle wounds for every one who died of disease or accident. Irish nationalists were thrilled with the exploits of the Irish soldiers in the war, believing that the reputation of all Irishmen benefited from the courage demonstrated by the Irish Brigade. "It has restored the somewhat tarnished military image of our race," declared the Fenian *Irish People.*

What benefits accrued to the Irish in America as a result of the Civil War? Unfortunately, very few. The hoped-for acceptance did not come very quickly. After the civil war discrimination against the Irish still continued. Many newspapers carried cartoons from time to time poking fun at the Irish. Anti-Catholic feelings were still very strong throughout the United States. Organisations like the American Protective Association promoted the idea that a papal conspiracy was plotting to overthrow American institutions. There was no great escape from poverty and the Irish still made up the bulk of the common labourers, dock workers, coachmen, draymen, waiters, cooks, barbers and servants in the cities.

Elsewhere, Irish workers poured into the mining industry and they dominated canal and railroad construction.

The Irish-Americans also failed in the liberation of Ireland. Too many of them never had a chance to fight for Ireland because they spilled their blood in an American war instead. The *Boston Pilot* lamented in 1863 that "We did not cause this war, (but) vast numbers of our people have perished in it." It declared emphatically that "the spirit for the war is dead! Our fighters are dead."

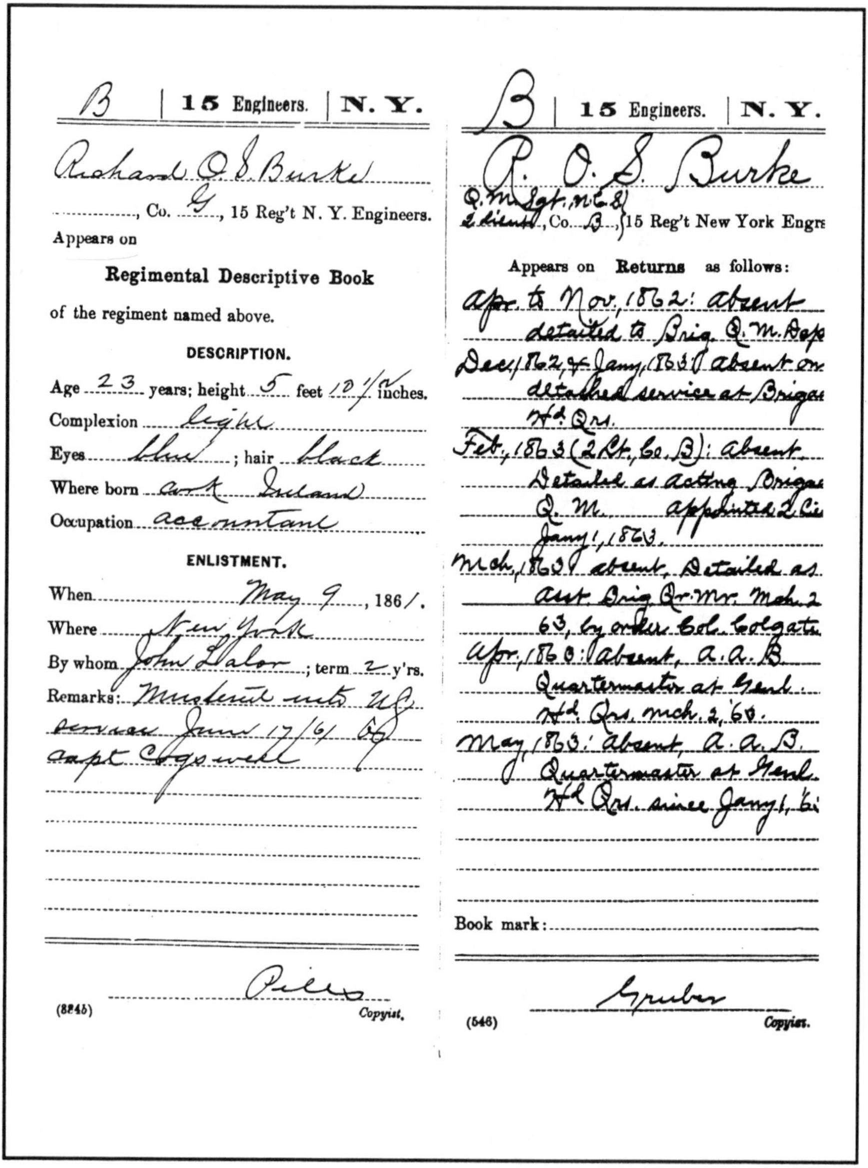

B | **15** Engineers. | **N. Y.**

Richard O. S. Burke

............, Co. G, 15 Reg't N. Y. Engineers.

Appears on

**Regimental Descriptive Book**

of the regiment named above.

**DESCRIPTION.**

Age 23 years; height 5 feet 10 1/2 inches.

Complexion light

Eyes blue ; hair black

Where born Cork Ireland

Occupation accountant

**ENLISTMENT.**

When May 9, 1861.

Where New York

By whom John Dalor ; term 2 y'rs.

Remarks: Mustered into U.S. service June 17/61 by Capt Cogswell

(8845) Pillis Copyist.

B | **15** Engineers. | **N. Y.**

R. O. S. Burke

Q.M. Sgt. N.C.S. / 2 Lieut., Co. B, 15 Reg't New York Engrs

Appears on **Returns** as follows:

Apr. to Nov. 1862: absent detailed to Brig. Q. M. Dep

Dec. 1862, & Jany. 1863: absent on detached service at Brigade Hd. Qrs.

Feb. 1863 (2 Lt. Co. B): absent. Detailed as acting Brigade Q. M. appointed 2 Lieut. Jany. 1, 1863.

Mch. 1863: absent. Detailed as Asst Brig Qr. Mr. Mch. 2 63, by order Col. Colgate

Apr. 1863: absent, A. A. B. Quartermaster at Genl. Hd. Qrs. Mch. 2, 63.

May 1863: absent, A. A. B. Quartermaster at Genl. Hd. Qrs. since Jany. 1, 63

Book mark: ............

(546) Gruber Copyist.

*Part of Ricard's Civil War Record*

## CHAPTER 16

# RICARD AND THE FENIAN RISING

When the American Civil War broke out on April 12th, 1861, Ricard did not delay in joining the Federal Army. As he states in his autobiography he first joined the 15th New York Light Infantry. This enlistment was declared illegal. Ricard immediately enlisted in the 15th New York Regiment of Engineers on May 9th, 1861 in New York. Soon after joining he saw action at the first battle of Bull Run where he was colour bearer for his regiment. Here the Federal Army suffered defeat and retreated to Washington. While in Washington his regiment underwent training as an engineer unit where Ricard made rapid progress in the Engineering School and soon became very proficient.

He served right through the four years of the Civil War, taking part in the siege of Yorktown in 1862, the Battle of Gloucester, the fierce fighting of the Seven Day Battle from Mechanicsville to Malvern Hill and at the Battle of Franklin's Crossing. He was present at the crossing of the Rappahannock to attack Fredericksburg. The 15th New York Engineers under Lt. Michael McGrath and of which Burke was a member were charged with building a second bridge across the river on December 11th, 1862. Building started at 3am on a cold foggy night. Wooden planks were laid over the sides of long narrow punts connecting the plain at the foot of Stafford Heights with the southern fringe of Fredericksburg. Work proceeded until 6am. At this stage the fog cleared and the Confederates opened fire on the bridge builders. At 8.15 the final section was being laid when heavy enemy fire forced the engineers to retire briefly.

More than once in the course of this terrible struggle, Burke owed his life to his extraordinary presence of mind. He was travelling with a party of mounted men through the enemy's country, and happening to cross a little hillock with a single orderly in advance of the main company he knocked at the door of a farmhouse. An old man appeared on the threshold. Burke asked

*Bridge built in 24 hours by the Engineering Corps of the Federal Army.*

*A view of the earthworks in front of the city of Petersburg, Virginia.*

him had he seen any of the grey jackets pass. The old man said he had not and invited Burke to come in and share whatever he had to offer. Burke dismounted and noticed something suspicious about the old man. He was in fact manoeuvring to get Burke seated with his back to the door. Burke did not fall for the ruse. He ordered the old man to open the door and three Confederate soldiers were lurking inside. Burke summoned the rest of the party and, as he was as magnanimous as he was brave, pardoned the old man and permitted his would-be assassins to escape.

In 1863 he was assigned to the staff of the Chief Engineer at General Grant's Headquarters at Petersburg, Virginia. One of the most notable sieges of the war was at Petersburg and here Burke was in charge of fifteen miles of earthworks in front of the city, as General Grant tried to subdue the Confederate Army under General Robert E. Lee. The siege dragged on through the winter of 1864. Eventually, Lee's lines became too thin to hold. 'No food, no horses, no reinforcements.' To avoid shedding more blood, Lee surrendered at Appomattox Courthouse on April 9th, 1865, and effectively brought the war to a close.

Burke made rapid progress in the Union Army, first as Quarter Master Sergeant in August, 1861, as a lieutenant on January 1st, 1863, then as captain and the rank of Colonel by brevet was confirmed on him just before he was mustered out of the service at Fort Barry, Virginia, on June 13th, 1865. He had gone through the whole war without a scratch, but on the day of the mustering out, the men of his company celebrated too wisely and were firing off their rifles indiscriminately, when a bullet grazed his hand, inflicting a slight wound. While in the army he joined the Fenians in New York before his regiment left for Washington and helped to organise several circles in the Army of the Potomac - Grant's Army in the east - and he, himself, was the head of one of these circles - The Brothers Sheares' Circle.

After leaving the army he went to New York and reported to John O'Mahony, then Head Centre of the Fenian Brotherhood. While he was waiting instructions he worked as a bookkeeper in a publishing house. A few months later he travelled to Ireland and

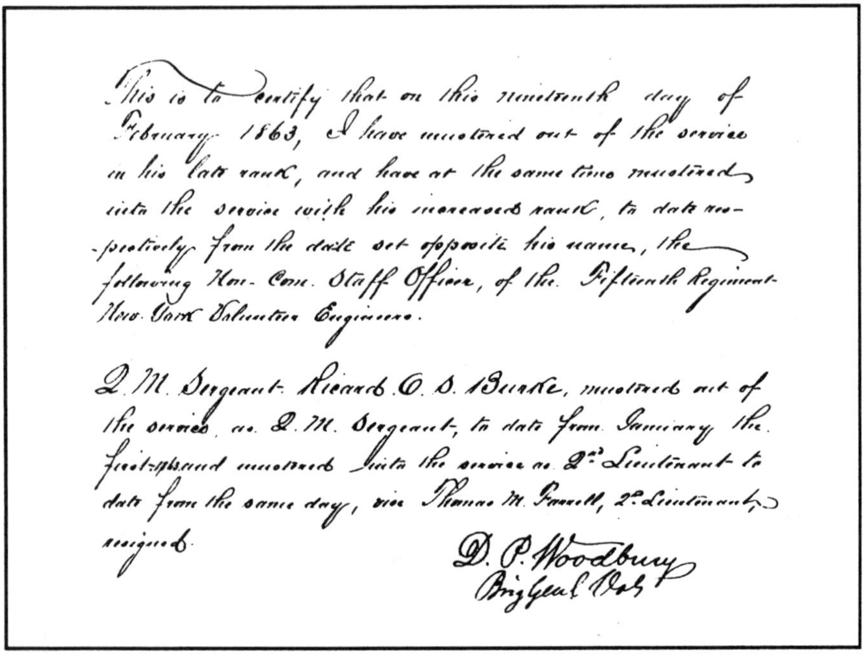

This is to certify that on this nineteenth day of February 1863, I have mustered out of the service in his late rank, and have at the same time mustered into the service with his increased rank, to date respectively from the date set opposite his name, the following Non-Com. Staff Officer, of the Fifteenth Regiment New York Volunteer Engineers.

Q.M. Sergeant Ricard O.S. Burke, mustered out of the service as Q.M. Sergeant, to date from January the first, and mustered into the service as 2nd Lieutenant to date from the same day, vice Thomas M. Farrell, 2nd Lieutenant, resigned.

D. P. Woodbury
Brig Genl Vols

*Ricard's Promotion to Lieutenant.*

reported to Colonel Thomas J. Kelly. In December, 1865, he went to England with the instructions to buy arms for the Fenian Movement in anticipation of a Rising. He set up business in Birmingham under the name of Edward C. Winslow - Merchant and Commission Agent. He made extensive purchases and between December 25th and January 13th, 1866 the total amount paid out by him was about £2,000. These arms were stored in Liverpool for delivery to Ireland. Packages were shipped from Liverpool to Cork addressed to Daly & Co., Drapers. These were seized in Cork by the police and on being opened they were found to contain arms which were identified as having been sold to Burke in Birmingham.

After the passing of 1865, which Stephens had declared to be the "Year of Action", matters became stagnant in Ireland in 1866 awaiting news from Stephens in America. In July, 1866, Burke was in Liverpool again on Fenian business. It is difficult to actually trace Burke's steps at this period, but he was frequently going to and from America for Fenian purposes and he was in constant communication with the leading Fenian leaders of the period. He also visited Ireland in 1866.

At the beginning of 1867 Burke returned to London accompanied by some of the American officers. He lodged at Tavistock Street with Godfrey Massey who later turned informer and gave evidence at Burke's trial. It was this group of American officers, Burke included, who finally decided on a date for the Rising, first in February and finally in March. When this date was decided upon Burke was sent to Waterford to take charge there.

**THE WATERFORD FENIANS**

In his book, *"Recollections of an Irish Rebel,"* John Devoy describes the Fenian Rising in Waterford as follows:

"Colonel Ricard O'Sullivan Burke was assigned to the command of Waterford in the Rising, but less than fifty answered the call. As they were too few in number and short of arms to do anything effective, Burke marched them into Tipperary to effect a junction with the men there, but when he got across the border the next day the 'Tips' were all scattered, so he had to send them home without any attempt at a fight."

But to judge the Waterford Fenians on this fiasco is to ignore the very real potential of the movement there. Relative to the population and in particular, to the number of Catholics in the population, Waterford was not in the first rank of Fenian counties. The cities of Dublin and Cork were, without doubt, the strongholds of the Fenians followed closely by Tipperary and Limerick. But, based on the number of arrests after the passing of Habeas Corpus Suspension Act, the next group of Fenian centres included Waterford, Kilkenny, Carlow and Clare. There was a strong circle of Fenians based in Waterford City. One reason for this was the fact that, shortly after the founding of the Fenians, Waterford was one of the first recruiting grounds visited by Stephens, Luby and Joseph Denieffe.

"On my arrival in Dublin, Luby was sent to the South while Stephens and I went on to Waterford. At that time we did not make much headway in the city of Waterford, but it afterwards became a stronghold of national activity. John Dillon, who kept an extensive wheelwright business, became one of the leaders, and for many years was the 'center' of the city. He was a most prudent and conservative man but, at the same time, an intense Nationalist, and carried on his work with such secrecy and precision that the Government remained completely in the dark regarding the existence of the organization until towards the close of the movement.

"Denis B. Cashman was another of the leading spirits in Waterford. He was chief clerk for a legal firm and had a wide circle of friends among whom he instilled his patriotic principles. W. K. Hearn, Terence Kent, John Kenny, John Topin and P. J. Donahue were also prominent leaders in Waterford." (A personal narrative of the Irish Revolutionary Brotherhood by Joseph Denieffe.)

The suspension of habeas corpus led to the arrests of hundreds. Every Irish-American who could be found was imprisoned. In Waterford the arrests were mainly in the city and were drawn from a wide range of trades such as draper's assistant, clerk, coach builder, etc. John Dillon was arrested prior to the passing of the act on February 16th, 1866. His successor as local 'center', Edward Kenny of Francis Street, was arrested three weeks later. William Hearn stayed free until 1868 when he, too, was arrested. These arrests and those of thirteen other leading local Fenians deprived the movement in Waterford of effective leadership and it is no wonder that so few answered the call in March 1867.

The importance of Waterford in the overall plans of the Rising is perhaps best reflected in the assignment of Burke to command in the area. But weakened by arrests and almost without arms and betrayed by spies, it is easy to understand why there was such a poor turn out. Many of those who did were arrested by the vigilant R.I.C. as they wandered the roads in March, 1867. On

March 7th the police reported the arrest of three 'suspicious' characters on the road between Portlaw and Carrick-on-Suir.

The importance of Waterford may be gauged from the reaction of the authorities. The main weapon that the authorities used in combating the rebels was the flying column. Six of these columns were formed in early March, 1867, based in Tipperary Town, Cork, Thurles, Ennis, Carlow and Waterford. Each column consisted of infantry and cavalry and the Waterford column was commanded by Major Bell of the 6th Regiment. In a review of their activities in April. 1867, Strathrairn (Commander-in Chief, Ireland) commended their activities, especially the Waterford column, which had been involved in the affray at Kilclooney Wood where Peter O'Neill Crowley was killed. He noted that the Thurles, Tipperary and Waterford columns had made long, rapid, surprise marches, often through six feet of snow.

As for the attempted Rising in Waterford in March 1867, it is clear that there were a significant number of men who, though ill-armed and badly prepared, were ready to rally at Kilmacow on that wet, snowy night. Whether the number was 50 (Devoy). 150 (Waterford Mail, 8/3/1867) or more than 300 (Police Reports) is not important. What is important is that Waterford had its share of 'Bold Fenian Men' who were prepared to strike a blow for Irish freedom.

## THE "ERIN'S HOPE" EXPEDITION

The most romantic episode of American Fenianism, and one that caused serious international complications between Great Britain and the United States was the "Erin's Hope" expedition. It was the outcome of an urgent letter to John O'Mahony in New York from Colonel Thomas J. Kelly written from Dublin on March 15th, 1867, in which he wrote: "Aid before two weeks and Irish Independence is a fixed fact. ... Don't believe a tenth of the vile newspaper reports about complete suppression - utter routs - overwhelming defeats. ... A landing in Sligo at the present time would be of infinite service. That section has been reserved for just such an event, and if Fortune should only guide our ships in that direction it would just suit our purposes."

Thus began the saga of the "Erin's Hope" which John Devoy describes "as a romantic incident and an illustration of the confusion and inefficiency into which the movement had fallen owing to the Split." The manner in which the vessel was acquired forms an interesting part of the whole episode. The ship, originally called the "Jacmel Packet", was built in Medford, Mass. in 1861 and registered in Nassau, Bahamas. Its owner, John Dawes, was apparently using her to run arms to the Mexican Republicans. The ship arrived in New York on December 13th, 1866, and she was carrying 5,000 stand of arms, including a quantity of breech loading rifles, several hundred Spenser repeaters, three small field guns and a quantity of ammunition. When nobody claimed the cargo the ship fell to the port collector of customs, Henry Smythe. The Fenians obtained the "Jacmel Packet" sometime between March 15th and April 12th, 1867. The collector of customs was neither an Irishman nor a Fenian, but the Brotherhood was given the vessel. The financial affairs of the Fenians were not in a healthy state, so, presumably, they acquired the ship for a consideration.

*The 'Erin's Hope'*

On April 13th, 1867, the ship, still called the "Jacmel Packet" and without clearance papers, at first set course for the West Indies. She was commanded by Commander Kavanagh of Waterford origin and was joined by 35 volunteers led by Brigadier

Kerrigan and including the inevitable informer, D. J. Buckley. Occasionally during the first week of the voyage they hoisted the British flag whenever another vessel hove in sight. But on Easter Sunday, April 21st, the Fenians felt safe and decided to re-christen the ship. Buckley related the story of this event.

*Erin's Hope Monument at Helvick Head, Co. Waterford.*

"On Eater Sunday, the green flag with a sunburst was hoisted some time before noon. At the hoisting there was a salute of different guns fired, after which, the orders delivered to John F. Kavanagh in New York, commanding him to land the arms in Ireland, were read by him. It was signed by Captain Powell of the Navy, also Colonel James Kelly. They were to be landed at Sligo, if possible. Vessel newly christened that day, "Erin's Hope" by John F. Kavanagh."

On April 20th, a Fenian named Hayes left New York for Ireland to inform Colonel Thomas J. Kelly of the sailing of the "Erin's Hope" and to arrange that on her arrival she should be boarded by an agent from the shore with information as to the state of the country and orders to guide the landing expedition. This task was given to Ricard O'Sullivan Burke.

Burke's adventures while waiting for the vessel to arrive were of the most extraordinary kind. He went to Sligo posing as an American and dressed in all the style of Yankee fashion and gave his name as Waters. He stayed in the Imperial Hotel for a short time. During his stay he was chiefly engaged in travelling about the country as an artist making sketches of the different places of antiquity in the area and along the coast of Sligo. His fine, gentlemanly manners and splendid figure enabled him to impose himself on the local gentry, including magistrates, as a gentleman of leisure travelling for pleasure. He was the guest of two or three of them, dined at their tables, was introduced to their friends and allowed to shoot and fish on their grounds. Their suspicions were never once aroused and it was only at the trials later that they learned of their guest's identity, through the testimony of Buckley.

The progress of the "Erin's Hope" across the Atlantic was delayed as she ran into bad weather and her sails were all in a poor state. Eventually, she arrived in Donegal Bay on May 20th. Shore signals were expected but not seen. The ship continued to cruise between Sligo and Donegal for two days. Burke, eventually, came out in a cutter and explained how the arrangements for signal contact had broken down. He informed them that the Rising had been suppressed more than two months previously and that there was no hope of taking Sligo as originally planned. He branded the enterprise as foolhardy and advised the Fenians to proceed to Cork.

No contact was made with Fenians ashore from Toe Head in Co. Cork and Kavanagh sailed his ship along the County Cork coast. A mutiny threatened at this time. Water and provisions were running low, so the Fenians decided by a vote of twenty two to ten to return to the United States, However, on June 1st, another change of plan occurred off Helvick Head in Waterford.

The Americans landed at Ring Strand. They were seen by the coastguard who immediately informed the police. Most of them were captured in the vicinity of Dungarvan. They were all fine athletic men aged between eighteen and twenty six. All of them possessed the dash of soldiers with the smartness and independent manner of citizens of the great Republic. All were comfortably and many respectably dressed. Their manner and address exhibited a superior intelligence. Their "cut" was decidedly Yankee and some wore the unmistakably square-toed shoes and chin tufts, with luxuriant moustaches. The ladies of Dungarvan treated the prisoners to dinner during their stay in the town.

The prisoners gave the following names:- Michael Fitzgerald, Carrigtwohill, County Cork; Michael Green, Massachusetts; Denis O'Connor, Cork; William F. Millen, New York; Jerry Murphy, Cork; Arthur Downey, New York; James Lawless, do; Daniel Lee, Castleconnell, Co. Limerick; John Harly, from America, but declined to say from what part; Robert Kelly, do; John Rooney, New York; William C. Nugent, Boston; Laurence Doyle, New York; John Cade Fitzsimons, Co. Longford; John Cade, England; Michael J. Greene, America; Jeremiah Murray, Cork; William Sheehan, Nelson Place, Cork; Augustine A. Costelloe, Philadelphia; Daniel J. Buckley, Patrick Cogan, Michael Fitzgerald, Robert Kelly and Andrew J. Leonard, all of New York; Michael Walsh, Queenstown and Patrick Roche, Cork.

Two more Americans were arrested near Youghal - General William Nagle and Captain John Warren. These two were considered to be the leaders of the expedition. They were transferred to Cork Jail to await trial. Two more were arrested between Carrigtwohill and Midleton and were remanded in Midleton.

On June 12th, the prisoners were transferred from Dungarvan to Waterford. As they left Dungarvan they were given an enthusiastic farewell. Women were actually shedding tears in torrents. The prisoners returned thanks to the ladies on repeated occasions as they left the town. A huge crowd cheered the prisoners as they marched from Ballynaneesha cross-roads to Waterford city jail. When the two prisoners arrested near Midleton arrived in Waterford, they, too, were greeted by a huge crowd. Stones were thrown at the police who then charged the crowd, killing one person, David Walsh, and wounding many others.

**Fate of the Prisoners**

Colonel William J. Nagle and Captain John Warren were brought to trial for treason-felony on October 25th. Nagle, a native born American citizen, applied for a jury *de mediate linguae* - one half citizens and one half aliens. This caused a poser for the judges and the trial was adjourned to Sligo. The only way he could be tried was with a jury of six American citizens who then happened to be in Sligo and six natives. The six American citizens couldn't be found and Nagle was released in May, 1868.

Warren also applied for a similar jury, but this was refused. He was sentenced to fifteen years penal servitude but was released in 1869. The others were also tried and given long prison sentences. However, the bulk of them were released in 1868 and the remainder in 1869.

Meanwhile, as no signal was received from shore and after a further delay to allow for all eventualities, the "Erin's Hope" returned to New York with its cargo arriving there on August 1st with a number of those on board sick. So ended the attempted invasion of Ireland which had been advocated by different revolutionary societies in the United States since 1848. The promised fleet had shrunk to one small vessel and it came at a time when the last flickering flame of revolt had long since been quenched by Britain. The cruise of the "Erin's Hope" proved conclusively that an expedition could have been sent from America to Ireland. In reality it was two years too late. 1865 was 'the year of action' and it was let slip by. (Incidentally, this attempted landing of arms at Helvick was the first of three attempts here at different periods in our history.)

## CHAPTER 17

# THE MANCHESTER RESCUE

After the failure of the Rising in March the Fenian organization still existed on a formidable scale. A general Convention of the I.R.B. was held in Manchester in late July or early August, 1867. About three hundred delegates came from Ireland, England, Scotland and Wales. Chairman of the Convention was Captain James Murphy, of the 20th Massachussetts Infantry Volunteers and Ricard O'Sullivan Burke was Secretary. Colonel Thomas J. Kelly was unanimously chosen to fill the position of Chief Executive of the Irish Republican Brotherhood. Captain James Murphy was placed in charge in Scotland; Captain Mackey in southern Ireland; Edmund O'Donovan in northern Ireland and O'Sullivan Burke was to give attention to England and to any special duty that may have arisen.

Kelly and his aide, Timothy Deasy, had attended a meeting called by the Circle officers of Manchester. Early on the morning of September 11th the policeman on duty in Oak Street, Manchester noticed four men loitering in suspicious circumstances in the doorway of a shop. When challenged by the policeman two of the suspects escaped and the other two, Kelly and Deasy, were arrested and charged with loitering under the Vagrancy Act. The two gave their names as Williams and Whyte and claimed to be Americans. The magistrate could find no cause to hold the two for anything but loitering with a possible three day imprisonment, when a policeman asked that the two be held long enough to see if either had ties with the Fenians.

Back in their cell, Kelly and Deasy realised they were in a very serious predicament. Their real names were soon known to the police possibly because they had already been recognised by the informer, Corydon. (John Joseph Corydon turned informer in 1867. Previously, he had been secretary of a Fenian Circle in the Irish Brigade in the Army of the Potomac. When his regiment was disbanded he offered himself for service in Ireland. It was due to the information he leaked that the earlier attack on Chester Castle was frustrated. He is quoted as saying that he turned informer in order to expose a pack of swindlers.) The police were overjoyed at their good fortune, for now they had in their hands the two men they had been trying to capture for a long time. A week later, on September 18th, the most important Fenian action of the year was fought in the streets of Manchester.

Although there are a few different accounts of the rescue it seems that Captain O'Meagher Condon was responsible for organizing the rescue under the direction of O'Sullivan Burke. In an account written by Burke and published in the "Gaelic American" he states, "A telegram reached me in London advising me of serious trouble in Manchester and asking me to go there at once. I started for Manchester by the first train. I found on arriving in Manchester a very serious situation. Chief Executive, Colonel Thomas J. Kelly, and one of the two American officers, Captain Timothy Deasy, were in the hands of the enemy. The Centres and Sub-Centres of the local organizations had made great progress in the procuring arms and ammunition and otherwise getting ready to rescue these two officers should I so direct, when I had looked the situation over. After I got to Manchester, Captain Michael O'Brien, who had served in a civil capacity with me in the Engineer Corps of the army, and later with me in England in 1866, gave me complete information as to the local situation.

"On the evening of September 17th, a final meeting prior to any action was called. At this meeting the following men of the local Circles volunteered to undertake the rescue:

"James Lavery, John Neary, Thomas O'Bolger, Peter Ryan, William Melvin, Michael Larkin, Timothy Featherstone, Charles Moorehouse, Peter Rice, William Philip Allen, Patrick Bloomfield, John Stoneham, Joseph Keeley, John Ryan, James Cahill and the two American officers, Michael O'Brien and Edward O'Meagher Condon.

"From these volunteers I called for two men who were willing to undertake extra hazardous duty. Of those who volunteered I selected Thomas O'Bolger and Peter Ryan. I advised the larger

*The rescue of Colonel Thomas Kelly and Captain Timothy Deasy.*

*Bellevue Prison*

body as to their conduct at and after the rescue, particularly dwelling upon the condition governing duty that no life was to be taken unless the taking of it was necessary to the success of the rescue, then it was to be taken without an instant's hesitation. After arranging to have the main body of the volunteers meet at the designated place to get more arms and ammunition in the morning, and privately instructing the two special volunteers as to the duty they were to do, and directing them to meet me near the Court House at which our officers (the prisoners) would again appear on September 18, this meeting was closed and all went quietly to their homes."

According to Burke, O'Brien was to cover the retreat and O'Meagher Condon was instructed to see to the safety of Kelly and Deasy once they were rescued. On the morning of the 18th the main body of the volunteers, in ones and twos, made their way to the point selected for the supply of more arms and ammunition. The prisoners appeared in court that morning and the police had been warned of a possible rescue attempt and some extra precautions were taken. The prisoners were remanded again and then conveyed in handcuffs in the prison van to Bellevue Gaol. After passing up Hyde Road beyond the railway bridge the police van was stopped by the selected band of Fenian volunteers and surrounded. They forced the police to get down. Inside the van with the two Fenians and the other prisoners was Police Sergeant Brett. When called upon to surrender, he refused. Attempts to batter in the roof with stones were not successful. As time was running out, one of the Fenians fired through the ventilators. Brett, who was trying to get a glimpse at what was happening outside was hit and mortally wounded. This had the desired effect. One of the women prisoners took the keys from Brett and passed them through the ventilator. Immediately, Kelly and Deasy, still in handcuffs, were released. Still in their handcuffs the two men made their way over the wall, across the railway line and to safety. Though a reward of £300 was offered for the capture of the two prisoners they were never recaptured. By mid-November both had arrived safely in New York.

Burke, himself, did not take an active part in the actual rescue. He stayed near the Court House "and made my headquarters at the Red Lion Inn, nearly opposite the Court House. O'Bolger and Ryan were sent into the Court House to watch everything and advise me of the progress of affairs, coming to the Red Lion Inn for that purpose. About three o'clock I was advised of the identification by a police official of our two men and their remand in jail, and the passing of the prisoners into the van. O'Bolger and Ryan were to watch the actual entrance into the van of the two prisoners, and then precede the van in a cab and give the signal agreed upon. A great crowd of people had gathered in the area in front of the Court House. I passed among them, keeping my eye on the Court House door. But I soon returned to my headquarters, as I thought the detectives were showing interest in the crowd. Going through the crowd, just after the van had left, to get a cab, I noticed quite a commotion. Immediately the detectives caught at several of the crowd, myself among them, but greater commotion near me alarmed the officers in plain clothes and I managed to break away from them, dodging through the crowd, and made my escape by side streets. When I got to Hyde Road crowds of people were in the road, and going to where the crowd was thickest, I soon learned from the excited people that 'the Fenians had shot a whole lot of people and murdered the police.' Further inquiries, made as a newspaper man, soon gave me the information of the success of the rescue."

Fifteen minutes was the time occupied to set Kelly and Deasy free, but in this short space an act was accomplished which shook the whole of the British Empire to its foundations. The rescue threw England into a panic of fear and rage. The movement she thought was dead and buried after the unsuccessful Rising of March was still alive and its spirit unbroken. All during the night of the rescue a raid upon the Irish quarters went on and large number of Irishmen rounded up - most of them merely because they were Irish and others just happened to be in the neighbourhood at the time of the rescue. Four of those who took part in the rescue bid stood trial for murder, William Philip Allen,

Michael Larkin, Michael O'Brien and Edward Condon. A fifth, Thomas Maguire, an Irish Marine, was also charged with the other four though he had never been near the scene of the rescue in his life.

An eye witness account of the capture of Allen was published in the *Cork County Eagle* on November 30th, 1907. John Quinn, aged 12, happened to be playing in a field some distance from the road where the rescue of Kelly and Deasy took place, when he was startled by loud shouts of 'Murder,' 'Fenian,' 'Stop him.' He saw a young man, somewhat slightly built, with black coat, light trousers without a cap, and a red kerchief round his head from which blood was copiously streaming. In swift pursuit was a number of policemen, who were, however, not gaining on him. In his flight he passed near a place where workmen were engaged in making bricks. The police shouted to these men to aid them in the capture. One threw a brick at the fugitive; it missed its aim. Another brick thrown with great violence struck him in the arm, but did not impede his flight. A third shot at him with a brick which struck him in his already wounded head, had the desired effect. It felled him to the ground and before he had recovered consciousness he was handcuffed and in the hands of the police, from whose custody he was never more to escape.

The trial began on October 28th and on that day huge crowds gathered outside the Court House and on every day during the trial. A military force of nearly 2,000 men as well as large numbers of armed police stood guard around the court house as well as escorting the prison van. The prisoners appeared in the dock in irons and it was felt that the outcome of the trial was a foregone conclusion particularly as it was held in Manchester where popular feeling against the men in the dock ran high.

The case, which was tried before Mr. Justice Blackburne and Mr. Justice Mellor, was opened by the Attorney General, Sir J. S. Karslake who emphasized the legal rule under which several men could be found guilty for a murder committed by one of their number. .All of the accused denied they fired the fatal shot. First to give evidence was Constable Yarwood who identified all five

*Michael O'Brien*

*William Philip Allen*

*Michael Larkin*

*Sergeant Brett*

including Maguire who was later to produce a cast-iron alibi. Constable Shaw also identified the prisoners and said it was Allen who fired the fatal shot. A hairdresser, John Griffiths, gave evidence that he saw Allen point the gun at the lock of the van and he also identified Maguire. As the trial progressed witness after witness identified the accused and in many cases identified Allen as the man who fired the shot which killed the policeman. However, a few witnesses referred to someone other than Allen as having been closely involved in the shooting incident. The cross examination revealed the prejudice among many of the witnesses.

Witnesses were then called for the accused. Elizabeth Perkins, a widowed sister of Maguire, said he didn't get up that day until 3.30pm and didn't leave the house until seven that evening. Neighbours testified that they had seen him that day between 3.30 and 4 pm. In his address to the jury the Attorney General hoped the conviction of the five men would have the effect of deterring anyone with Fenian tendencies of upsetting the British Constitution. In his summing up, Mr. Justice Blackburne stressed that the use of violence in the rescue made the offence murder. He advised the jury that there was strong evidence that the shot was fired with the intention of killing Brett.

The jury retired at 6.15 pm on the fifth day. At 7.30 they returned to give their verdicts - Guilty in every case. The sentence was death by hanging.

**William Philip Allen**

William Philip Allen was born in Tipperary the son of a Protestant father and a Catholic mother. His father, Tom Allen, worked in the Bridewell in Bandon as custodian until he joined the R. I. C. He was stationed in Thurles, but, for some reason, he didn't like the police force, and because of his great love for Bandon, he resigned and returned to Bandon with his wife and two year old son and resumed his old job in the Bridewell. When young William Philip Allen was 14 years old, he was apprenticed to a carpenter. At the age of 16 he emigrated to Manchester and at the age of 18 he was executed as one of the noble-hearted three. His mother was present at the execution but died shortly after returning to Bandon. Old Tom lost his job at the Bridewell because of his son's activity in the Fenians, but he lived for ten years after, then died a pauper and is buried in Kilbrogan graveyard. The night before he died he became a convert to the Catholic faith.

**Michael O'Brien**

Michael O'Brien was born in Ballymacoda in County Cork. He was apprenticed to a draper in Youghal. Then followed a spell as an assistant in a leading drapery store in Cork City before emigrating to the United States. He joined the Union army at the outset of the Civil War and served in the same regiment as Thomas Kelly. He returned to Cork after the war and was active in Fenian circles there. At one stage he was tried in Liverpool for having in his possession a number of rifles, but he was acquitted. As a result of this and a warning that followed the incident, the American Government did not intercede for him when he was sentenced to death as he had failed to follow their advice.

**Michael Larkin,**

Michael Larkin, an older man, was born in Lumagh in Co. Offaly. He worked for many years as a tradesman and in 1858 he went to England. There he was caught up in the Fenian movement.

When sentenced each of the five addressed the court. Allen in his speech said:

"My Lords and Gentlemen - No man in this court regrets the death of Sergeant Brett more than I do, and I positively say, in the presence of the Almighty and ever-living God, that I am innocent, aye, as innocent as any man in this court. ... I say positively and defiantly, justice has not been done me since I was arrested. If justice had been done me, I would not have been handcuffed at the preliminary examination in Bridge Street; and in this court justice has not been done me in any shape or form. I was brought up here, and all the prisoners by my side were allowed to wear overcoats, and I was told to take mine off. What is the principle of that? There was an obvious object in that; and I say positively that justice has not been done me. ... ...

"And now with regard to the other means by which I have been identified. I have to say that my clothes were kept from me for four hours by the policemen in Fairfield Station, and shown to parties to identify me as being one of the perpetrators of this affair on Hyde Road. Also in Albert Station a handkerchief was kept on my head the whole night, so that I could be identified the next morning in the corridor by the witnesses. I was ordered to leave on the handkerchief so that the witnesses could more plainly see I was one of the parties alleged to have committed the outrage. ... My name, Sir, might be wished to be known. It is not William O'Meara Allen. My name is William Philip Allen. I was reared in Bandon, in the county of Cork, and from that place I take my name. I am proud of my country, and proud of my parentage. My Lords, I have done."

*Maid of Erin Statue, Bandon.*

Condon was the last to speak. "I do not accuse the jury, but I believe the jury was prejudiced. I don't accuse them of wilfully wishing to convict, but prejudice has induced them to convict when they otherwise would not have done. We have been found guilty, and, as a matter of course, we accept our death as gracefully as possible. We are not afraid to die - at least I am not."

" 'Nor I, nor I,' repeated the other convicted men.

"With regard to the other prisoners who are to be tried afterwards, I hope our blood at least will satisfy the craving for it. You will soon send us before God, and I am perfectly prepared to go. I have nothing to regret, or to retract, or take back. I shall only say, GOD SAVE IRELAND!"

*Manchester Martyrs' Memorial Card*

As he spoke these words, his companions with one step, advanced to the front of the dock, and stretching their hands upwards, cried out earnestly, "God save Ireland." This exclamation was a rallying cry of the Irish nation from then on.

Efforts were made to get the death sentence commuted. Maguire's case was reviewed immediately and after an inquiry the Government admitted there had been a mistake and he was pardoned. The United States Government intervened on behalf of Condon and he was reprieved. In England, where a powerful section of the public demanded a sacrifice, the pardon of Maguire and the reprieve of Condon were considered deplorable exhibitions of weakness. As already stated the United States did not intervene on behalf of O'Brien because of a previous involvement with the police.

And so on the cold grey morning of November 23rd, 1867, Allen, Larkin and O'Brien were led out to die. Huge crowds, the likes of which had never before attended a Manchester execution, thronged the area around the jail. Allen was the first to appear, and although he was deadly pale, he walked with firm and steady tread. Next came O'Brien followed by Larkin. As the three men stood before the crowd capped and pinioned, their words, 'Lord Jesus have mercy on us,' rang out. The bolt was drawn and the three bodies fell. A subdued hum of terror and surprise ran through the crowd.

*Allen Memorial,*
*Kilbrogan Cemetery, Bandon.*

The execution of the three was a signal for a great burst of anger and revulsion. The 'Nation' issued a black-bordered edition on November 30th and most of the Irish papers including the Freeman's Journal condemned the executions roundly. "We have no desire to revive past animosities, but we must say that no policy tends so much to re-create discord and hate as the sacrifice on Saturday. It was not a display of strength, but of weakness instigated by anger and fear." *(Freeman's Journal, November 28th, 1867.)*

In Manchester nearly 3,000 people marched in a funeral procession as a mark of protest, many wore green. Similar demonstrations or funeral processions were banned in many English towns for fear of disturbances. In Cork 12,000 marchers took part in a funeral procession. In Bandon, the home town of Allen, a funeral procession which bore any empty coffin went from the town to Kilbrogan Cemetery where prayers were offered for those who had been executed. A commemoration ceremony is held in Bandon each year on November 23rd. A huge demonstration took place in Dublin on December 8th. Three hearses, bearing the names of Allen, Larkin and O'Brien, followed by mourning coaches and cabs, were at the rear of the procession.

The three bodies were buried in quicklime in Salford Jail. When the jail closed the remains were transferred to Strangways prison.

*Plaques on site of Bridewell, Bandon.*

# CHAPTER 18

# RICARD IS ARRESTED

On November 20th, 1867, the Fenians were dealt another severe blow when Ricard O'Sullivan Burke was arrested in London. The most prominent Fenian in England and Ireland, his loss was felt to be almost as serious a blow to the organization as had the arrest of Kelly. After the Manchester rescue he again assumed the guise of a businessman in Birmingham with the intention of continuing his purchase of arms. He was in London in November staying at 7 Tavistock Street. Staying in the same house was John Devany, a police spy, who identified Burke to the police.

On the night of November 20th, Inspector Thompson of Scotland Yard was in Clarendon Street, Saint Pancras with Devany and he was later joined by a police constable. They saw Burke who was accompanied by Joseph Theobald Casey and they followed them into Woburn Square. When Devany identified Burke, Thompson tapped him on the shoulder and said, "I am Inspector Thompson of the detective police and hold a warrant for the apprehension of Ricard Burke for serious crime. I know you to be Ricard Burke and must take you into custody. You must consider yourself my prisoner and must accompany me to the nearest police station." Burke denied he was that person and said his name was George Berry, a medical student, and demanded to see the warrant which the inspector did not show him. When the two policemen laid hold of Burke, he struggled and protested as they pushed him a short distance. Casey then intervened and struck Thompson a few blows.

Burke then walked quietly as far as the corner of Russel Square. Again he demanded to see the warrant and, once again, Thompson refused to show it to him. He protested again and wrenched himself free and ran about half a dozen yards. Casey tried to prevent the inspector from following Burke. Thompson then drew a revolver and threatened Burke, "By God, Burke, if you attempt to go away I will fire on you." A crowd then gathered and Casey

*Cells in Clerkenwel House of Detention.*

and Burke tried to excite the people to interfere. Thompson then called a cab and with Burke inside drove to Bow Street police station where Burke was detained. Casey followed in another cab and he was also detained. Devany was sent for and, when asked, he pointed to the prisoner and said, "This is Ricard Burke."

Burke was charged with treason felony and Casey was charged with assaulting police officers. Both were remanded for trial. While awaiting trial they were sent to the Clerkenwell House of Detention.

The House of Detention was used mainly for prisoners awaiting trial. It was surrounded by a wall twenty five feet high which was three feet thick at the base. The exercise yard, where Burke, Casey and the other prisoners exercised every day, was 100 feet long and 60 feet wide. Conditions in the House were no worse than in any English prison and prisoners awaiting trial did have certain privileges. They could, if they so wished and if they had the money, have their meals sent in to them. This was most welcome as the meals inside were anything but appetizing - one pint of oatmeal gruel for breakfast, one pound of bread for dinner and one pint of oatmeal gruel for supper. (Burke did have a slight problem about his meals. When he was arrested he had in his possession a five pound note which was taken from him. When he asked for its return as he needed it to buy food, the request was refused. He had to apply to the examining magistrate for its return. He, however, did not return the actual note but ordered the police to give the prisoner five sovereigns instead.) The prisoners were not allowed to speak to each other day or night. Despite these somewhat harsh regulation Ricard Burke had no complaints about his detention. In a speech at the end of his trial he said: "Then, as a preliminary to the observations I have to make, I wish to say that since the period of my arrest, and since I have been confined in various prisons - Bow Street, the House of Detention, Newgate, Warwick Gaol, the King Street station-house, and other places - and I have received from all the officials, from the governor down to the lowest warder, the most unvarying kindness; and I desire to record my gratitude to these gentlemen for such an extension of kindness towards me." It was during this period that Burke wrote his autobiography.

**The Clerkenwell Explosion**

In no way deterred by the executions in Manchester, plans were made to free Burke from Clerkenwell prison as he was regarded as essential to the success of the organization after the collapse of the March Rising. Contact was made with the two Fenian prisoners through Catherine Barry, Ricard's sister, and Mrs. Anne Justice, a friend of Casey's. The escape plan suggested by Burke was simple and straightforward. The yard in which the prisoners exercised each day between 3 and 4 pm was separated from the street by a high wall. He advised the placing of an explosive charge in a trench in a weak section of the wall which he had noticed. When the explosive charge was in place a signal was to be given to the prisoners, then, in the confusion after the explosion, the two prisoners were to rush through the breach where friends would be waiting with horses to convey them away from the prison as quickly as possible.

Captain James Murphy made most of the arrangements for the rescue and he was assisted by Michael Barrett and Jeremiah O'Sullivan. Gunpowder was purchased in small quantities and brought to the Clerkenwell area. (The use of dynamite had not yet been perfected.) However, as in the past, an informer obtained all the details of the plan and passed on the information to the police in Dublin. As a result of this information security at the prison was increased.

The first attempt to rescue the prisoners was made on December 12th. A barrow with a beer cask packed with gunpowder was placed against the wall by Murphy and his two companions, a white ball was tossed over the prison wall as a signal to Burke and Casey that the charge was about to be fired. The warders saw the ball and presumed a child had accidentally kicked it over the wall - nothing new. Burke pretended to have a stone in his shoe and in a protected area near the wall he attempted to remove it, all the time waiting for the explosion. The

***Entrance to House of Detention.*** *(Courtesy Islington Public Library)*

***Aftermath of the Clerkenwell Explosion.*** *(Courtesy Islington Public Library)*

fuse was lit, spluttered and went out. It was lit a second time and, again, it went out. A third time the fuse was lit and for the third time it went out. It was then decided to abandon the attempt and the conspirators wheeled the barrow away. Burke must have been wondering why the explosion had not gone off and must have been very frustrated.

It was decided at a Fenian meeting that night to try again the following day. However, the Governor of the prison, fearing some attack, cancelled the normal period of exercise for the prisoners and kept them in their cells. On Friday 13th, the barrel of explosives was placed against the wall once more and the fuse was lit. This time it did not go out and the barrel exploded. A hole was blown in the wall but to no avail as Burke and Casey were in their cells at the other side of the prison.

Unfortunately, most of the blast effect went across the road and a row of slum dwellings collapsed and fires broke out. The place was in chaos as women and children screamed and glass, bricks and mortar littered the street. Barrett and O'Sullivan raced to the breach in the prison wall hoping to meet the two prisoners hurrying out to meet them. But, when they peered into the yard the place was empty. So all three beat a hasty retreat and tried to make their escape.

There was confusion and panic in the streets and lanes around Clerkenwell. The newly formed London Fire Brigade was soon on the scene and quickly put out the flames. The walls were shored up to prevent them collapsing. Firemen worked hard to clear the debris and search for victims. Three persons were killed and over one hundred were injured. Over four hundred houses in all were damaged. The dead were Minnie Julia Abbott (7), Sarah Anne Hodgkinson (36) and William Clutton (47). The next day Martha Evans (65) died of injuries. Later two others, - Humphrey Evans (67) and Martha Elizabeth Thompson (11) - died of their injuries. All six are buried in the one grave in Finchley Cemetery. A relief fund was opened for the victims by the Rev. Robert Maguire, vicar of the Anglican Church of St. James, Clerkenwell. A total of

£10,073 - 14 - 2 was collected and the bulk of it was spent in compensating those who suffered injuries or damage to property.

The tragedy enraged the British not only against the Fenians but also against the Irish living in the larger cities of England. The American Ambassador in Britain, Charles Francis Adams, described the mood in England following the explosion: "It may be doubted whether at any time since the discovery of the scheme of Guy Fawkes, there has been so much panic spread among families throughout the community at this time ... The consequences may be serious, not so much to the perpetrators of these offences as to the multitudes of the very class which they are supposed to befriend. I think it would now be unsafe for Irishmen to attempt to hold a meeting for any purpose in any large town in England. The chief sufferers will be those least contemplated at the outset."

Rumours spread like wildfire through London and all England. The Fenians were doing this or attempting to do that. The attack was condemned in all the British newspapers. In the United States even the New York 'Herald', which up to this had been friendly towards the Fenians, now condemned the Brotherhood. In its edition of December 29th, 1867, it called the Brotherhood a "cut-throat organisation" and predicted its speedy demise. The explosion caused confusion and increased dissension among the Fenian Brotherhood in America where the organisation was already split.

A reward of £400 plus a free pardon was offered for information about the Fenians involved. Despite the help of informers the British police were not highly successful in their search for the organizers. Among those arrested in London was Patrick Mullany, a tailor and a member of the Fenian organisation, originally from Dublin. After much questioning he agreed to tell everything he knew. Another tailor, John Vaughan, offered his services when he heard about the reward. Eventually, after weeks and weeks of looking for further evidence, six people stood trial for the murder of Sarah Anne Hodgkinson. They were Michael Barrett, Timothy

Desmond and his brother, William, Nicholas English, John O'Keeffe and Ann Justice.

**The Clerkenwell Trials**

The case, which opened in the Old Bailey on Monday, April 20th, 1868, was heard by two judges, Lord Chief Justice Cockburn and Baron Bramwell. Leading the prosecution, once again, was the Attorney General, Sir J. B. Karslake. The accused lacked money to pay for a top class defence team. Appeals were made in Irish papers for money to pay a defence team and these produced enough money to pay young lawyers just beginning their careers. It must be said that they performed remarkably well and won five of the six verdicts.

Mullany, now a key witness for the prosecution, gave a detailed account of the planning and implicated Murphy (not on trial) and Barrett as being the main movers in the rescue attempt. John

***Arrival of the accused at Bow-Street Polic Court.***
*(Courtesy of Islington Public Library)*

*Three of the accused: Desmond, Allen and Ann Justice.*
*(Courtesy of Islington Public Library)*

Vaughan implicated Timothy Desmond who told him (Vaughan) on December 13th that he was going to take part in the attack on Clerkenwell Gaol that evening. Many other witnesses were called who testified to seeing the prisoners at the scene of the explosion. But under cross examination the weakness of the conflicting evidence was pointed out. It was also pointed out by the defence lawyers that the identity parades had not been conducted in an impartial manner.

On the completion of the prosecution's case, the defence lawyers pointed out that no evidence had been given to connect Ann Justice with the explosion. Both judges agreed, the case against her collapsed and she was discharged. Next case to collapse was the one against John O'Keeffe and he was also discharged. The case against Nicholas English and the Desmond brothers began to look very weak. Michael Barrett, who had been implicated by Mullany, stated he was in Glasgow at the time of the explosion and he offered an alibi and produced witnesses to support it. The prosecution produced witnesses who said they saw Barrett in London in November, 1867. In his summing up the Attorney General attacked Barrett's alibi and Lord Chief Justice Cockburn in his address to the jury told them they would have to decide on the credibility of the various witnesses with regard to Barrett's alibi.

***Examination of the Prisoners.*** *(Courtesy of Islington Public Library)*

***Removal of the Prisoners.*** *(Courtesy Islington Public Library)*

The jury, having spent two and a half hours considering their verdict, returned a verdict of guilty against Michael Barrett and found the other three not guilty. He was sentenced to death with the Chief Justice adding there was no hope of reprieve.

Despite many requests for a reprieve or a re-trial, on May 25th, Michael Barrett was told that the Home Secretary had rejected all pleas for mercy and the execution would take place the following day. On May 26th Michael Barrett was executed - the last public execution in England. The following extracts are taken from the *London Express.*

"The Fenian convict, Michael Barrett, was hanged this morning in front of Newgate gaol. His demeanour was unaltered to the last, and those who heard his speech from the dock saw another striking illustration of the coolness, resolution, and fortitude he then displayed. Those most conversant with executions declared that no convict ever met his doom with more signal courage than the unhappy man who suffered this morning; and the *'Good bye, Barrett,' 'God bless you, Barrett,'* yelled from all portions of the crowd, showed that the popular sympathies were roused. ......

"Calcraft, the hangman, smiling disagreeably, and looking, in black skull cap, and good black broad-cloth surtout and suit, more repulsive than if he had worn the insignia of his dreadful office, smirked and fawned on those officials on the scaffold as he passed down the stairs and slouched by them to pull the bolt. He had been greeted by a terrific storm of hisses and yells while in view of the people, and seemed nervously anxious to hurry out of their sight. Though growing old, and with bleached locks and a snow-white beard, he is a powerfully built muscular man, whose callous matter-of-fact handling of the ropes, straps, and paraphernalia of violent death, cannot be seen without a shudder....

"Both Calcraft and Barrett each had a horrible noisy reception when they appeared. The persistent burst of groaning became appalling when the hangman was recognised. *'Let's put him there instead!' 'Shame,' 'Down with him,' 'Bah, bah, murderer, bah,'* are but a few of the articulate sounds heard from the windows of the Old Bailey and ringing in the doomed man's ears at the supreme

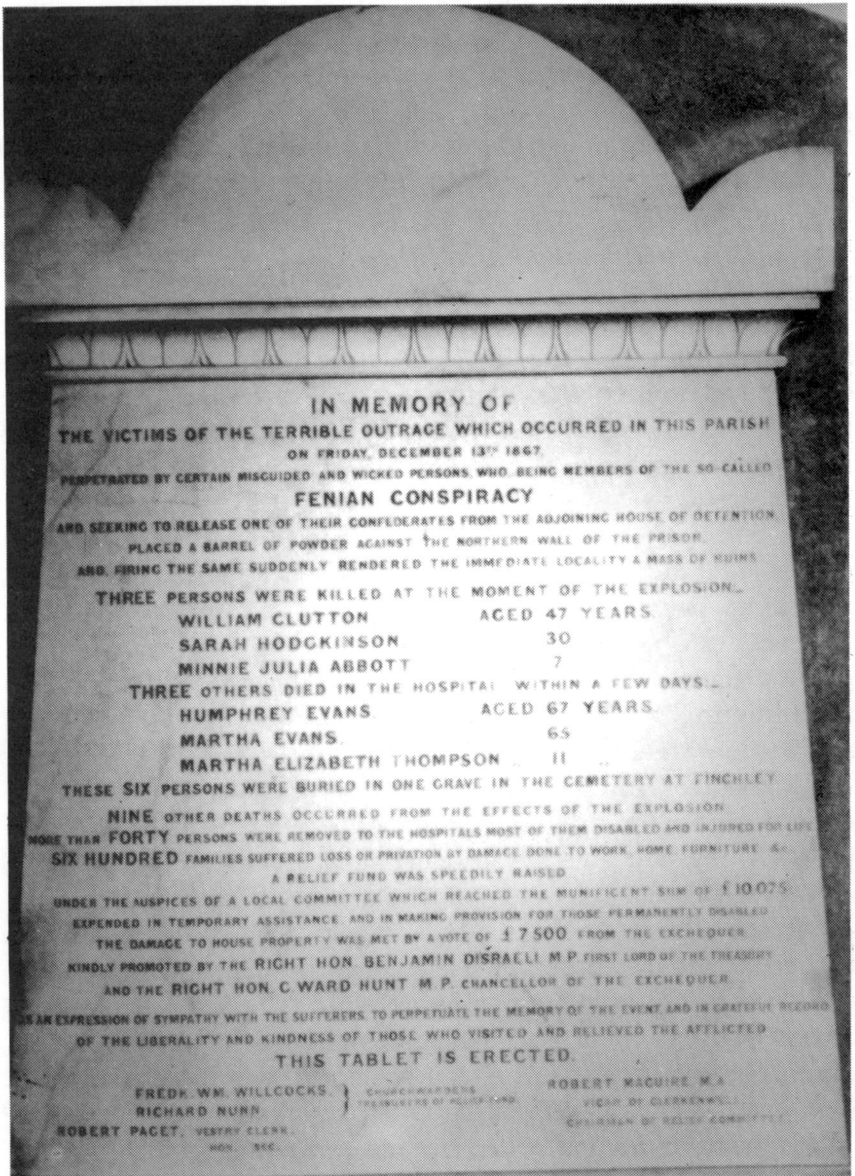


*Memorial Plaque in the Church of St. James, Clerkenwell.*

moment. But even these were lost in the excited and congratulatory cheers and handclapping for Barrett. *'Bravo, Barrett.' 'Good bye, Barrett.' 'Never mind 'em, d—-n them'* were mixed with cheers as hearty as ever followed hero to the battle-field. …

"Hanging over the railing immediately opposite the gallows, and supported on either side by a female friend, stood the half fainting figure of a young woman four or five and twenty. Her decent demeanour and modest air won even upon the brutal natures round her, and a couple of London roughs kept back their comrades by entreaties, and, when necessary, by blows. Whatever her relationship or knowledge of Barrett may have been, there could be no doubt of the genuineness of her emotion this morning. Deadly white, with clenched lips, and hands which clung to the wooden barrier before her with the tenacity of a drowning man, she succeeded in controlling herself until the drop actually fell. When Barrett appeared on the scaffold the women supporting her redoubled their consolatory efforts; and her bleached face and wistful air became intensified in their expression. But when his face was covered, she gave way, and at the fatal moment fell prostrate, and lay in a passion of hysterical grief, deaf to the noises and blind to the sights near her, and conscious only of the gallows and its doubtful mission. … …

"The horrors and brutality of an execution crowd have been so often described that an enumeration of some of the features absent this morning will give the reader a more accurate understanding of the scene than an attempt to elaborate detail. There were comparatively few women, little violence, few fights, and no robbery to speak of. Up to 6 o'clock the assemblage was scattered and sparse. At seven the people standing did not cover Newgate Street, and it was not until nearly eight that the more distant approaches were filled. The ragged element was far less common than ever. Take away the little tatterdemalions of five years old and upwards who gambolled up and down, over and under the barriers, and mocked and gibed at the windows, and in the face of death, and it was not, by comparison, a disreputably dressed crowd. They hated the hangman more than his victim, and yelled him down accordingly. ... Much disappointment was expressed by the tavern-keepers and window-letters at the smallness of the crowd and the slackness of demand throughout the night; and the preachers who energetically foretold the wrath to come in unbroken succession and with failing lungs from the north-east corner of the Old Bailey at an early hour. ...

"But the last public hanging in England found abundant testimony, were any needed, of the expediency of the recent changes in the law. An incarnation of evil passions and perverted sympathies, it showed neither real pity for the criminal nor horror of his crime. The bastard pride in his animal courage and the brutal delight that he died game, made the law and its ministers seem to them the real murderers and Barrett to be a martyred man."

The Clerkenwell explosion was a disaster for the Fenians and they lost a lot of public sympathy which had been generated by the Manchester executions. In later years Jeremiah O'Sullivan blamed Ricard O'Sullivan Burke for the catastrophe as he had ordered too much gunpowder. However, it must be said, that when Burke planned the strike, the explosives were to be placed in a trench in the road where the workmen were laying pipes. The trench, however, was filled in on December 10th - two days before the first rescue attempt was made. Though he had planned the bombing, Burke and his companion, Casey, were very lucky not to have been in the exercise yard that afternoon. It is probable that they would have been killed by the force of the explosion. Then, on the very next day after the Barrett trial and in the very same courtroom, Ricard Burke went on trial on a charge of treason-felony.

## CHAPTER 19

# TRIAL AND CONVICTION

When Burke and Casey were arrested their examination before the magistrate at Bow Street extended over a few weeks. Burke, well dressed, who said his name was George Berry, was placed at the bar upon a charge of treason-felony, and John Theobald Casey was charged, conjointly with Burke, with assaulting a police officer. Burke was represented by Dr. Kenealy, a lawyer of ability who had been born in Cork and emigrated to London to concentrate on languages and law. He took part in Chartist activities and in 1848 defended two chartists who were among the hundreds who were arrested at that time.

After the Clerkenwell explosion he very quickly withdrew from the case. The examination of the prisoners was resumed on December 14th, the day after the explosion. *The Morning Star* reported that: "Not withstanding the additional interest which might have been supposed to have attached to the case of Burke and Casey in consequence of the disastrous attempt to rescue them on Friday evening, there was rather less crowding in the street and at the entrance of Bow Street police-court and certainly less exhibition of excitement in anticipation of the examination of these prisoners on Saturday morning than on former occasions. There was, indeed, a crowd of some two or three hundred persons in Bow Street opposite the court and a few small knots of Fenian sympathisers hung about the street corners and bars of public houses gossiping over the one engrossing topic of the explosion. Even amongst these there was a general tone of reprobation for its purpose and so terribly destructive to the unoffending.

"Burke and Casey were brought up in the van (which was well guarded) at an early hour and locked up in the cells of the court."

Before the case proceeded Dr. Kenealy begged leave "to make a statement of the reasons why he felt bound at this stage to withdraw from the position of counsel for the defence. When originally instructed, the case presented itself to him under features that gave him great reluctance to appear, but he was so earnestly solicited by the prisoners' friends that he consented to do so, believing that when so solicited counsel ought not refuse to accused persons the best assistance in their power to give. And therefore, though his own sympathies were entirely opposed to those of the persons supposed to be favourable to the prisoners, yet he consented to undertake their defence, and would have fought it to the end, doing his best for the prisoners with the utmost impartiality he could exercise as to the difference of views. But the dreadful proceedings of last night had so influenced his mind that he could not bring to the case that attention which a counsel ought to devote to the cause of his clients. He did not intend to impute that the prisoners had any complicity in the crime of last night, but he could not disguise from himself that those who instructed him might be probably supposed to sympathise with that outrage, and that it was their duty to satisfy him that they, at least, were not concerned in that act. As they had not done so, he must commit the defence of the prisoners to other hands. If prisoners will have counsel, they must not have recourse to violence. If violence is used they cannot have me, at least, for their counsel."

When Dr. Kenealy withdrew, Ricard Burke said he regretted deeply that such an occurrence should have taken place as it seemed to brand him as a criminal before the court. He thanked Dr. Kenealy for his kindness and consideration who, he felt bound to say, had acted without even a retaining fee. But he felt he must protest against any imputation that any part of the responsibility of what had occurred on the previous day should rest on his shoulders.

Before leaving the dock at the end of that day's examination, Casey said: "Sir, I must ask leave to declare here my entire abhorrence of the crime that was committed yesterday. I cannot find words to express what I feel - my horror that such a crime should be committed by any person whatever."

When Dr. Kenealy withdrew as counsel for the defence an appeal for funds for the defence was made in the 'Irishman.' A letter from London dated December 22nd and signed Justitia appeared in that paper on December 28th.

*To the Editor of the 'Irishman'*

*Sir*

*The readers of the 'Irishman' are already aware of the base and paltry way in which "loyal" Dr. Kenealy abandoned his clients, Burke and Casey, at Bow Street leaving them to the mercy of a magistrate and Crown Prosecutor. ...... Now, in as much as Mr. Merriman has been instructed to appear for Colonel Burke and Casey, it will be necessary to indemnify him in the expenses he has to incur, and in order to carry out this object, I have today learned that a committee was organised last week here in London to collect subscriptions towards meeting the expense of counsel, but they had to abandon the project in consequence of finding a place to meet in without being dogged by those sleek and oily-tongued gentlemen who are recently so fond of making everybody's business their own. ...... I trust you shall not consider it presumptuous of me to ask you to lay the case of our fellow countrymen before the Irish people. ...... As all meetings here, social and political, are forbidden, a committee would be powerless to act in concert, though not, I expect, individually."*

Commenting on the letter the *'Irishman'* had this to say: "We earnestly hope that the suggestion in the above letter will be promptly acted upon. Colonel Burke and Mr. Casey by the unprecedented conduct of their counsel, Dr. Kenealy, having abandoned their defence, are left without any legal assistance. The greatest criminals are allowed this as a right by English law. The law, however, while it provides counsel for murderers, denies the same privilege to men accused of a crime which they call treason-felony.... We have already received the following subscriptions:-

R. P. - £1; L. O'S - 10s; M. P. - 5s.

Many other subscriptions were received too numerous to mention. A Scottish Garibaldian - 2s; Friends in Fitzroy - £1 - 6 - 6:

Subscribers at Stockport - £1 - 7s: A Lover of Justice - 2s - 6d: One Who Fears Nothing - 1s; etc.

On the last day of the examination of the prisoners who now numbered three - Henry Mulleda, who had been arrested in Drogheda in March 1867 and held without trial since, had been added to the list of defendants, rumours had circulated of an intending attack on the prison van. Because of this, greater precautions were taken when bringing the prisoners to the court. Prior to the arrival of the van the road had been cleared by a strong force of police who formed two lines across the street - one at the Bow Street end and one a little above the police station. The van was escorted by about forty mounted police, armed with cutlasses and revolvers. The passages of the court were crowded with armed policemen, and a double reserve, also armed, was kept at the station.

The prosecution applied for the committal of the prisoners for trial on the charge of treason-felony. Although the overt acts took place in various parts of the country and in Ireland, the principal acts and the foundation of the substantial case against Burke were the purchase of arms at Birmingham and the prosecution asked that the trial be held in the county of Warwick. The examining magistrate, Sir Thomas Henry, agreed. Counsel for the accused objected to this on the basis that the prisoners were more likely to get a fairer trial in London than in Warwick, most of the witnesses were from London and then there was the expense of sending counsel so far. However, the magistrate did not entertain any of the objections and committed the accused for trial in Warwick.

When it became known that the prisoners were to be committed to Warwick the greatest excitement prevailed. Precisely at the appointed time of 1.15pm a large body of police, numbering 300, came out of the police-court and station. The foot police were all armed with cutlasses. Then the mounted escort galloped up. Then came the van. The prisoners, who were not handcuffed, were led from the cells - Burke being the first - and each was then handcuffed and locked in separate compartments in the van. On the signal being given, the van moved off rapidly surrounded by at least forty mounted men, all armed with cutlasses and revolvers. The destination was Euston Square Railway Station. The train of the Great Western Line arrived in Warwick at 6.15. One carriage was filled with armed police - 30 in number - escorting the prisoners. The local police assembled at each station down the line to keep guard. The event created great excitement in Warwick.

**Burke's Trial at the Old Bailey**

However, the trial of the three prisoners did not take place in Warwick but was transferred to the Central Criminal Court of the Old Bailey. The prisoners, Ricard Burke (35), alias George Berry, alias Edward C. Winslow, alias Wallace, no occupation, Joseph Theobald Casey (25), clerk, and Henry Mulleda (26) alias Shaw, carpenter, were charged with "feloniously and traitorously conspiring to deprive our Sovereign Lady, the Queen, of the style and royal name of the Imperial Crown of Great Britain and Ireland." The original indictment, which is over thirty feet long and written in neat handwriting, is still kept at the Old Bailey.

The presiding judges, Mr. Baron Bramwell and Mr. Justice Keating, took their seats on the bench at 10 o'clock and the prisoners were then called upon to plead. Burke and Mulleda pleaded not guilty and Casey also pleaded not guilty, adding, "I am a loyal man."

The counsel for the Crown were the Attorney General, the Solicitor General, Mr. Giffard, Q. C., Mr. Poland and Mr. Archibald. The counsel for the prisoners were Mr. Ernest Jones and Mr. McDonald for Burke; Mr. Pater for Mulleda and Mr. F. H. Lewis for Casey. The defence team was much stronger that at the previous trial. The American Government had instructed its Ambassador in England to obtain legal assistance for Burke and contributed £150 to his defence fund.

Even before the trial opened Ernest Jones went on the attack on Burke's behalf and applied for a jury de mediate linguae. This device whereby a jury would be composed of one half citizens and one half aliens was originally intended as a protection to foreigners residing in Britain, it was never intended for aliens speaking the same language. Jones produced an American passport granted to Burke as a citizen of the United States. Mr Baron Bramwell decided the evidence of a passport inadmissible because of the British theory of indefeasibility of allegiance, the law of England being that a native born subject could never shake off his allegiance and even though he renounced it in favour of a foreign power, it fastened on him again whenever he returned to the land of his birth in any part of the United Kingdom.

(When Ambassador Adams remonstrated about previous trials of American citizens, Earl Clarendon, Secretary of State for Foreign Affairs commented: "I told Mr. Adams that no British-born subject would ever or under any circumstances renounce or be resolved from, his allegiance to his sovereign.")

This request was not allowed. Burke was annoyed at this and said he wished to make a few remarks on the decision. Baron Bramwell refused this request also as the prisoner had counsel to speak for him. Burke then asked his counsel to withdraw which he did. However, when it was pointed out to Burke that the other two cases were tacked on to his and as the fate of those prisoners more or less depended on the decision that might be arrived at in his case, he decided to follow the usual course and allow his counsel to appear for him but under protest.

After the first witness, Inspector Thompson, had given evidence of arresting Burke, John Joseph Corydon, one of the approvers, was then examined by the Solicitor General. He said in evidence: "I was formerly in the Federal army of the United States and am 26 years old. The 'gentleman with the pen in his hand' (Burke) was also in the Federal army. I became a Fenian in 1862 and continued a Fenian until 1866 and attended Fenian meetings. Burke also attended these meetings at headquarters in New York. We had consulted about sending military men to Ireland and Burke was a party to this proposition. In 1866 Fenian meetings were held in Liverpool which Burke attended. At these meetings Burke was told off with Mulleda for the purchase of arms. In the early part of 1867 all the American officers - about twenty in number - met in Liverpool and at this meeting Stephens was ditched. The raid on Chester Castle was discussed and Burke was present during these discussions."

In replying to cross-examination by Earnest Jones, Corydon said: "I saw Burke paid some money in the summer of 1866 for the storage of arms. I was baptised in a place called Ballyragger in the county of Kerry. I call myself a Christian, I am not a Roman Catholic or a Protestant, but about half and half. (laughter) I cannot say how many times I have given evidence against different persons in this affair. The first man I gave evidence against was Colonel Halpin. I never was paid any money for that trial. All I have received was for my board and lodging. Of course I expect to get remunerated for what I have done in this matter. If I don't get it here I shall get it over the water."

John Devany, another approver, said: "In the year 1865, I was in New York and became a member of the Fenian Brotherhood. I attended Fenian meetings in America and saw the prisoner, Burke, at these meetings and he was a centre and a member of the Committee of Safety. The circle to which he belonged was called the Brothers Sheares' circle. I met him in London in 1866. He told me he had been in Ireland and that he had been 'doing the thing' in London and that he had passed himself off as Major Winslow of the Confederate Army."

Godfrey Massey, yet another approver, was the next witness. He had been arrested at Limerick Junction and had been easily persuaded to give information. Money was indeed an inducement, but it was also pointed out to him that he could get a long term of imprisonment and when he thought of his young bride whom he had recently married, it helped him to make up his mind very quickly. Like the other two informers, Massey had been in the Federal army and joined the Fenians. He knew Stephens, Captain Kelly and the prisoner, Burke. He had met him with Stephens at Fenian headquarters at 19 Chatham Street, New York. He gave details of Burke's work in getting arms and ammunition to Ireland.

During cross examination it came to light that he did not turn informer until he was 'sold' himself by Corydon.

After the evidence of the informers much of the trial was taken up with the testimony of Birmingham gun dealers. The chief witness here was George Kynoch, a dealer and manufacturer of firearms, of 45 Little Hampton Street, Birmingham. He first met Burke, whom he knew as Winslow, and Mulleda in December, 1865. On the 23rd of that month Burke bought two million military percussion caps and 250,000 caps for revolvers and paid £385 in cash. The following January he sold Burke a number of pistols and 500 rifles for which he received £1,385, again in cash He became very friendly with the prisoner and visited him at his place in George Street. There was a plate on the door on which '*E. C. Winslow, merchant and commission agent*' was engraved.

Evidence was then given that the prisoner, Burke, by the name of Edward C. Winslow, became the tenant of premises in George Street, where the firearms were delivered. He said that he intended to use the place as a branch house for a mercantile firm at New York and that the same firm had branches at Liverpool, Manchester, Glasgow and Paris. When renting the premises the prisoner was asked for references, and he said he was a stranger in Birmingham, and an arrangement was made that the rent should be paid quarterly in advance. The prisoner left without giving any notice, and the owners of the premises were compelled to gain admission by breaking the door open. Nothing was found in the place but an empty carboy which smelt strongly of petrol. There were also several bullet holes and a chalk mark which appeared to have been used as a target

Railwaymen from the London and North Western Railway were called to prove the circumstances connected with the removal of the firearms when these were sent to Liverpool. It was suggested that they were transmitted to Ireland. Various police officers from Ireland were called to give evidence on the incidents in March 1867 in Tallaght, Drogheda, Killmallock and Ballyknockan, Cork.

The prosecution case was carefully built up and the result was never in doubt. The one surprise that came at the end was when the Attorney-General announced that the case against Casey was being dropped and he was acquitted and he left the court. The jury retired at ten minutes past five and returned into the court after a deliberation of twenty minutes. Both prisoners were found guilty.

Mr. Avery, the clerk of the court, then put the usual questions to the prisoners, whether they had anything to say why judgment should not be passed upon them according to law.

Burke: I have a few remarks to make if I am permitted to make them.

Baron Bramwell: You are entitled by law to state anything you think proper why judgment should not be passed upon you.

Burke: I am not surprised at the verdict which the jury have arrived at, my lord; nor do I desire to impeach it. Under all the circumstances, and considering all the evidence that was brought forward, I could see that twelve reasonable men could arrive at no other conclusion. But there are other points, which, with your lordship's permission, I may touch upon without impeaching the verdict. I will not allude to the Attorney-General's conduct towards me during the past week, because he is not present, and I will, therefore, exercise more forbearance towards him than he used towards me; but I will briefly allude to some statements of the Solicitor-General in reference to my case. The learned gentleman, with his usual ability, has stated it was not the desire of the prosecution to try my case under any shadow of prejudice, but, if so, I would ask why he did not permit my case to be taken before that of the prisoners charged with causing the Clerkenwell explosion, although my attorney laid an affidavit before him, distinctly stating that my case would be bitterly prejudiced if the Clerkenwell case was brought on before mine. No prejudice! It has been most heinously prejudiced.

Baron Bramwell (interrupting): You have no right to make the observations you are now making. What you are entitled is to take an objection on any point of law if there is any,

Burke: I am bound to defend my character.

Baron Bramwell: You have no right to do that now. (Then proceeding to pass sentence.) I have informed myself what would be the proper punishment to pass upon you both and I have done so without taking into consideration at all the other case.

Burke: Pardon me, my lord. I understand you to consider that I have finished. I have concluded my remarks on that point, but I have something else to say.

Baron Bramwell repeated that he could only urge objections in law to judgment being pronounced upon him. He must accept the verdict of the jury as final. Burke continued to argue with the judge who finally lost his patience and said in a peremptory tone: "Silence. I cannot allow you to go on; I have borne with you long enough. I have made up my mind that no man who is convicted by the lawful tribunals of the country should afterwards be permitted to assail those tribunals and apparently have all the honours of the contest with him. I think many men have been tempted into the commission of crime by the expectation that they would have an opportunity of making an exciting speech when called up for judgment, and I think it would be a salutary alteration of the law without being allowed to do so, and I have determined that that shall be the case with you. I say I have inquired what sentence should be passed upon you, and I find that in Ireland, where they have had more experience in these cases than we have in England, the sentence that would probably have been passed upon you for this offence would have been fifteen years' penal servitude, and that sentence, with the concurrence of my learned brother, I now pass upon you."

# CHAPTER 20

# ENGLISH PRISON CONDITIONS

Treason-felony prisoners, when first sentenced, were sent to either Pentonville or Millbank prison where they spent nine months on probation. At the end of this period they were then transferred to another convict prison - usually Portland, Chatham or Portsmouth. Every time a prisoner entered a new prison he was stripped and searched. In these jails no distinction was made between the Fenian prisoners and the ordinary convicts except that they were kept apart when working. However, the Fenian prisoners objected to doing heavy work and work which they found degrading. When a Fenian prisoner refused to work he was reported and punished - usually solitary confinement. When this happened his comrades refused to work also. Eventually the prison officials came to the conclusion that it was waste of time punishing these Fenian prisoners and they ignored this breach of rule. This is quite evident from the records of Portland prison for 1870.

When admitted to prison each Fenian prisoner was supplied with a prison uniform the same as all other prisoners. It consisted of a woollen short coat, knickerbockers, stockings, shoes, shirt and cap. No matter how cold the weather was he wasn't given flannels (underclothes) except on the say so of the medical officer. These clothes were washed regularly and a prisoner never got the same clothes returned to him. At night time the prisoner slept in his shirt and flannels (if he had been issued with them.) He kept his outer clothes in his cell except when he was under punishment or if he was suspected of trying to escape. If this was the case, then, he had to put his body clothes outside his cell door and collect them again in the morning. The cap was never worn in the cell but was always hanging on the bell-handle.

The prisoner's cell measured 10ft by 7ft (approximately) and was furnished with a table, stool, bed, a tin box, a tin pint, a spoon, a plate and a knife. If the cell didn't have a water closet each

| — | FEBRUARY. | 1. | 2. | 3. | 4. | 5. | 7. | 8. | 9 | 10. | 11. | 12. | 14. | 15. | 16. | 17. | 18. | 19. | 21. | 22. | 23. | 24. | 25. | 26. | 28. |
|---|---|---|---|---|---|---|---|---|---|---|---|---|---|---|---|---|---|---|---|---|---|---|---|---|---|
| 5,360 | Thomas C. Luby | None | None | None | None | None | None | None | None | None | None | None | None | None | None | None | None | None | None | None | None | None | None | None | None. |
| 5,361 | John O'Leary | V. little | V. little | V. little | V. little | V. little | V. little | V. little | " | " | " | " | " | " | " | " | " | " | | " | | " | " | " | " |
| 6,331 | Michael Sheehy | " | Fair | Fair | Fair | Fair | Fair | Fair | Fair | " | " | " | " | " | " | " | " | " | V. little | " | | Little | Little | Little | " |
| 6,332 | Mortimer Shea | " | None | None | None | V. little | V. little | None | None | " | " | " | " | " | " | " | " | " | " | " | | " | " | " | |
| — | — | Fair | Fair | Fair | Fair | Fair | Fair | Fair | Fair | Fair | Fair | V. little | V. little | V. little | Fair | Fair | Fair | Fair | Fair | Fair | Fair | Fair | Fair | Fair | V. little. |
| 6,659 | Edward St. Clair | " | " | " | " | " | " | " | " | " | " | " | " | " | V. little | V. little | " | " | " | " | " | " | Little | Little | Little. |
| 6,683 | Patrick Walsh | " | " | " | " | " | " | V. little | None | None | None | None | None | None | None | None | None | None | V. little | " | " | " | " | " | None. |
| 6,742 | John McCafferty | None | None | None | None | None | None | None | " | " | " | " | Infy. | Infy. | Infy. | Infy. | Infy. | Infy. | Infy. | Infy. | Infy. | Infy. | Infy. | Infy. | Infy. |
| 7,020 | Patrick Doran | " | " | " | " | " | " | " | " | " | " | " | None | None | None | None | None | None | None | None | None | None | None | None | None. |
| 7,022 | William Mackay | V. little | V. little | V. little | V. little | V. little | V. little | V. little | " | " | " | " | Infy. | Infy. | Infy. | Infy. | Infy. | Infy. | Infy. | Infy. | Infy. | Infy. | Infy | Infy. | Infy. |
| 7,168 | Peter Mohan | Fair | Fair | Fair | Fair | Fair | Fair | Fair | Fair | Fair | Fair | Fair | Fair | Fair | Fair | Fair | Fair | Fair | Fair | Fair | Fair | Fair | Little | Little | Little. |
| 6,661 | George Brown | Infy. | Infy. | Infy. | Infy. | Infy. | Infy. | Infy. | Infy. | Infy. | Infy. | Infy. | Infy. | Infy. | Infy. | Infy. | Infy. | Infy. | Infy. | Infy. | Infy. | None | None | None | None. |

| — | MARCH. | 1. | 2. | 3. | 4. | 5. | 7. | 8. | 9. | 10. | 11. | 12. | 14. | 15. | 16. | 17. | 18. | 19. | 21. | 22. | 23. | 24. | 25. | 26. | 28. | 29. | 30. | 31. |
|---|---|---|---|---|---|---|---|---|---|---|---|---|---|---|---|---|---|---|---|---|---|---|---|---|---|---|---|---|
| 5,360 | Thomas C. Luby | None | None | None | None | None | None | None | None | None | None | None | None | None | None | None | None | None | None | None | None | None | None | None | None | None | None | None. |
| 5,361 | John O'Leary | " | " | " | " | " | " | " | " | " | " | " | " | " | " | " | " | " | " | Infy. | Infy. | Infy. | Infy. | Infy. | Infy. | Infy. | Infy. | Infy. |
| 6,331 | Michael Sheehy | " | " | " | " | " | " | " | Infy. | " | " | " | " | " | " | " | " | " | " | Little | None | None | Little | None | None | None | Little | Little. |
| 6,332 | Mortimer Shea | " | " | " | " | " | " | " | None | Little | Little | Little | Little | Little | Little | Little | Little | Little | " | " | " | " | None | " | " | Little | " | " |
| — | — | Little | Little | Little | Little | Little | Little | Little | Fair | Fair | Fair | Fair | " | " | " | " | " | " | Little | " | Fair | Little | Little | Little | Little | " | Fair | Fair. |
| 6,659 | Edward St. Clair | " | " | " | None | " | " | " | Little | Little | Little | Little | " | " | " | " | " | " | " | None | None | None | None | None | None | None | None | Little. |
| 6,698 | Patrick Walsh | None | None | None | " | None | None | None | None | None | Little | None | None | None | None | None | None | None | None | | | | | | | | | |
| 6,742 | John McCafferty | Infy. | Infy. | Infy. | Infy. | Infy. | Infy. | Infy. | Infy. | Infy. | Infy. | Infy. | Infy. | Infy. | Infy. | Infy. | Infy. | Infy. | Infy. | Infy. | Infy. | Infy. | Infy. | Infy. | Infy. | Infy. | Infy. | Infy. |
| 7,020 | Patrick Doran | None | None | None | " | " | " | " | " | " | " | " | " | " | " | " | " | " | " | " | " | " | " | " | " | " | " | " |
| 7,022 | William Mackay | Infy. | Infy. | Infy. | " | " | " | " | " | " | " | " | " | " | " | " | " | " | " | " | " | " | " | " | " | " | " | " |
| 7,168 | Peter Mohan | Little | Little | Little | Little | Little | Little | Little | Little | Little | Little | Little | None | None | Little | Little | Little | Little | Little | Little | None | Little | Little | Little | None | None | None | Fair. |
| 6,661 | George Brown | None | None | None | None | None | None | None | None | None | None | None | " | " | None | None | None | None | None | None | " | None | None | None | " | . | " | None. |

| — | APRIL. | 1. | 2. | 4. | 5. | 6. | 7. | 8. | 9. | 11. | 12. | 13. | 14. | 16. | 18. | 19. | 20. | 21. | 22. | 23. | 25. | 26. | 27. | 28. | 29. | 30. |
|---|---|---|---|---|---|---|---|---|---|---|---|---|---|---|---|---|---|---|---|---|---|---|---|---|---|---|
| 5,360 | Thomas C. Luby | V. little | V. little | Little | Little | None | None | None | None | None | None | None | None | None | None | None | None | None | None | None | None | None | None | None | None | None. |
| 5,361 | John O'Leary | Infy. | Infy. | Infy. | Infy. | Infy. | Infy. | Infy. | Infy. | Infy. | Infy. | Infy. | " | " | " | V. little | V. little | Little | Little | Little | " | " | Little | Little | Little | Little. |
| 6,331 | Michael Sheehy | Little | Little | Little | Little | None | None | None | None | None | None | None | " | " | " | None | None | None | None | None | " | " | None | None | None | None. |
| 6,332 | Mortimer Shea | " | " | " | " | " | " | " | " | " | " | " | " | " | " | " | " | " | " | " | " | " | " | " | " | " |
| 6,338 | — | Fair | Fair | Fair | Fair | Little | Little | Little | Little | Little | Little | Little | Little | Little | Little | Little | Little | Little | Little | Little | Little | Little | Little | Little | Little | Little. |
| 6,659 | Edward St. Clair | " | " | " | " | None | " | " | " | " | " | " | " | " | " | " | " | " | " | " | " | " | " | " | " | " |
| 6,698 | Patrick Walsh | Little | Little | Little | Little | " | None | None | None | None | None | None | None | None | None | None | None | None | None | None | None | None | None | None | None | None. |
| 6,742 | John McCafferty | Infy. | Infy. | Infy. | Infy. | Infy. | Infy. | Infy. | Infy. | Infy. | Infy. | " | " | " | " | " | " | " | " | " | " | " | " | " | " | " |
| 7,020 | Patrick Doran | " | " | " | " | " | None | None | None | None | None | " | " | " | " | " | " | " | " | " | " | " | " | " | " | " |
| 7,022 | William Mackay | " | " | " | " | " | Infy. | Infy. | Infy. | Infy. | Infy. | " | " | " | " | " | " | " | " | " | " | " | " | " | " | " |
| 7,168 | Peter Mohan | Fair | Fair | Little | Fair | None | Little | Little | Little | Little | Little | Little | Little | " | " | " | " | " | " | " | " | " | " | " | " | " |
| 6,661 | George Brown | Little | Little | " | Little | " | None | None | None | None | " | " | " | " | " | " | " | " | " | " | " | " | " | " | " | " |

| — | MAY. | 2. | 3. | 4. | 5. | 6. | 7. | 9. | 10. | 11. | 12. | 13. | 14. | 16. | 17. | 18. | 19. | 20. | 21. | 23. | 24. | 25. | 26. | 27. | 28. | 30. | 31. | June 1. | 2. | 3. |
|---|---|---|---|---|---|---|---|---|---|---|---|---|---|---|---|---|---|---|---|---|---|---|---|---|---|---|---|---|---|---|
| 5,360 | Thomas C. Luby | None | None | None | None | None | None | None | None | None | None | None | None | None | None | None | None | None | None | None | None | None | None | None | None | None | None | None | None | None. |
| 5,361 | John O'Leary | Little | Little | Little | Little | Little | Little | Little | Little | Little | Little | Little | Little | Little | Little | Little | Little | Little | Little | Little | Little | Little | Little | Little | Little | Little | Little | Little | Little | Little. |
| 6,331 | Michael Sheehy | None | None | None | None | None | None | None | None | None | None | None | None | None | None | None | None | None | None | None | None | None | None | None | None | None | None | None | None | None. |
| 6,332 | Mortimer Shea | " | " | " | " | " | " | " | " | " | " | " | " | " | " | " | " | " | " | " | " | " | " | " | " | " | " | " | | " |
| 6,338 | — | Little | Little | Little | Little | Little | Little | Little | Little | Little | Little | Little | Little | Little | Transferred. | | | | | | | | | | | | | | | |
| 6,742 | John McCafferty | None | None | " | None | None | " | " | " | " | None | " | " | " | None | None | . | " | " | " | " | " | . | " | " | " | " | " | " | " |
| 7,020 | Patrick Doran | . | " | None | " | " | None | None | None | None | " | None | None | None | " | " | . | " | " | " | " | " | " | " | " | " | " | " | " | " |
| 7,022 | William Mackay | " | " | " | " | " | " | " | " | " | " | " | " | " | " | " | " | " | " | " | " | " | " | " | " | " | " | " | " | " |
| 7,168 | Peter Mohan | " | " | " | Little | Little | Little | Little | Little | Little | Little | Little | Little | Little | " | " | " | " | " | " | " | " | " | " | " | " | " | " | " | " |
| 6,661 | George Brown | " | " | Little | None | None | None | None | None | None | None | None | None | None | " | " | " | " | " | " | " | " | " | " | " | " | " | " | " | " |
| 6,659 | Edward St. Clair | Little | " | " | Little | Little | Little | Little | Little | Little | Little | Little | Little | Little | " | " | " | Little | Little | Little | Little | Little | Little | Little | Little | Little | Little | Little | Little | Little. |
| 6,698 | Patrick Walsh | None | " | " | " | " | " | None | None | None | None | None | None | None | " | " | " | None | None | None | None | None | None | None | None | None | None | None | None | None. |

*Treason Felony Convicts – Record of Industry on the Public Works, Portland.*

prisoner had a urinal (pot) which he wasn't allowed to use at night. The bed, 7ft by 3ft, had a timber base, a horsehair mattress a half inch thick, a pillow of similar material, two blankets and a pair of sheets. In cold weather a third blanket might have been issued. Every morning the bedclothes had to be placed, nicely folded to a regulated height and width, on a kind of open cupboard which stood in the corner of the cell. The towel had to be folded in a particular manner with the bit of soap in the middle. These were all open to the view of the inspector who visited every morning and if he wasn't satisfied he threw them on the floor and the prisoner had to arrange them again. To annoy the prisoner some inspectors would throw the clothes on the floor a couple of times before he would be satisfied.

The spoon and plate were made of timber and from all the cleaning they were nearly white. A type of white dust and rags were supplied to clean these vessels. Prisoners lodged complaints that they had to use the same rag to clean the vessels as they did to clean the urinal. The tin pint sparkled from all the cleaning. Gruel, cocoa, milk and soup were taken from the pint. The knife consisted of a bit of tin four inches long. Each prisoner was issued with two leather knee caps which were to be worn when polishing the cell floor. This had to be done twice a week and finished off by rubbing the flags with a kind of soft white stone, known as 'holystone', so that when the cell dried it had a nice chalky appearance. If any of these things were not done properly then the prisoner was punished.

**DISCIPLINE**

For the general body of prisoners the discipline was very strict but there was some relaxation for the Fenian prisoners. This relaxation was not granted freely but was wrung from the authorities through protests. Compared to the other prisoners the Fenians were highly insubordinate in manner, in language and in general bearing. When being addressed by prison officers a prisoner had to remove his cap, stand with feet in the military position and had to be attentive. Saluting was not necessary except to the medical officer, chaplain, priest and governor. However, the Fenian prisoners didn't keep these regulations. The Governor of Portland Prison, George Clifton, told the Devon Commission on June 15th, 1870, "When I went around today to ask these prisoners for their reports, I did not expect any of them to salute me, but I did think, as an act of courtesy, that they would put their hands to their sides. They stood with their hands behind their backs. I have often been told by some of them, 'We shall treat you as so much dirt under our feet.' " The warders did not want to supervise the Fenian prisoners as they were often abused and called liars. There was not a very friendly feeling between the two groups and the Fenians often complained of insolent language and harsh treatment.

Prisoners had to remain silent at all times except when addressed by a prison official. However, this rule was relaxed for the Fenian prisoners. At work they were allowed to talk when it was connected with their duties. This rule was not observed either. With Ricard Burke in Chatham prison in 1868 were O'Donovan Rossa, William Halpin, Harry Mulleda, John Warren and Augustine Costelloe. Rossa describes their work periods. "Rick Burke and Harry Mulleda, who were undergoing their nine months term of probation, were sent out to us and our work was changed from grass picking to wood splitting. We were taken into an old shed where lime was stored, and, after each of us fixed a block for himself, we were supplied with small hatchets.

"A pile of wood lay convenient, and, after having sawn this into pieces about nine inches long, our duty was to cut it up into splinters about one inch square and tie it into bundles. This occupation was pleasant enough, unless you gave your fingers a touch of the hatchet, which occasionally happened to us all round.

"Colonel Warren chopped a piece off one of his fingers once, and, instead of our crying at his misfortune, some of us, not thinking he had given himself so wicked a stroke, were cruel enough to laugh at him, which did not at all please him. On the whole, we made ourselves as jolly as possible, and, as we were allowed to joke and tell stories, we passed the time pretty pleasantly. 'Twas a paradise to me compared with the life I previously led, and I look back now with a kind of affectionate longing for the stories and the prison society of Rick Burke and Halpin."

On Sundays the Fenian prisoners were allowed to talk during the exercise period as long as they did not make too much noise. Again this rule was not observed. When O'Donovan Rossa was in irons for thirty five days in Chatham the two cells over his were occupied by Rick Burke and Harry Mulleda. They conversed with each other by knocking on the wall. As both Burke and Mulleda were working - picking oakum - Rossa had to talk to each of them in turn.

**LETTERS**

When a prisoner entered jail for the first time he was permitted to write a letter telling his relations where he was. He was granted the same facility when he was transferred to another jail. While on probation, which lasted nine months, he was allowed to write and receive just one letter. After completing his probationary period and provided he was of good conduct for at least two previous months he advanced to the third class and was then allowed to write and receive a letter every six months. As a second class prisoner the period between each letter was four months and as a first class prisoner he could write a letter every three months. Promotion from class to class was based on conduct and industry. Loss of merit marks could result in a prisoner being demoted in class right back to probation with a resultant loss of letter writing privileges.

Every letter written by and to the prisoner was read and any letter containing public news was withheld. If a letter written by a prisoner contained any criticism of the prison or its officials it was withheld. Eventually this regulation was changed and the offending pieces were blacked out. If a letter of a death announcement or some such serious matter arrived the prisoner could not see it until the time arrived that it was due. However, the information contained in the letter was communicated to him and nothing more.

**VISITS**

The prisoner was allowed visits by family and friends on the same basis as letters. The visits always took place in the presence of a warder or a deputy governor or some other officer and each visit lasted twenty minutes or, in exceptional cases, thirty minutes. The Fenian prisoners complained that it was next to impossible for them to have visitors as all their relatives lived in Ireland and the cost of the journey to England would have been beyond their means. As a result of complaints the regulations on letter writing were relaxed slightly for these prisoners. Ricard Burke was not as badly affected as some of the others in this matters. His sister, Catherine (Kate) Barry, lived in London and visited him whenever she was allowed. His brother, Richard, from Coachford, Co. Cork, also visited him.

**DIET**

The diet in each prison varied very little. In Chatham the diet was as follows:

***Breakfast***

| | |
|---|---|
| 1 pint of cocoa containing | ¾ oz of cocoa<br>2 oz of milk<br>¾ oz of molasses |
| Bread : | 11 oz |

***Dinner***

*Sunday:*

| | |
|---|---|
| 1 pint of soup containing | 4 oz pork<br>4 oz pease<br>¼ oz vinegar<br>½ oz onions |
| Bread : | 5 oz |

*Monday and Saturday:*

| | |
|---|---|
| 5 oz beef without bone after being cooked | With its own liquor flavoured with ½ oz onions and thickened with 1⅛ oz of flour and any bread and potatoes left on the previous day and ¾ oz pepper per cent. |

Potatoes: 1 pound     Bread:  5 oz

*Tuesday and Thursday:*

| | |
|---|---|
| 1 pint of soup containing: | 8 oz shins of beef<br>1 oz pearl barley<br>2 oz fresh barley<br>2 oz fresh vegetables<br>1 oz onions. Thickening same as above. |

Cheese: 2 oz     Potatoes: 1 pound     Bread :  5 oz

*Wednesday:*

| | |
|---|---|
| 5 oz of mutton without bone after being cooked. | With its own liquor and flavoured and thickened as above. |

Potatoes: 1 pound     Bread :  5 oz

*Friday:*

| | |
|---|---|
| 1 pound of suet pudding containing | 1½ oz suet<br>8 oz flour<br>6 oz water |

Potatoes: 1 pound    Bread : 5 oz

*Supper*

1 pint of gruel
8 oz bread.

A prisoner had to be two years in prison and free of reports before he became entitled to tea for supper.

There were many complaints about the diet. When the prisoner got his food, which was pushed through a trap door 5 inches square, he could lodge a complaint. Usually the food was there and then examined and weighed. Sometimes, if a prisoner was constantly complaining, he would be left waiting until all the other business was done. There were complaints of entrails of fowl and mice and droppings in the food. The meat was often bad and the suet rancid. The bread often was not properly baked - if it was then the prisoners would complain of light weight.

Brian Dillon, (of whom more later), in a submission to the Commission on July 22nd, 1870, had much to say about the food. "The dietary at the prison (Woking), except when a director is expected or upon such rare occasions as the visit or expected visit of the Commissioners, has been always inferior. Prisoners who complain of food here are called 'troublesome'. Not long ago, at the beginning of May, I believe, the tea was so very bad that at least a great many men in the hospital ward returned their breakfast tea; it was, in truth, more coloured water. The cheese one Sunday was so surpassingly bad that whole wards of prisoners went to the cook-house to return it. I showed mine to the warder through the trap-door of my cell. He said, 'It's all the same,' and passed on. I did not carry my food to the cook-house. My pride, my self-respect revolted against the degrading humiliation of voluntarily standing in line amongst thieves, waiting like a pauper until my bit of cheese was examined.

"This is an accurate description of the beefsteak given to me six days out of every seven from 25th September, 1869 to 17th May, 1870 - a short thick junk or lump of beef, burnt as black as your hat on one side, the other side raw, red, bloody and uncooked; or a similar junk burnt black on all sides, and as white and dry as a chip when cut. The puddings are scarcely ever free from a sprinkling of soot more or less thick. Because of my illness I have been placed on chicken; a wing or a leg falls to my share generally, so dirty and covered with 'penfeathers', that I spend some time every day picking them out before I attempt to eat. The chicken broth was mere hot water, having neither the taste nor colour of chicken broth. The milk is seldom unadulterated by water; in fact it is well known prisoners seek the situation of cooks, not to cook, but to plunder. This accounts to some extent for the small chops, watered milk and puddings without egg or sugar."

The Devon Commission in its report on Diet: "We inquired with care and minuteness into the dietary of the several prisons visited and the quality of the food, personally inspecting, in many instances, the provisions in store, tasting the food when dressed, and testing it in the rations of individual prisoners. We see no reason to doubt that, in the vast majority of instances, the food is wholesome and good of its kind. ... We have on some occasions observed that the bread did not appear to have been thoroughly leavened, and that the dough had not fully risen; and we also noticed, in some instances, that the bread was not sufficiently baked. ... The tea supplied to certain classes of prisoners also attracted our attention; it appeared to us to be of inferior character, owing to its being too long in the cauldron before use.

"With reference to the allegations that such foreign substances as a mouse, entrails of fowl, or other refuse, have found their way into the prisoners' diet, we have to observe, that if such articles got accidentally into the soup cauldron a few hours before the soup

Medical [illegible]
certificate
as to this prisoner's
present state of health

No. 341c.

Convict Establishment,

Chatham

Convicts are permitted to write one Letter on reception, and also at invervals of 3, 4, or 6 months, according to the class they may be in. They may also receive one Letter (prepaid) at the above named periods. Matters of private importance to a Convict may be communicated at any time by Letter (prepaid) to the Governor, who will inform the Convict thereof, if expedient.

In case of misconduct, the privilege of receiving or writing a Letter may be forfeited for a time.

All letters of an improper or idle tendency, either to or from Convicts, or containing slang or other objectionable expressions, will be suppressed. The permission to write and receive Letters is given to the Convicts for the purpose of enabling them to keep up a connection with their respectable friends, and not that they may hear the news of the day.

All Letters are read by the Governor or Chaplain, and must be legibly written on the ruled lines, and not crossed.

Neither clothes, nor any other articles, are allowed to be received at the Prison for the use of Convicts, except through the Governor. Persons attempting otherwise to introduce any article to or for a Convict are liable to Fine or Imprisonment, and the Convict concerned is liable to be severely punished. Convicts are not allowed to have Money, Books, or Postage Stamps sent to them while in Prison.

A Visit of twenty minutes duration allowed every 3, 4, or 6 months, according to class, between the hours of 10 a.m and 4 p.m., not on Sundays.

F & T 17,500 8—69

was served, they would be boiled down into a condition in which they could not be recognised. ...... It must be admitted as barely possible that, in transition from kitchen to prisoners' cells, by accident or design, a foreign object of small size might find its way into a convict's ration. An object supposed to have been a mouse was on one occasion detected in a prisoner's ration. On careful examination it was found to be a small piece of cowhide with the hair on."

**WORK**

All healthy prisoners were required to do hard labour. This involved clearing and trenching land, hewing and dressing stone, etc. Work started at 7.30am and continued until 5pm with a break of an hour for dinner. The Fenian prisoners, eventually, refused to do this heavy work and were then given lighter work such as tailoring, knitting socks, splitting wood, weeding, cleaning bricks, etc.

**PUNISHMENT**

The usual punishment for a serious infringement of the rules was solitary confinement and a bread and water diet for three days. This could be extended to twenty eight days by order of a prison director with a penal class diet every fourth day. When on bread and water a prisoner got 8oz of bread and 1 pint of water at 5.30am and the same at 5.30pm. The cell was sparsely furnished with no mattress on the bed and no stool or seat of any kind. The only book the prisoner was allowed was the Bible. The prisoner was visited every hour of the day and night by a warder and had to answer, "I'm all right," when questioned which he did even when he had managed to get some sleep. He was allowed no exercise, no letters, no visits, no news and even could not attend mass.

For less serious infringements a prisoner could be fined so many "marks." When a prisoner was sentenced, every day of the prison term was put down against him as six marks. He was told that if he was obedient and worked hard he could earn eight marks a day. Thus if the term of imprisonment was twenty days - 120 marks - he could work out this 120 marks in fifteen days. In

***House of Detention, Clerkenwell showing exercise yards.***
*(Courtesy Islington Public Library)*

other words he got a quarter off for good behaviour. However, what frequently happened was that a prisoner worked hard for fourteen days earning his eight marks per day. Then his officer would report him for some trifling offence such as looking at another prisoner, or, indeed, for some imaginary offence. For this he could be fined as many marks as would put him back to his original sentence.

**COMPLAINTS PROCEDURE**

A prisoner had the right to complain to the governor about the warder's behaviour to him. The governor was bound to investigate the complaint. The prisoner was questioned in the presence of the governor and the warder in question. He could not call on any other prisoner to support his testimony. It was always the prisoner's word against the warder's and the warder's word was always accepted.

The prisoner then had the right to appeal to the prison director who had to investigate the complaint. However, if the prisoner was undergoing a term of punishment when the director visited the prison, then, his appeal would not be heard. The prisoner had the right of appeal right up to the Home Secretary, but this could only be made once in the twelve months no matter how serious the matter was.

**EXERCISE**

Each prisoner was allowed one hour's exercise each day. In each exercise yard were circular flagged pathways around which the prisoners walked four paces apart, hands by the side, eyes looking straight ahead. If a prisoner was detected attempting to pass a whisper or sign of recognition he was immediately sent to his cell and held under report for punishment. Prisoners were reprimanded for having their hands behind their backs with one stuck into the sleeve of the other in an attempt to keep warm. Hands had to be at the side, so the prisoners walked around with hunched shoulders and their hands shrugged up to keep them warm.

## CHAPTER 21

# RICARD'S PRISON LIFE

Such was the prison system that Burke was admitted to on 30th April, 1868. After sentencing, he was confined in Newgate prison until May 2nd when he was transferred to Millbank jail to begin his nine month's probationary period. However, having spent only sixteen days in Millbank, he was transferred to Chatham on May 18th and remained there until December 10th, 1869. He was admitted to Woking Invalid Prison on that date and on March 28th, 1870, he was sent back again to Millbank. On May 1st he returned to Woking and finally on August 30th he was transferred to Broadmoor Asylum.

Let us look then at this young man - just thirty years of age - an American Colonel of Engineers - as he begins his sentence of fifteen years penal servitude in an English jail. The London correspondent of The Irishman in his letter published on February 18th, 1868, says:- "Let me say that prison officials are loud - now that their temporary scare is over - in praising the calmness and gentlemanly manner of Colonel Burke, all the while he was immured in that hideous Bastile. Burke was habitually self-possessed and self-subdued. His iron tenacity of character, his determination to put up with what he could not help, first amazed, and then charmed his jailers. I heard a lady, who casually saw him while in confinement, as he paced the dismal rounds of the exercise yard: 'If there is but one gentleman in the world, that is he.' "

John Augustine O'Shea, editor of Burke's autobiography, wrote from Paris on May 2nd, 1868:-

"What I do know of my own knowledge and whatever else concerning his career I have gathered from others is to his honour.... He was robust, tall, cast in one of nature's symmetric moulds. I despair of being able to put this man before you as he appeared to me. Picture to yourself a bold, frank, free bearing - bearing of a cavalier; a face of Irish type, with dancing light in the

| General Register Number. | Name and Aliases and Trade. | Date and Place of Birth. | Married or Single and Number of Children. | Name and Residence of Family or Next of Kin. | Date and Place of Conviction—Crime with Particulars. | Previous Convictions and Character. | Religion. | Education. | | Transfers from Date of Committal. | | Remarks. |
|---|---|---|---|---|---|---|---|---|---|---|---|---|
| | | | | | | | | Read. | Write. | Prison. | Date of Reception. | |
| 14 | Charles Underwood O'Connell (clerk). | Frankfort, King's Co., Ireland. | Single - - | Uncle, Dr. O'Connell, Kilmallock. | 14th December 1865; Special Commission, Cork; Treason-felony; 10 years penal servitude. | Nil - | Roman Catholic. | Both | - - | Mountjoy -<br>Pentonville -<br>Portland -<br>Millbank -<br>Chatham - | 14th Dec. 1865<br>16th Jan. 1866<br>14th May 1866<br>20th May 1868<br>15th March 1869 | |
| 15 | John alias Capt. John M'Clure (book-keeper). | 17th July 1845; Dobb's Ferry, WestchesterCo., New York State, United States. | Single - - | Father, Mr. D. M'Clure, Dobb's Ferry, Westchester Co. | 2nd May 1867; Special Commission, Cork; High Treason; death commuted to life penal servitude. | Nil - | Roman Catholic. | Yes | - - | Millbank -<br>Portland -<br>Millbank -<br>Chatham - | 4th July 1867<br>21st April 1868<br>20th May 1868<br>15th March 1869 | |
| 16 | William Halpin, alias Jno. Hart (civil engineer). | 1824; declines to state. | - - - | Friend, Mr. J. F. O'Donnell, 45, Amwell Street, London, E.C. | 25th October 1867; Special Commission, Dublin; Treason-felony; 15 years penal servitude. | Nil - | Roman Catholic. | Yes | - - | Kilmainham -<br>Millbank -<br>Chatham - | —<br>29th Nov. 1867<br>19th Aug. 1868 | |
| 17 | Jeremiah O'Donovan (Rossa) (publisher of "Irish People" newspaper). | 4th Sept. 1831; Rossenbury, Co. Cork, Ireland. | Married, five children. | Friends reside at Skibbereen and Clonakilty, Co. Cork. | 13th December 1865; Special Commission, Dublin city, Dublin; Treason-felony; life penal servitude. | Nil - | Roman Catholic. | Yes | - - | Mountjoy -<br>Pentonville -<br>Portland -<br>Millbank -<br>Chatham - | 13th Dec. 1865<br>23rd Dec. 1865<br>14th May 1866<br>20th Feb. 1867<br>24th Feb. 1868 | |
| 18 | Patrick Lennon (cork cutter). | 1843; Dublin - | Single - - | Brother, 159, Capel Street, Dublin. | 10th February 1868; Dublin Special Commission; Treason-felony; 15 years penal servitude. | - - - | Roman Catholic. | Imperfectly | - | Millbank -<br>Dartmoor - | 26th Feb. 1868<br>30th Dec. 1868 | |
| 19 | Richard Burke, alias Geo. Berry, alias Edward C. Winslow, alias Wallace (soldier). | New York - | Single - - | Cath. Berry, 6, Harriet Street, Lower Marsh, Lambeth. | 6th April 1868; Central Criminal Court; Treason-felony; 15 years penal servitude. | - - - | Roman Catholic. | Well | - - | Newgate -<br>Millbank -<br>Chatham -<br>Woking -<br>Millbank -<br>Woking - | 6th March 1868<br>2nd May 1868<br>18th May 1868<br>10th Dec. 1869<br>28th March 1870<br>May 1870 | |
| 20 | Peter Mohan (carpenter). | 4th Feb. 1837 - | Married, two children. | Amelia Morgan, Disney Street, Red Cross Street, Bow. | 4th May 1868; Central Criminal Court; Treason-felony; 10 years penal servitude. | Nil - | Roman Catholic. | Imperfectly | - | Newgate -<br>Millbank -<br>Portland - | 8th April 1868<br>12th June 1868<br>15th April 1869 | |

*Ricard's Prison Record*

grey eyes, and thin lips, plastic, yet firm, that lifted betimes with the ready smile, and revealed a glistening row of white teeth. Crown the head, squarely set on broad shoulders, with Antonious curls, crisp and close, and dark brown in hue. The large forehead with its brows well developed, bespoke intellect; the bronze tinting over forehead and face, with freckle groups motting it to olive here and there, showed that here was no dangler of the boudoir, no dandy airing his fine graces over the pavement or carpet. No; there was a Dantonesque strength in that man, and the weather stains on his cheeks, and the hard pliant hand that stretched forth to grasp yours convinced you that he had been where things needed to be done, and could do things at will... I found him well informed, agreeable, full of bonhomie, a racy raconteur, ...."

Mr. John Rowland Gibson, Fellow of the Royal College of Surgeons and medical officer of Newgate prison, in evidence before the Devon Commission on 16th August, 1870, said he could remember Ricard Burke well when he was an inmate of that prison from March 6th, 1868, to May 2nd of the same year. He seemed perfectly sound in mind; there was no question of that. He never refused his food during that period. His health was good and he was well nourished. He was always quite calm, well sustained, never excited. He was ever ready to enter conversation with anybody. Mr Gibson concluded his evidence with this comment. "I recollect how well composed he was. There was a nice gentlemanly manner about the man."

Burke did not have an easy life in prison and was very ill for a long period and was also of unsound mind - whether real or feigned. One of the prison doctors, Dr. Burns of Chatham, maintained that Burke was feigning insanity in the hope of an early release. Two other prison doctors, Dr. Cambell of Woking and Dr. Meyer of Broadmoor Lunatic Asylum, did not agree with Dr. Burns's diagnosis. Burke also claimed that an attempt was made to poison him but that he detected it in time.

Early in 1869, Ricard was taking some medicine for a slight pain in the chest and, occasionally, for intestinal worms which the quality of food gave rise to. He felt terrible pain in the spine and back and head after most doses. But it was not until November 23rd that he found he had mercury in his system. On that day, Dr. Steele, the assistant surgeon, visited him while at work where Burke complained of a slight pain in the head. He took three doses of the stuff prescribed by Dr. Steele which from all the symptoms, he concluded, was some compound containing a portion of mercury. He was attacked with convulsions, occasional vomiting and he suffered from a violent pain in the stomach - hot, raw, strong pain in the heart and larger blood-vessels. Dr. Steele, to humour Ricard, said he would give him some white of egg as an antidote. He continued to get worse, took fits of not eating and refused all medicines. One day he said to a fellow prisoner:- "I would like to lie down in old Kinneigh by the side of my brother, Dan, and that father from whom I learned the principles I glory in." In December he was so ill that his death was hourly expected and he received the last rites from Fr. O'Sullivan, the Catholic chaplain. At one stage, Karl Marx interrupted a meeting of the First International to announce that a report of Burke's death had been received. With his physical and mental condition in a very poor state he was removed to Woking Invalid Prison on December 10th, 1869, where his health still continued to be a cause of concern,

(According to the Encyclopaedia Brittanica symptoms of mercury poisoning include a metallic taste and excessive production of saliva; an inflation of the membrane of the mouth; loosening of the teeth; pain, numbness in the extremities; loss of weight and appetite; and mental and personality changes marked by depression and a tendency to withdraw. All these symptoms Burke complained of.)

Burke's sister, Kate Barry, was very concerned about his health and frequently made representations to the Secretary of State for the Home Department, Mr. Bruce, and to Mr. McCarthy Downing, M.P. for County Cork. In February, 1870, she wrote to Mr. Bruce expressing her concern and alarm about her brother's health. "I am informed that he is very low and that his physical health has of late become impaired, in addition to the heavy calamity which has ruined his mind." The reply from the Home Secretary included a copy of a letter from Dr. Meyer of Broadmoor Asylum which stated:-

"Sir - After careful examination of the prisoner, I am of the opinion that he is of unsound mind. I have been chiefly led to this conclusion by Burke's general appearance and demeanour, by his extravagant ideas of his own powers and knowledge, and by his exceedingly defective memory. My view of the case is supported by the evidence of the medical officers of the prison, as well as the warders in charge of the prisoners."

About the same time, early February, 1870, as she was making representations to the Home Secretary, Kate Barry, accompanied by a George Haslam, visited Ricard in Woking prison. Haslam has left this account of the visit:-

"After a journey attended with considerable difficulties which need not here allude to, Mrs. Barry and myself arrived at the prison, which is situated in a wild, bleak and comfortless common, at nightfall, and after the stipulated hour for visiting." They were met by the Governor who kindly relaxed the rule and allowed the visit to take place.

"Burke was attired in a pair of high-low shoes, blue worsted stockings, with red wings, drab knee-breeches, brown cloth vest, a smartly made grey over-coat, 'topped' with a villainous looking Glengarry woollen chaput. He entered the room in a wild, excited and nervous manner as though impressed with fear. Instead of being placed behind the wooden railings at the end of the apartment, the under-governor motioned Burke, in a conciliatory manner, to be seated on a chair beside Mrs. Barry and myself, near the fire, which he did. After looking around him with a vacant and idiotic stare, the convict settled his gaze upon Mrs. Barry, who opened the conversation with an inquiry as to her brother's health. It was some time, however, before Burke appeared to recognise his sister, when, in answer to her repeated inquiry he exclaimed in an excited manner, 'That he was as strong as a bull.' ... Suddenly he jumped up from his chair and standing behind it, exclaimed in a

# Facsimile of Letter from Prison

N.B.—The Convict's writing to be confined to the ruled lines of these two pa[ges]

Chatham Prison October 28th. 1869

Dear Dick

Pardon silence since reception of yours—the interval of six months between the times of writing explains ~~my~~ conduct. I am glad to hear all ~~are~~ well, I sincerely trust they will continue so. Love to them—space forbids the insertion of names; you know all those to whom I wish to be remembered. A portion of your letter was cancelled, doubtless it related to the amnesty agitation, and on this head we have been joked soundly; by all accounts we ought to be quietly domesticated in New York now, so often have we been assured by visitors and correspondents that we were to be liberated "next Feby." "next May", or "certainly when Parliament opens". We took all these statements with very great latitude, indeed, for though suggested by a sincere interest in our welfare, they came from a world by no means infallible; hence we, having never credited these statements, are not disappointed. My health is far from well. The Doctor assures me that "it is nothing serious"; I cannot, however, deny the evidence of my senses, nor do I see any prospect of recovery under existing circumstances. I commenced this life with a fixed resolve to employ all means of improvement obtainable, and devoted any time left me to careful study of the physical sciences, intending to make one of them a special pursuit when I again reached the world. My health however has made a partial relaxation from such studies a necessity and I season my reading time now with lighter matter—I would give much for a copy of Molière, Swift, Hood, Carleton, Banim or Cervantes, I have not seen a Spanish book for three years. The library does not contain anything of this nature.

I am glad to know you consider your boys so full of promise. At any expense have them educated not only in mere school acquirements but in broad generous principles; guard their minds from everything that tends to bigotry of any kind, and above all, religious bigotry. A boy who grows up without education, and in that state is to contend against

28. 10. 69

**:—In writing to the Convict, direct to No.** 9711 Richard Burke

the future, to win his own bread, is like a soldier sent without arms or ammunition to meet a well-equiped and armed enemy – defeat is a certainty. ~~If I will have the happiness of seeing them and you, I expect to find them well advanced, as well Mrs~~ B's folks in London – and by the way Dick, Kate is poor, works very hard, must do so to keep some kind of a roof over her head, and I pledge myself to return any aid you may give her from time to time, if God grants me health, liberty, and any kind of a field for labor.

This Winter promises to be a biter: last one was bad enough, but evidently this coming one will be far more intense. Impoverished blood and a reduced system ~~[illegible]~~ are well calculated to heighten its effect. It is not a pleasant prospect to contemplate.

I have written several letters regarding my case, but a strange fatality seems hang over them. Wrote to New York – no answer; to O'Shea Paris – no answer; to the authorities at Washington – no answer; and, on the 6th of last July to Kate with the same result. This, you perceive has not a tendency to add to my peace of mind, however I'll imitate Micawber, and lie 'on my oars, until something "turns up." There are many dear friends, both in England and Ireland from ^or of^ whom I'd like to hear, but as you don't know them, I suppose I must do without that happiness. Write soon, and long. I am entitled to obtain any news relating to myself be it domestic [redacted]. Love and fond remembrance to the family, relations and friends. I am, Dear Dick, ever faithfully Yrs.

R. Burke.

Dear Kate: Send this letter to Dick. Why did you not write as I asked? Have you done what I requested? I send authority for a visit with this, come yourself and bring ~~with you~~ any of the family [redacted] who conveniently can accompany you. Tell Ellie and Mary I expect they have been studying hard during the last two years. Love to them, Kate, Lou and all the folks. Remembrance to Mr Edwards & Dick Butler as well ^as to^ Dr K, who had my ring. Ever faithfully Yrs.

R Burke.

## Transcription of Letter from Prison

*Chatham Prison,*

*October 29th, 1869.*

*Dear Dick,*

*Pardon silence since reception of yours, the interval of six months between the times of writing explains my conduct. I am glad to hear all are well, I sincerely trust they will continue so. Love to them - space forbids the insertion of names - you know all those to whom I wish to be remembered. A portion of your letter was cancelled, doubtless it related to the amnesty agitation and on this hand we have been joked soundly; by all accounts we ought to be quietly domesticated in New York now, so often have we been assured by visitors and correspondents that we were to be liberated "next Feby", "next may" or "certainly when Parliament opens". We took all these statements with very great latitude indeed, for though suggested by a sincere interest in our welfare, they came from a world by no means infallible, hence we having never credited these statements, are not disappointed.*

*My health is far from well. The Doctor assures me that "it is nothing serious", I cannot, however, deny the evidence of my senses, nor do I see any prospect of recovery under existing circumstances. I commenced this life with a fixed resolve to employ all means of improvement obtainable and devoted any time left me to careful study of the physical sciences, intending to make one of them a special pursuit when I again reached the world. My health, however, has made a partial relaxation from such studies a necessity and I season my reading time now with lighter matter - I would give much for a copy of Moliere, Swift, Hood, Carlton, Banim or Cervantes. I have not seen a Spanish book for three years. The library does not contain anything of this nature.*

*I am glad to know you consider your boys so full of promise. At any expense have them educated not only in school acquirements but in broad generous principles, guard their minds from everything that tends to bigotry of any kind and above all religious bigotry. A boy who grows up without education and in that state is to contend against the future to*

*win his own bread, is like a soldier sent without arms or ammunition to meet a well-equipped and armed enemy - defeat is a certainty.*
*If I will have the happiness of seeing them and you I expect to find them well advanced. Mrs. B's folk in London and by the way, Dick, Kate is poor, works hard, must do so to keep some kind of roof over her head and I pledge myself to return any aid you may give her from time to time, if God grants me health, liberty and any kind of field for labour.*
*The winter promises to be bitter, last one was bad enough, but evidently it will be far more intense, impoverished blood and a reduced system calculated to heighten its effect. It is not a pleasant prospect to contemplate.*
*I have written several letters regarding my case but a strange fatality seems to hang over them. Wrote to New York - no answer, to O'Shea , Paris - no answer, to the authorities at Washington - no answer, and on the 6th of last July to Kate with the same result. This, you perceive, has not a tendency to add to my peace of mind, however, I'll imitate Micawber and lie on my oars until something "turns up."*
*There are many dear friends both in England and Ireland from or whom I'd like to hear, but as you don't know them I suppose I must do without that happiness. Write soon and long. I am entitled to obtain any news relating to myself, be it domestic or --(censored)--. Love and fond remembrance to the family, relations and friends. I am, dear Dick,*

*Ever faithfully yours,*
*R. Burke.*

*Dear Kate,*

*Send this letter to Dick. Why did you not write as I asked? Have you done what I requested? I send authority for a visit with this, come yourself and bring with you any of the family who conveniently can accompany you. Tell Ellie and Mary I expect they have been studying hard during the last two years. Love to them, Kate and Tim and all the folks. Remembrance to Mr. Edwards and Dick Butler as well as to Dr. K. who had my ring.*

*Ever faithfully yours,*
*R. Burke.*

fierce tone, 'Kate, I should have been at liberty before this, yes, long ago, but for the aristocrats. Kate, I hate them as I hate hell's fire.' We all persuaded him to be calm and resume his seat, his sister reminding him most pathetically that he was not wont to curse in such a manner. ... On asking the Colonel how long he had been at Woking, and the date of his removal from Chatham, his memory was a perfect blank. He could not remember when he had last received a letter from his sister, and, turning to the Governor, inquired in a diffident tone if he might write a letter, to which that official replied that he might write and receive a letter any time on asking permission from the Directors of the Convict Prisons. This assurance seemed to relieve Burke's mind greatly. The Governor, in Burke's presence, said the latter was supplied daily with port wine and stout, with a liberal quantity of food, to which Burke assented, but added that, the 'little doctor was all right, but the big doctor was his enemy.' As far as I could make out, it appears that the 'big' doctor referred to by Burke was the medical officer at Chatham, and the 'little' doctor is the one at Woking.

"In conclusion, without expressing any opinion as to what treatment Burke was subjected to at Chatham, I may tell you without the slightest reserve that the poor fellow's reason is now affected - his memory is utterly gone, and his ways, manner and language that of an insane man. He was in that state on being sent to Woking, in addition to which his health was then in a shattered condition. Since he has been at Woking his physical condition is improved most wonderfully, no doubt through pleasant companionship and improved rations, but his mental condition is still a wreck."

On March 10th, 1870, Kate wrote to her brother, Richard, in Coachford, enclosing correspondence between Mr. McCarthy Downing and Secretary Bruce and asking him to send it to the Cork papers. This correspondence was published in the Cork Examiner on March 17th. Bruce's final reply to McCarthy Downing on the matter held out no hope of an early release.

## Facsimile and transcription of letter from Kate Barry to her brother in Coachford.

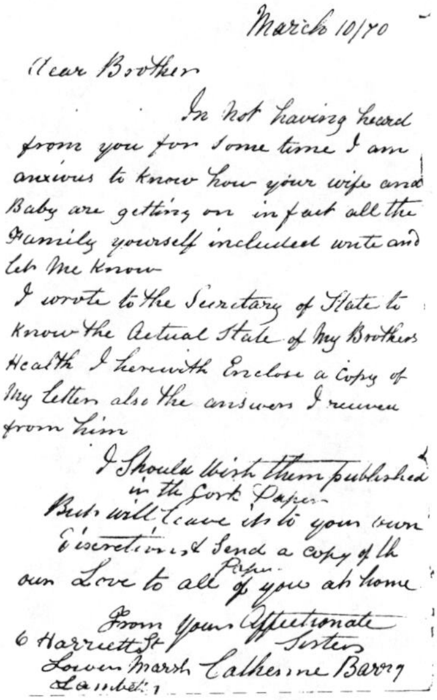
March 10/70

Dear Brother

In not having heard from you for some time I am anxious to know how your wife and Baby are getting on infact all the Family yourself included write and let Me Know

I wrote to the Secretary of State to Know the Actual State of My Brothers Health I herewith Enclose a Copy of My Letter also the answers I receive from him

I Should wish them published in the Cork Paper But will leave it to your own Discretion I Send a copy of th Paper

our Love to all of you at home

From your Affectionate Sister

6 Harriett St
Lower Marsh
Lambeth

Catherine Barry

*March 10/70*

*Dear Brother*

*In not having heard from you for some time I am anxious to know how your wife and baby are getting on in fact all the family youself included write and let me know.*

*I wrote to the Secretary of State to know the actual state of my brothers health. I herewith enclose a copy of my letters also the answers I received from him.*

*I should wish them published in the Cork Paper but will leave up to your own discretion. I send a copy of the paper.*

*Our love to all of you at home.*

*From your affectionate sister*
*Catherine Barry*

*6 Harriett St.*
*Lower Marsh*
*Lambett*

*Greetings from Newgate. (This photograph was taken in Cork on the occasion of Ricard's visits to that place on Fenian business)*

My Dear Sir: - I greatly regret I am unable to recommend Burke's discharge.

It is true that he has exhibited symptoms of insanity and that in ordinary cases I might be justified in recommending him to the mercy of the Crown. But this case wasn't an ordinary one; for not only was he a conspirator of a desperate character, but his complicity with the Clerkenwell explosion which had it been effected as designed by him would have caused much loss of life even more disastrous than it actually incurred, makes him, even in his present condition, an improper recipient of pardon."

**BURKE'S MENTAL HEALTH**

As already mentioned, Dr. Meyer of Broadmoor Asylum considered Burke to be of unsound mind. The 'big' doctor referred to by Burke, Dr. John Burns, M.D., Medical Officer, Convict Prison, Chatham, gave evidence before the Devon Commission on August 16th, 1870, concerning Burke's health when he was in Chatham. He was in a very healthy state when he arrived there in May, 1868. He observed a change in Burke's health soon after a visit by Mr. McCarthy Downing, M.P., in March, 1869. From then on Burke began refusing food and became emaciated. He complained of poisoning and described accurately the symptoms of biochloride of mercury. The doctor wondered how he knew these until he discovered Burke had been studying 'Pownes Chemistry.' Dr. Burns declared that Burke was rational in every way, the most intelligent of all the Fenian prisoners and his mental faculties were excellent. He also felt that if Burke had more work to do his mind would be more occupied in his work and less about his personal feelings. When asked to comment on Dr. Meyer's opinion of Burke, Dr. Burns stated:- "I feel perfectly certain that his mind was not affected when he left Chatham Prison. If his mind is affected it must have been after he left Chatham." On further questioning, he felt the prisoner was labouring under the condition of hypochondriasis, (thinking of his own personal discomforts and little annoyances of life) but it was slight.

The 'small' doctor referred to was Dr. John Cambell, M.D., Medical Officer, Convict Prison, Woking. His evidence to the Commission on 29th June, 1870, may be synopsised as follows:- "He has been very strange in his manner and very confused. He is more reduced in weight, but I understand that arose from his refusal to take his food. He is not competent to make a statement and always turns away from me and avoids me in every possible way. He is inclined to be excitable and cannot give a connected answer. At present I think he is a man of weak mind but I should not say that it is a decided case of insanity. I would say the man is labouring under dementia. He doesn't converse with his room mates and has shown a great dislike for medicine. Here he is on a low hospital diet with chop and potatoes, porridge and milk, bacon and eggs, pudding and half pint of porter. When he refused the chop I ordered him some chicken broth which he is now taking."

Ricard, himself, appeared before the Commission on two occasions, the first being on June 19th, 1870. Prior to this appearance Captain Harris, Deputy Governor, asserted that Burke's mind was so affected that he could not attend the inquiry. The members of the Commission, however, adjourned to the prison infirmary and took Ricard's evidence as he lay in bed. Here are some of the questions he was asked at the first interview.

**3644.** Have you anything to say? I'll see. *(Rolls the clothes about himself and turns to the wall.)* By-and by; by-and by.

**3651.** Can you not answer a civil question? Let me alone, I tell you. I won't stand it any more from any of you (sitting up). I don't interfere with any of you. You, let me alone; stand off from me, or, by God, I'll make you. *(Lies down.)*

**3653.** Won't you answer? — Let me alone, I tell you; I know you are all my enemies, every one of you. You would roast me; you would roast me alive.

**3667.** What prison is this? — Do you suppose I am a damn fool or an ass, that I don't know these things? I know all things accurately. I have a most thorough, accurate knowledge of everything.

**3670.** Have you any complaints to make of your food or medicine? — I won't take their medicine from them; no damned mixture either. Do you see that? *(Pointing to a speck on one of his fingers.)* I won't take as much medicine as that; not if I went to ten thousand hells, not so much as that (emphatically).

**3675.** Are you in good health now? — Oh, you let me alone; first rate. You see me here; I am strong, strong, every way strong; nothing the matter with me in any particular; nothing the matter with me in any way. I can stand anything.

**3676.** And do you eat? — Eat! I don't want to eat; eat be damned. I want my friends; I want my friends. I want Tom again.

**3688.** Is this milk yours *(showing him a vessel of milk)*? Why didn't you drink it? — What is that? *(pointing to the scum on it).*

**3689.** That is only from boiling of it? — You can't cheat me.

**3690.** Was this milk sent to you this morning? – *(The prisoner turned away and gave no answer. As the Commissioners were leaving the room he looked towards the door and said,* "Upon my soul, I don't want them.")

Just over three weeks later, on July 22nd, Ricard appeared before the Commission again, this time accompanied by his friend Tom, Colonel Tom Bourke. A selection of the replies he made indicates that he was still as confused as ever.

**8322.** Do they give you good meat. Is the meat pretty good? — Oh, I don't care about such things. This damned stuff.

**8326.** You have been walking to-day? — I am not sure.

**8340.** Have you any complaint to make of the medical treatment you get in this prison? — I don't want anything at all with the doctor. I don't want anything to do with them, in the smallest trifle.

**8342.** Have you any complaint against the doctor? — They all hate me, every one of them; doctors, they all do.

**8351.** We are here to do you good; and if there is anything wrong done to you we will try to have it rectified? – *(Prisoner walks about making guttural sounds.)*

**8354.** Do you remember how long you are in this prison? — Of course I know all about everything about me.

**8360.** How many prisons were you in, in this country, altogether? — Oh, I don't care about these things. I don't care about these matters. These things don't trouble me a damn bit. I don't pay attention to these trifles. They are not important; quite unimportant.

**8390.** You have no friends you wish to write to? — I have no friends at all.

Colonel Thomas Bourke was very concerned about the state of Ricard's health, both of body and mind, and he wrote to the Commission requesting an interview,"to lay before the Commissioners in as brief a manner as possible, an account of the treatment to which my poor dear friend and fellow prisoner, Colonel Ricard O'S. Burke, has received since his removal from Chatham Convict Prison to this prison (Woking) in the month of December, 1869, bereft of reason and broken down in health." His evidence to the Commission on August 13th can be summarised as follows:-

"He came here to Woking on December 10th, 1869. He was standing at the foot of the stairs here. I had not the slightest knowledge of his mind being affected, I merely heard that a political prisoner had come to prison. I looked at him and I really did not know him, he was so changed. So I ran up to him and I took him by the hand and said, 'Rick, how are you?' He looked at me. I said, 'Don't you know me, Tom?' 'Oh, yes,' said he, 'I know you well; I am all right.' I was awfully affected at the time. I did not know what in the duece to make of the matter. We went out into the yard. I spoke to Mr. Mulcahy, (a Fenian prisoner), and those others of the friends who were with him in the room. I asked what they thought of him. They told me they thought he was completely gone,

"His recollection - his memory seems to be completely gone; any facts that he should know. Previous to this unfortunate occurrence he was the most playful and jovial man I ever met - a man of strong will, strong mind, vigorous mind. He has a peculiar mania for books. I have seen him go over all the cells and bring a book from every ward and put them under his bed and secrete them under his pillow.

"He is very particular about what he puts into his mouth. He will look at it and is very suspicious about everything. The very name of a doctor enrages him. Talk of a doctor and he immediately loses temper and will curse and swear and medicine he will have nothing to do with. He doesn't write letters. He gets the paper and says, 'We will write to Kate.' Then he would write 'Kate'; then he would say he would go out or see about the books. He has received two letters since he came here and he gave both of them to me to read them for him.

"I think the man is insane. The life of this man is really at stake. I think the Commission will have done much if they preserve it."

It was probably as a result of this impassioned plea that Ricard was transferred to Broadmoor Asylum two weeks later.

(If Ricard was feigning madness, he put up a very good performance.)

DEVON COMMISSION: After many calls for an inquiry into allegations made respecting the treatment of prisoners in England, for the crime of treason-felony, the Home Secretary eventually set a commission of inquiry in May, 1870. This commission was chaired by the Right Hon. Earl of Devon and it became known as the Devon Commission. The other members were Hon. George Charles Brodrick, 32a, Mount Street, Grosvener Square; Stephen Edward De Vere, Esq., Monare, Foynes, Limerick; R. D. Lyons, Esq., M.D., 8 Merrion Sq. West, Dublin and E. H. Greenhow, Esq., M.D., 77 Upper Berkley Street, Portman Square, London.

**The terms of reference of the Commission were:-**

1st. Whether there is anything in the treatment, diet, or discipline of the convict prisons to justify any charge of unnecessary severity or harshness towards the prisoners confined therein, or neglect of the conditions necessary for the due preservation of their health; and

2ndly Whether the treason-felony prisoners have been subjected to any exceptional treatment in any way, or have suffered any hardships beyond those incidental to the condition of a prisoner sentenced to penal servitude.

The first meeting was held on May 24th at 6 Westminster Chambers, Victoria Street. In all the Commission met 63 times, the last meeting on Tuesday, September 20th. The Commissioners visited Pentoville, Millbank, Dartmoor, Woking, Chatham and Portland prisons and heard testimony from eighty one witnesses, including eighteen prisoners.

In their report the Commissioners, on the whole, were satisfied with conditions in the prisons. With reference to the second point the following is their report on Ricard O'Sullivan Burke:-

*Ricard O'Sullivan Burke*

**143.** We have with great care and anxiety inquired into the case of Ricard Burke.

**144.** He was convicted at the Central Criminal Court in London on the 6th of April 1868, and was sentenced to 15 years' penal servitude. He was received into Newgate on the 6th of March 1868. We find by the statement of the medical officer, Mr. Gibson, that he was considered of sound mind on his removal from that prison. He was transferred to Millbank on the 2nd of May 1868, and was thence removed, after a sojourn of 16 days, to Chatham prison. Mr. Glover, medical officer of Millbank, states that Ricard Burke did not manifest any peculiarities while in that prison in May 1868 such as to constitute in his opinion symptoms of insanity. He states that he saw him often, and at each visit found the prisoner writing, and so absorbed in thought that he scarcely noticed his entry into the cell. When questioned, he returned perfectly rational answers, although he was somewhat impatient and absent in manner.

**145.** From the 18th of May 1868, to the 10th of December 1869, Ricard Burke was an inmate of Chatham prison.

**146.** The medical officer, Dr. Burns, has been examined by us in regard to the mental and bodily health of the prisoner during the period just referred to. He states that he considers him to have been a strong, healthy man, and possessed a very remarkable intelligence. About May 1869, Dr. Burns states that he observed a decided change in Burke's demeanour immediately subsequent to a visit which he then received. He refused his food, and became peculiar in manner; Dr. Burns attributes this changed demeanour to malingering on the part of the prisoner, the origin of which he appears to trace to hopes of his release inspired by the parting words of his visitors, to the effect that they soon hoped to see him out of prison. Dr. Burns states that no reference to the prisoner's health was made at this interview. He finally states his opinion to be that the prisoner was labouring under hypochondriasis during the latter period of his location at Chatham prison.

**147.** On the 10th of December 1869, Ricard Burke was transferred to Woking invalid prison. He was under the charge of the principal medical officer, Dr. Cambell, until the 28th of March 1870. Dr. Cambell states that his opinion has been from the first, and still is, that the prisoner is of unsound mind. In a special report to the directors, under the date of December 21st, 1869, Dr. Cambell says, *"The medical report states that he has been losing flesh for some time, and that there was a decrease of 18 pounds on the 18th inst.; that he had delusions about his medicine containing corrosive sublimate, and that poison had been introduced into his food, and that his behaviour was otherwise uncertain."* In January 1870, Dr. Cambell held two consultations, by the instruction of the directors, with the late Dr. Meyer, of the Broadmoor lunatic asylum, who visited and examined the prisoner at Woking on two occasions, January 3rd and 10th, 1870. This gentleman placed on record his opinion, which has since been made public, that Ricard Burke was then of unsound mind.

**148.** For the purpose of further observation the prisoner was sent to Millbank on the 28th of March 1870, and until the 1st of May 1870 was for the second time under the care of Mr. Gover, medical officer of that prison.

**149.** Mr. Gover has been examined by the Commissioners, and he stated that, while he could not affirm that the prisoner was then of sound mind, he was not prepared to say that he was insane.

**150.** The prisoner was sent back to Woking on 1st May 1870, and has been since under the care of Dr. Cambell.

**151.** Dr. Cambell has been repeatedly examined by us, and his opinion, at all times the same, is given in his final answer on August 13th, 1870, that he considers Ricard Burke to be of unsound mind. This opinion as he informs us he repeated to the directors in August 1870, in a special report.

**152.** We have ourselves at our visits to Woking had interviews with Ricard Burke. We have taken evidence, as to his general state, of the warder specially in charge of him, who states that he always considered him of unsound mind, and who gave evidence as to the kind and amount of food used and returned by the prisoner. We obtained a record of the food he has returned unused. We have examined treason-felony convict, Thomas F. Bourke, who is stated to have most influence over the prisoner, and whose statements in regard him will be found in the minutes of evidence.

**153.** Captain Harris, Deputy-Governor, and from the time of the sitting of the Commission Acting-Governor, of Woking prison stated in his evidence that Ricard Burke was not, in his opinion, of sound mind, or in a fit mental state to give evidence before the Commission. The same opinion was expressed by the Rev. Mr. O'Leary, the visiting priest.

**154.** In view of all the circumstances of this very peculiar and painful case, we thought it right at our sitting of August 13th, 1870, to read to Captain Harris a resolution which the Commission had arrived at, that it would be desirable that Ricard Burke should be placed in association with some of the treason-felony prisoners who are known to have influence over him.

**155.** We have finally to report that, so far as we have had opportunity of forming judgement, we are of opinion that treason-felony convict, Ricard Burke, is not of sound mind, and that his case demands the immediate consideration of the authorities as to his future location and treatment.

**156.** We have also to call attention to the opinion of Dr. Cambell who thinks that it would be advisable to remove the prisoner from Woking.

# CHAPTER 22

## CHRISTMAS HOLIDAYS IN PRISON

## *Sketches, Real and Imaginary in Prose and Verse.*
## *By Ricard O'S Burke.*

(As well as writing his autobiography in prison Ricard O'S Burke wrote some sketches entitled "Christmas Holidays in Prison." Some of these were real, some were imaginary. These were published in five parts in The Irishman between April 4th, 1868 and May 23rd, 1868. The sketches, with some explanations, have been edited by the authors.)

"Christmas in prison! What a world of thoughts these three words embrace and convey to a reflective mind. On the anniversary of that great day when he entered upon his suffering pilgrimage to Calvary, to free man from a thraldom thousands of years in duration, it is hard for one to be denied one glance of the bright blue sky, the rich and gladsome earth, forbidden to breathe the fragrance of nature. While here, shut off from the congregation of men, because one obeys the Heaven-born instinct of his own soul, the deathless principles of justice and right, how vividly the words of Job rush to the mind: — 'They have shut me up with the unjust man, and have delivered me into the hands of the wicked.'...

"Christmas in prison! Spending what George Francis Train would call 'Humanity's Fourth of July' in a narrow, damp, cheerless cell in Millbank (prison). Everything within seems *doomed*, and is cold, and oh! so clammy to the touch. ...

"Even Ireland, poor, suffering, outraged, tortured land, even she for a time ignores her many injuries - no light task - and yields to the joyous influence of this happy season" (He imagines what it is like in Ireland, a blazing fire, merry laughter, hearty songs, sports like 'Blind Man's Buff', stories of the hard times long ago.) "Closer around old Uncle Con draws the group of listening faces as story after story rich and replete with incidents that speak to their hearts, is related. We have a glance at red Ninety-Eight - the days of Lord Edward and Master Robert, God rest their sowls, - down through the years of the fearless Rapparees, and we linger over Forty-Eight and its scenes. Thus, in company with the long ago, the hours fly by quietly, the night grows old, and the mirth and rejoicing of the Christmas gradually blend into calm, peaceful repose."

(Back to reality.) "Christmas in prison! I think of that interesting Frenchman who wrote three volumes on a turn round his chamber; and in far different mind I go round and round my narrow cell feeling what an ecstasy of relief it would be if one could but go just twelve paces in a straight line and back, and not to be thus eternally twisting like our footed friends in Van Amburgh's. ... How cold the flags are: they never before felt so cold to me: they have no boards here. Everything inside my little house is so dull, cold, and drear; not one pulse of warmth or comfort inside its four square walls. I look out through the 'inspection,' warder passes with a blunderbuss. I turn away and resume my habitual walk around my cell. 'Dinner for you, No 1,' said the warder, who unheard by me, had opened the door and entered my cell, 'You had better take it while hot - exercise will be in a few minutes more,' and he laid a small white bundle on the table and left me alone once more. I turn to the table, open the bundle, and place the contents upon it. It is no prison fare, but made up from the table of a poor but contented home. (As an unconvicted prisoner, Ricard was allowed to have his food sent in from outside.)

"Duck, goose and a host of etceteras with names to me unknown, are there, and this, what is this? Guinness in Millbank? Yes, by Jove. Who complains now? Who says we suffer? ... I wonder if George Arnold was in prison when he sang -

Here
With my beer
Alone I sit,
While golden moments flit?

"I am plying knife and fork in good aldermanic fashion, thinking of others who have no Christmas dinner but that on the 'dietary.' The cold air and long fast have made my appetite keener. I wonder what the old folks at home are doing just now? Do they keep that nook by the fireside for me? Will I ever fill it again? These and similar thoughts chase each other through my brain. I lose sight of Millbank, and am off there in — ." (Ricard is off once more on another flight of fancy to New York and a dash along Bloomingdale in a snug a piece of workmanship as ever followed horse.)

(Part Second of Sketches) "The last three or four days have passed gloomy enough, the nights sleepless and restless. During these nights everything seems to have conspired against one's slumbers. Have you ever heard a convict bell? … How the hours toll out in a dull, dead, monotonous sound, that drags itself along for minutes, until it dies away in a long 'dong' that is most annoying. Hang it! I have learned to hate it already, and whenever this bell strikes I feel inclined to rush to the window, raise it, and, like De Quincy, cry 'Police' only this is a prison on the *separate system* where talking or screaming would be at once treated as insanity. You cannot open the window if you would, and the police are most conveniently at hand. … I think I understand why joy bells were invented, though never having the occasion to use them. Are convict bells made for the reverse purpose? The bell is determined to always sharpen your senses. It seems to say, at its every stroke, ha! Ha! only two hundred and ninety thousand hours more - that's all. …

"I draw the water bucket, which serves me also as a seat, close to the wall beneath the window, stand upon it and rest my arms upon the wall, and look through the window out upon the day, or what is intended to be the day. Mercy how it snows! .... The convicts promenade even through the snow. They seem to like it, and step in each other's footprints as they follow around the yard and look up at my window as they pass. Under other circumstances this spectacle, dummy figures in grey and black with a small cylinder of brown and red wool close over their heads, would delight me who so love the ludicrous. What a full expressive and painful chapter of life may be read in their faces as they pass! I think of many comrades and friends who, during the past two years, have stepped from comfortable homes to prison, from prison to the dock, the grey suit and the convict establishment on the separate system, to public works at Millbank, or the quarries, and I search anxiously through these grey ranks, as round and round each man goes passing my window with an upward leer, for the lynx eye of the warder is always on them in that yard, but I see no face I know, not one in all those that pass.... Lame and mutilated men are among them - mere wrecks and remnants of manhood! I suppose being unable to earn any bread they look upon prison life as their natural state, and limp along one by one - a faint expression of melancholy contentment in their wan faces. Old men, too, bowed down by the weight of fifty winters, drag themselves by my window endeavouring vainly to keep up with younger feet. Sad! crime and the grave in company."

(Part Third of *Sketches*) "Back once more to the narrow cell, cold walls, and gloomy prospect, fast becoming friends and familiar. I had spent the earlier part of the day at Bow-Street Police Court. The preliminary examination is still dragging its weary length along, and was remanded once again for seven days. Whirled home, for I call this place by that endearing name, in the van guarded by forty mounted police. 'Halt!' and your humble servant is received by the chief warder, who stands on the door-step, a smile on his full round face. 'To No. 1, Bryce.' He hands me over to the warder - my warder - and here I am at last, safely lodged in the old place. I am beginning to like it too. The spare furniture seems to welcome me back again. The polished brasses that I guard and tend so carefully look up to me with a welcoming glow in their bright faces - they seem glad. We'll get on better together in future, I think ...."

In the rest of *Sketches* Ricard gives an account of an imaginary party held in his cell which was attended by all the Fenian prisoners. In come General Tom Burke, Ricard's old friend, followed by Halpin, Luby, O'Leary, McClure, Captain Deasy, Col

T. J. Kelly, Larry O'Brien, O'Connor, Bucher, Profell, "Irish Bohemian", McCafferty, Costelloe, Professor M., Brophy, Kickham, Col. O'Riordan, Flood, Condon, Beecher, Burton and a host of others including the victims of the Special Commissions since 1865. One notable absentee was O'Donovan Rossa who was otherwise engaged in another part of the prison. All the visitors carried baskets and hampers and chairs etc.

" 'Boys,' said Kelly, 'we won't have any confounded formality nor frigid ceremony here to night. I propose the editor of the old People take the head of the table - come, O'Leary, flourish a carving knife.'

" 'All right, boys,' says John O'Leary as he rose and walked up to the head of the table without any ceremony, 'this is the happiest moment of my life. Come, fill your glasses and I'll give you all a toast instead of Grace Before Meals. My toast will not be *Our Sovereign Lady, the Queen,* nor the ministers, nor the parliament. No, my toast will be none of them; but, boys, I drink this to the health of the promoter of industry, a patron of the arts, an affectionate father, a loving, faithful husband, a true friend, a worthy man, an estimable citizen. Boys, I drink this to - myself.' And emptied his glass, while a roar of laughter rose along the table.

"You ought to see how the carving knives are playing, how turkey, duck, and partridge lose member after member; how the luxuries began to grow beautifully less, as they were attacked by sturdy weavers of prison grey, whose appetite two years of training had fully developed. The hum of conversation, occasionally broken by requests for this or that article; the clattering of bright blades as their owners -

Like reapers descended to the harvest of death;

with an occasional loud laugh at some piece of extravagant drollery, plainly tell us how serious is the work at hand. ..."

Having eaten their fill the party continued with lively conversation interspersed with songs, all written by Ricard, and stories which are probably based on fact. Frequent references were made about the notorious Judge Keogh and Halpin told Ricard he was lucky to escape his clutches. There was much discussion between the "Irish Bohemian" and the rest on life in Paris - (Ricard did spend some there and knew the set-up among the Irish.) Halpin gave a long account of an incident which happened in Dublin when he and B —— were there in which Burton and some girls were involved. Larry O'Brien recounted an incident involving William Kirwan, a Fenian, which happened in Clonmel when he was in prison there.

Kirwan used stroll around the town each day and talk with the old folks and do some flirting with the youngsters. He was on the most agreeable terms with the police and used accompany the "flying columns." One day Gore Jones, J. P., came up to the "flying column" a few miles north of Tipperary town. He demanded to know who Kirwan was. Kirwan told him he was a reporter for a London newspaper and Gore Jones asked to see his credentials. Kirwan produced some papers from his pocket and handed one to Gore Jones. He read it carefully and finished with a grunt of triumph as he felt he had caught an impostor as R —— emphatically refused Kirwan's offer to report for the paper. Kirwan was well able and asked Gore Jones if he had seen the word over at the bottom of the page. Jones turned the paper over, read it and handed it back remarking at the same time 'all correct, sir.'

The others at the party wanted to know how Kirwan had got away with it. Larry explained that Kirwan had copied the hand writing and on the back of the sheet had written, - 'P.S., - Since writing the foregoing, circumstances have arisen to lead us to reconsider the matter, and, as the importance of reliable intelligence from Ireland is now apparent, we accept your offer and terms, and enclose an order for five pounds. Let us hear from you in time for our next issue.' The letter was signed R —— .

Every so often during this imaginary party a guest was called on to sing. All the songs were written by Ricard, himself .

## HURRAH FOR THE NEXT WHO DIES

We meet 'neath the sounding rafter;
And the walls around are bare,
And they echo our peals of laughter,
It seems that our dead are there!
Then stand to your glasses - steady,
We drink to our comrades' eyes;
One cup to our dead already -
Hurrah for the next who dies!
Not here are the goblets flowing;

Not here is the vintage sweet;
But cold as our hearts are growing,
And dark as the doom we meet.
Then stand to your glasses - steady,
One cup to our dead already —
Hurrah for the next who dies!
...... etc.

## SEE, THE SPOILERS COME

See, the spoilers come
In pride, and pomp, and vaunted glory,
Those oft made our home
But ashes, black, and cold, and gory.
Oft our fathers bled,
No more they'd wear the badge of slaves -
Hear the martial tread!
O'er our martyr'd dead!
Profaning now their sacred graves!
...... etc.

Long the scourge we've felt;
Too long endured its burning feeling;
Long entreating knelt
For justice o'er, in vain, appealing,
Now no more we bend;
Our vile insatiate tyrants scorning
God the right defend!
Soon the night shall end
And usher Freedom's brilliant morning.

## FILL HIGH, TO-NIGHT, BOYS

With ruby nectar, boys, fill high!
Drink to the cause for which we die;
And, comrades to each sparkling eye
That gilded hours too soon gone by.
Fill high to-night to patriot hearts
That for our Motherland have bled;
And drain your goblets, boys, to all
Who in their foosteps tread!
And drain your goblets, boys, to all
Who in their footsteps tread!

.........

Now, comrades, yet again! - fill high!
The last with you to-night I give:
None but the willing hearts to die
Deserve with men on earth to live -
To our land! Oh! comrades, still
In her true cause ever endure;
And not with wine your goblets fill,
But nature's beverage pure!
And not with wine your goblets fill,
But nature's beverage pure!

**HURRAH FOR THE BARRICADES!**

There's a voice of thundering tones,
Obey it the haughtiest must;
It crushes the mightiest thrones,
And tramples their crowns in dust!
See the tyrant's cheeks grow pale,
As scatter his lured brigades
Like chaff in the maddest gale -
The voice of the Barricades!
Then, whenever the despot's hand
Any manhood's right invades -
From God and our native land!
Hurrah for the Barricades!
Hurrah!
Hurrah!
Hurrah for the Barricades!
...... etc.

## HOPE ON, HOPE ON

Oh, Erin fair, hope on,
The doubting ne'er aught noble won.
Strive for your right against all foes,
E'en, though the night 'round darker grows,
At last the day e'er sheds its ray,
And pass our darkest hours away:
As rise the moon so chaste and bright
From ocean's bed in tempest night,
So wilt thou glide
O'er thy troubled tide,
With purest beauty teaming,
Over the wild waves gleaming,
Far to thine exiles beaming,
Joy of a home at last!
With purest beauty teeming,
Over the wild waves gleaming,
Far to thine exiles beaming,
Joy of home at last!
...... etc.

## ONE AFTER ONE

Since first came our Keogh 'tis two years and more,
And one after one since we came to the fore,
The juries they met, and each job was soon done,
'Tis purty this goin', boys, one after one!

"Ten years, take O'Connell for wearing the green,
Invading the realm of our Lady, the Queen;"
"We'll exchange our prisoners ere ten years are gone,"
'Tis purty this goin', boys, one after one!

"Here nothing to mitigate your guilt appears,
We now give you, Halpin, your fifteen long years"-
"Fifteen for Ireland - your lordship add on,"
'Tis purty this goin', boys, one after one!

... ... ...

You, Burke, you're a black one, we know you of ould,
The rest of your years our fine prisons shall hould,"
"We'll trot out your quarries, I'm ready, come on,"
'Tis purty this goin', boys, one after one!

We meet here to-night, boys, all who pass'd away,
And look through the window of this prison grey,
And there see behind us, how others come on,
'Tis purty this goin', boys, one after one!

**TALK WE OF LIBERTY!**

Talk we of liberty!
Bondsmen of love are we;
Down on bended knee,
Slavery ruling.
Woman's pure, love-lit eye
Ruby lip, balmy sigh,
Our vaunted mastery,
Ever subduing.
These, when love found me,
Wreathed he round me,
Who would unbound be
From his sweet chains!

Man ever toil away,
Building your coming day;
Hark! what the Fates ere say,
All idle dreaming.
Weak is our boasted might
Bow'd in love's spirit light,
One glance from beauty bright,
Vanish our scheming!
These, when love found me,
Wreath'd he round me,
Who would unbound be
From his sweet chains!

## THE CONVICT GREY

They tell us that we are base and vile!
Have souls that pierced all grades of guile,
And bear the taint; ha! ha! you know
How little we heed the sland'rous blow,
Our laugh and song
Shall echo along
The corridors' gloomy way!
Our hearts are free
Here though bound are we
And wearing the convict grey.
Comrades up! hip! hip! hurrah!
A manly garb is the convict grey!

Not ours the life to cringe nor fawn,
In servile heart, on purple lawn,
Nor envy we the ermined great,
To finish their webs, and rot in state!
The glory that falls
On their proud palls
Is a feeble transient ray;
Our duty and faith
Defy e'en death,
Though wearing the convict grey.
Comrades, up! hip! hip! hurrah!
A soldier's garb is the convict grey!

" 'Get up, No. 1, and go to bed.'

" 'Up, bed, go to bed! Oh, yes, yes, warder, thanks, I'll go to bed.' I rose up from the little table. The warder had entered, failing to waken me by the grating of the bolts when being withdrawn. (The fantasy is over.) I undress and turning down the clammy sheets, overcoming a strong inclination to shudder, I lie down in the bed. Desiring a little sleep I turn my face to the wall."

## CHAPTER 23

# FREE! AT LAST

Many efforts were made in an attempt to force the British Government to free the Fenian prisoners. Questions were asked and resolutions passed in the American House of Representatives on behalf of the prisoners. Burke, because of his American citizenship, was a particular concern to the American-Irish. For a long time Gladstone withstood the pressure to release them.

With regards to Burke his solicitor, Josiah J. Merriman, wrote to the United States Ambassador, the Hon J.L. Motley, requesting his intervention and the intervention of the American Government on behalf of his client. The legal ground on which the application rested was the refusal of Mr. Baron Bramwell, the trial judge at Burke's trial, to allow Burke a jury *de mediate linguae* as an alien. The application for a mixed jury was made to ensure that he got a fair trial. If the British Government accepted the particulars of Ricard Burke as recorded by the Devon Commission where his place of birth was given as New York, then he should have been allowed a mixed jury. The appeal to the United States Ambassador did not bring a new trial.

After the failure of the Fenian Movement to achieve a successful rising many groups both in Ireland and England combined to plead for amnesty for the Fenian prisoners. The Amnesty Movement in Ireland in 1869 was headed by Isaac Butt, Q.C. and J. Nolan was secretary of the movement which had offices in the Mechanic Institute in Dublin. Huge meetings were held up and down the country beginning with a meeting of 30,000 in Limerick and culminating in a gigantic demonstration of 300,000 in Dublin in October. At all these Amnesty Meetings resolutions were passed calling on the British Government to grant an amnesty to the Fenian prisoners.

Many amnesty meetings were held in County Cork in the autumn of 1869. There was a huge meeting in Bandon on Sunday, October 11th. *The Cork Examiner* describes it thus:-

"The 'ancient and loyal borough of Bandon Bridge,' was the theatre of a demonstration yesterday such as had never been seen there within the memory of the 'oldest inhabitant.' It was often the scene of election excitement, but the dull old town was never as excited as yesterday. The excitement was of an unusual kind in Bandon. There were no opposing factions - no cries of Tories and Liberals. The colours of orange and green were entwined yesterday in rosettes on men's breasts and ribbons on women's bonnets. From an early hour the town was astir, people coming in from the country on foot, and in car, every one bearing some emblem of the national colour. The ordinary morning train from Cork brought about five hundred, and the special train at one o'clock about treble that number; and the West Cork line from Skibbereen and Dunmanway conveyed about six hundred.

"There were four musical bands in the town. The first that arrived was that belonging to the Cork Working Men's Association. They drove from Cork and were received on their arrival by an immense crowd who cheered them lustily. As the church services were not over at the time, they passed through the town without playing and proceeded to Kilbrogan cemetery, where a beautiful ornament has been erected to the memory of Allen, Larkin and O'Brien, and there all knelt and prayed for the repose of the souls of the Manchester martyrs. The next band that arrived was the Blackpool band, the members of which were arrayed in handsome uniform - green sashes over dark clothes and caps trimmed with gold and green. The splendid band from Clonakilty next arrived in a long car, five other cars following it all filled with good looking young men.

"About three o'clock the several bands met at the Bridge where a procession was formed, which proceeded through the town to the place of the meeting known as 'The Hill.' An immense concourse of people followed it through the streets. At the top of 'The Hill' was erected a platform, from which the speakers addressed the meeting. The multitude assembled on the large sloping green was estimated from twelve to fifteen thousand, and it was decidedly one of the most orderly gatherings, large or small, that we have ever witnessed. In fact, from morning to night there was not a single case of riotousness or drunkness, and even the rigidly righteous of the town could scarcely have had their feelings violated."

The Hon. Secretary, Mr. T. Lynch read an apology for non attendance from T. McCarthy Downing, M.P. The chairman of the meeting was Henry Hassett, J. P., Woodlands, who was introduced by Rev. Mr. O'Keeffe, C.C., Bandon. Father O'Keeffe delivered a long speech which was cheered and booed at the appropriate points. The first resolution, "That as the British Government has declared through the Prime Minister that Ireland shall, in future, be ruled in accordance with the feelings of the Irish people, we publicly declare that it is the wish of the Irish people that the political prisoners be immediately and unconditionally released." was proposed by J. C. Hurley at the end of a lengthy speech and was seconded by Patrick Foley who also delivered a lengthy speech. Two further resolutions were proposed. - "That we believe the immediate and unconditional release of these men would tend more than any other act of the British Government to promote good feeling between the two countries." and "That no boon or favour, promised by the British Government, will satisfy the people of Ireland, while the political prisoners are in prison." Needless to say all resolutions were passed unanimously to loud cheers.

The Amnesty meeting in Skibbereen was held on Sunday, September 5th and was presided over by P. W. Johnson, Kanturk. In the course of a long and eloquent speech the chairman had this to say about the amnesty meetings and the political prisoners.

"The meeting was for amnesty - free and unconditional. *(prolonged cheering and cries of 'that's the shot')* He had been, as they were aware, an humble instrument of the Mallow meeting. There, on the banks of the Blackwater, in his native town, rose the cry of amnesty. It rolled along till it came to the blacksmiths of Limerick *(a voice - 'cheers for them' - loud cheers)* They echoed it from bank to bank of the lordly Shannon, it swept on through historic Clare, invigorated with the recollections of O'Connell - of him who never fawned to ask but always demanded justice. *(loud cheers)* It swept on through the city of the western tribes where it gathered freshness from the breezes borne across the Atlantic from the land of freedom. *(cheers)* It reverberated from the walls of the unconquered city. *(cheers)* The people's thunder was next heard on the banks of the storied Boyne amid the fruitful valleys and smiling plains of Meath. *(cheers)* And to-day the people, the power and pride of rugged Carberry, in their simple grandeur, had assembled to protect the flag of amnesty - free and unconditional. *(cheers)*

A Voice — They may keep it any other way. *(renewed cheers)*

The chairman continued to say they had assembled to pronounce again the ultimatum declared at Mallow, 'we want our brothers back again.'

A Voice — Nothing else will do. *(cheers)*

The chairman declared they had their gentle Kickham, (cheers) but they wanted their honest Rossa. *(cheers)* "Dublin wanted the learned Luby. *(cheers)* Tipperary wanted the proud O'Leary. *(cheers)* The men of Duhallow wanted their brave John Keneally, the man whose noble utterances in the dock, when asked to plead guilty, they all remembered. *(hear, hear, applause)* They wanted their guileless Bryan Dillon. *(cheers)* They wanted their noble Burke, *(continued cheers)* - in a word they wanted them all, and would be satisfied with no less. *(loud cheers)* What was their object? *(a voice - A good one. And cheers)* They rose in a noble cause. *(enthusiastic applause)* Their's was no empty seeking for paltry place, no self-interested struggle for emolument. *(no, no, and cheers)*"

The amnesty agitation continued and eventually Gladstone granted an enquiry - the Devon Commission. Then on December 20th, 1870, five prisoners were released conditionally - the prisoners were not permitted to live in Ireland for the duration of their sentences. Supporters of Amnesty charged Gladstone with a breach of faith, alleging that he had promised unconditional pardon. The *Irishman* commented that the prisoners had been given "exile, not amnesty." However neither soldiers nor the men convicted for the rescue of Colonel Kelly in Manchester were included in this amnesty. This meant that Ricard Burke still languished in Broadmoor.

The released prisoners - O'Donovan Rossa, John Devoy, Charles O'Connell, John McClure and William Halpin - sailed to America on the ship "Cuba" and they were known as the "Cuba Five." They got a tumultuous welcome in the United States and were received by President Grant on February 22nd. "He asked if any among them were American citizens. To this the answer was made that none present were citizens, but that R. O'S Burke and E. N. Condon, two Americans, were yet in prison and they desired to bring their case before the President at the proper time. To this the President replied that they could do so and that whatever was proper to be done by the government would be performed." *(The Nation)*

Richard Burke travelled to Broadmoor to see his brother. Though he was to note that the officials of that establishment were rather lenient and kind to Ricard, he still continued his efforts to have him released. Through the good offices of John Francis Maguire, M. P., he intimated to the Home Secretary that he would assume guardianship of his brother if he was released. Eventually all the efforts made on Ricard's behalf by the Amnesty Movement,

***Cuba Five***

***From left to right:*** John Devoy, Charles Underwood O'Connell, Harry Mulleda, Jeremiah O'Donovan Rossa and John McClure.

the American Government and Richard, himself, were successful and his family, friends and fellow republicans were delighted when the following letter was received by Mr. Maguire.

*Whitehall 22nd June 1871.*
*Sir - Mr. Secretary Bruce having had before him your application on behalf of Ricard Burke, a treason-felony convict now under detention in Broadmoor Criminal Lunatic Asylum, I am directed to acquaint you that under all the circumstances Mr. Bruce proposes upon receiving an assurance from you that Burke's brother is willing to receive and take care of him, to advise his release on license upon terms similar to those granted in the case of Bryan Dillon. The condition of the prisoner's license will therefore be that, "So long as the license shall remain in force the holder shall present himself on the first day of January every year to such person and at such place as may be mentioned in any order requiring him to do so in England or Scotland by one of Her Majesty's principal Secretaries of State or in Ireland by the Lord Lieutenant or other Chief Governor of Ireland." - I am, sir, your obedient servant.*

*A. J. O. Liddell*

*John Francis Maguire, M.P.*

The necessary assurances from Richard were forthcoming and immediately forwarded to the Home Secretary. Richard also intimated that it was his intention to have his brother conveyed quietly home and avoid all public display with the liberation. On receipt of them Ricard Burke was eventually released on Friday, July 6th, 1871. His health was a grave cause of concern to his sister and she felt he could not travel home to Ireland unaccompanied. She sent a telegram to her brother, Richard, asking him to come to London immediately to attend Ricard on his journey home. Richard Burke wasted no time and travelled to London immediately to bring his brother to Coachford and they were accompanied on their journey from England by their sister Kate and arrived in Cork on Sunday July 9th where they were met by another brother, Con O'Sullivan Burke. Even if a welcome home

## Facsimile and transcription of the letter announcing the release of Ricard.

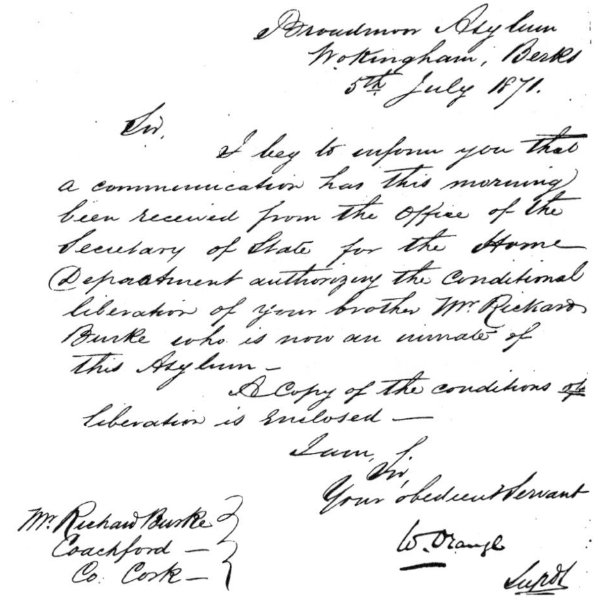

Broadmoor Asylum
Wokingham, Berks
5th July 1871.

Sir,

I beg to inform you that a communication has this morning been received from the Office of the Secretary of State for the Home Department authorizing the Conditional liberation of your brother Mr. Rickard Burke who is now an inmate of this Asylum –

A Copy of the conditions of liberation is Enclosed —

I am, Sir,
Your obedient Servant
W. Orange
Supdt

Mr. Richard Burke
Coachford –
Co. Cork –

Broadmoor Asylum,
Wokingham, Berks.
5th July, 1871

*Sir,*

*I beg to inform you that a communication has this morning been received from the Office of the Secretary of State for the Home Department authorizing the conditional liberation of your brother, Mr. Rickard Burke, who is an inmate of this Asylum.*

*A copy of the conditions of liberation is enclosed —*

*I am, Sir,*
*Your obedient Servant,*
*W. Orange.*
*Sup.*

*Mr. Richard Burke,*
*Coachford,*
*Co. Cork*

reception was allowed by the family, the state of Ricard's health didn't permit him to receive a public ovation and so the homecoming was a very quiet affair.

"Colonel Ricard O'Sullivan Burke, one of the most distinguished of the political prisoners, arrived in this city by the mid-day train on Sunday (July 9th, 1871) from Dublin. He has been released from Broadmoor Convict Lunatic Asylum on conditions similar to those under which Brian Dillon was amnetised - his brother, Richard Burke, of Coachford, undertaking to take charge of him until the gallant soldier's health is thoroughly re-established. Colonel Burke looks well, considering the terrible ordeal he has gone through, and there is every prospect that his native air will soon restore him to vigour. His arrival in this city was entirely unexpected, his friends being anxious to avoid the excitement of the great popular welcome he would otherwise receive. After visiting some friends in the city he left in the evening for his brother's residence in Coachford." *(Cork Herald)*

"On Sunday, Ricard O'Sullivan Burke, the Fenian Colonel, arrived in town, having been set at liberty by the Government and permitted to reside in the country among his friends, in consequence of his mental affliction. He was accompanied by his sister, Mrs. Barry of London, and his brother, Mr. Richard Burke, Coachford. The Colonel looks better than the accounts given of his health would lead one to expect; but he is not the strong spirited young fellow of the bright intellect that he was a few years ago, when his appearance and demeanour elicited the praise of the judge who condemned him to imprisonment. His constitution has been very much shaken, and the intellect is affected, but neither irretrievably so, and it is hoped that, in a short time, both mind and body will be restored to their former state of health. Colonel Burke was considered to be the most remarkable man amongst the political prisoners. His life, which was sketched at the time of his trial by one apparently on very intimate terms with him, forms a romance in itself. Though a young man, he has travelled to the most distant countries, and there is scarcely a clime under which he has not lived. His time was not spent unprofitably for he acquired a knowledge of several languages, and could speak as fluently in the Spanish, French and Italian as in the English language. Besides being a linguist, he is a painter and a poet, and the productions of his brush and pen have been commended by those who would withhold praise were it not due. Mr. Burke left last night for Coachford, where he will remain for some time. We sincerely hope that the original vigour of his mind and of his body may be restored to him." (Daily Telegraph)

*Guy's Pictorial Guide.*

# HOTEL, COACHFORD, CORK.

RICHARD BURKE, Proprietor.

THIS Hotel has been newly fitted up for the accommodation of Tourists. It is situated at the Coachford Terminus of the Cork and Muskerry Light Railway. The Village of Coachford itself is in the centre of a country containing splendid views of the scenery of the river Lee.

The salmon fishing along this part of the river Lee is the very best, and is much patronised by anglers from all parts of the United Kingdom.

In the tributaries of the Lee adjoining the village the trout fishing is excellent.

There is a Bath room attached.

TERMS MODERATE.

*Richard Burke's establishment in Coachford where Ricard spent two years convalescing. 1871-1873*

## CHAPTER 24

# RICARD AND HIS FRIEND, BRIAN DILLON

The terms of Ricard's release were laid down as in the letter of June 22nd, 1871, to John Francis Maguire, M.P. He had to present himself on the first day of January every year to a certain person at a certain place as long as the licence remained in force and this licence remained in force until the expiry of his prison sentence, i.e. in 1883. If he broke the terms of his licence he could be re-arrested and then would serve out the remainder of his sentence.

He spent about two years in Coachford with his brother, Richard, and his family. As far as he was able, he spent practically all his time in the open air fishing and shooting, until his health was completely restored. The River Lee abounded in fish and it was along its banks, in the fresh air, Ricard tried his luck with rod and line. He also visited his relatives in Slieveowen and Seanacashel in the parish of Kilmichael. Here he had plenty of opportunities to pass the time in the open air fowling. The wild birds of Mid-Cork must have wondered where this excellent marksman had come from.

Recovery was slow but steady and eventually he was restored to full health. His one public appearance during this period was at the funeral of Brian Dillon on August 25th, 1872. Ricard's health had improved so much in the preceding fourteen months that he was able to act as pall bearer at the funeral and also deliver the funeral oration. Indeed no more suitable person than Ricard could have been chosen to perform this task as both he and Brian had been inmates of Woking prison at the same time and were well acquainted with each other.

**Brian Dillon**

Brian Dillon was born in the parish of Glanmire, near Cork City, in 1830 and was one of a family of seven. In his early childhood a sad occurrence marked him out as the 'favourite' of his parents. He was involved in a serious accident - a heavy fall - which resulted in curvature of the spine and general ill-health. He grew only to a height of four feet ten inches and this deformity of his back added greatly to his prison suffering in later years.

While he was yet young the family moved to a house near the corner of Old Youghal Road and Ballyhooly Road in Cork - a junction which shortly afterwards became known as 'Dillon's Cross' - and here his parents opened a tavern. Brian's parents provided him with a good general education and sent him to the Cork School of Art, where he studied for several years and became quite talented with brush and pencil. In the early 1850s he went to work as a clerk in the office of Mr. W. R. Coppinger, Solr., 58 South Mall and he soon became a valued member of the staff there.

From boyhood he had been an ardent nationalist. He joined the Tuckey Street 'National Reading Rooms', a society of patriotic Corkmen, of which, at one time, Michael O'Brien (one of the Manchester Martyrs) was secretary. In 1858 he joined the Fenian Movement and in the years that followed Dillon threw himself heart and soul into the organising of Fenianism in Cork. Amongst the principal meeting places for the Fenians were Geary's public-house in North Main Street, a drill room in Barrack Street, a blacksmith's forge off Bishop Street and the premises of the Coopers' Society in Domnick Street. By 1865 Dillon had come to be recognised as the principal 'Center' of the organisation in the city.

On the night of September 15th, 1865, Dillon, with six others, was arrested. Many more arrests followed in the succeeding weeks and all the more active members were returned for trial to the Special Commission due to sit in December. On December 18th Brian Dillon went on trial at Cork Courthouse and was defended by Isaac Butt, future founder of the Home Rule Party. The case against Dillon was based largely on the unscrupulous lies of the informer, Warner. He was found guilty and sentenced to ten years penal servitude.

Now began the long martyrdom for Brian Dillon. From Cork Jail he was transferred to Mountjoy. Having spent a month there he was transferred to Pentonville jail in England having had a dreadful journey across the Irish Sea handcuffed to John Casey, (the "Galtee Boy"), who was prostrate with sea-sickness and diarrhoea. The cold of Pentonville affected Dillon very much and in May, 1866, he was transferred to the hospital wing of Woking Convict Prison which was to be his home for the next four and a half years. Life was hard there and it is vividly described by Walter McGrath in his excellent booklet, *"A Cork Felon"* published in 1952.

Brian Dillon was released on licence on February 8th, 1871, having spent nearly six years in jail. Though he was very seriously ill, he nevertheless participated in the tumultuous welcome that awaited him when he arrived in Cork on Monday, February 13th. When the train arrived it seemed at first glance that every man, woman and child in Cork had turned out to welcome him. He travelled in triumph from the station to Dillon's Cross through vast crowds with bonfires blazing.

Despite the tender care of his aged mother and many friends, his health continued to deteriorate. By the summer of 1872 he was far gone in tuberculosis and on Saturday evening, August 17th, 1872, surrounded by his family and friends, he died at his home in Dillon's Cross.

Immediately the sad news of his death became known plans for a big public funeral were made. It had been decided to build a vault at the family burial-ground in Rathcooney, using some of the stones from the house in which Brian had been born. As this would not be ready for a few days, the remains were privately buried in a temporary resting-place at St Joseph's Cemetery, Turner's Cross. The organising committee looked around for a suitable person to deliver the funeral oration, and who better than Brian's prison companion, Colonel Ricard O'Sullivan Burke, who was then living in Coachford.

The funeral was the greatest seen in Cork since the remains of Terence Bellew McManus had been borne through the city ten years before. When the cortege moved off, headed by the Barrack Street Band, the crowd was estimated to be eight thousand strong and this included trainloads from Limerick and Tipperary. All

Brian Dillon

Plaque on Brian Dillon's house.

Unveiling of plaque on Brian Dillon's house, 1909.

wore mourning emblems on the left arm - crepe tied with green and white ribbons. The six pall bearers were all released Fenians - Colonel Ricard O'Sullivan Burke, J. S. Casey (the "Galtee Boy"), Captain James O'Connell, P.F. Barry, Jeremiah O'Donovan of Blarney and W. O'Sullivan of Limerick. At Rathcooney the crowd was so dense that considerable difficulty was experienced in getting the coffin to the grave.

When the burial had taken place, Col. Ricard O'Sullivan Burke stepped forward and, in a voice trembling with emotion, delivered his oration.

"We have assembled here today to pay a sad tribute of esteem and respect to the memory of our departed friend, Brian Dillon. It has been requested of me to bear public testimony to his worth, and most cheerfully do I add my voice to the many that assert the singular purity and steadfast patriotism of his life. As an Irishman swayed by the broadest and most generous principles, the prominent part he took in the Irish Republican Brotherhood is already generally and widely known. It is not necessary to allude to any of the special causes that gave rise to the Organisation of which our late friend was so self-sacrificing a member. He saw, on the one hand, a generous people adhering with sublime tenacity to the indestructible right of national independence; and on the other hand, a government that even if charitably considered, was remarkable for the readiness with which it adopted the expedient of exceptional legislation to deny the rights, to refuse the privileges, to scoff at the traditions, to insult the Faith, to slander the reputation, of that people.

"With him, reflection was decision, and decision action; and throwing himself into the ranks of the popular cause with the zeal and earnestness of his nature, we find him in '59 and '60 working with a fixity of resolution that justly won the esteem of the national party, of which he soon became the guiding spirit in the South of Ireland. This, then, was his position in Irish politics when he was first visited by the chief organiser of the Irish Republican Brotherhood, for Brian Dillon was a true Irishman, a genuine republican and an able organiser even before the coming of James

Stephens, who, recognising his merit, readily appointed him, in conjunction with others, to conduct the affairs of the national organisation in the city and county of Cork.

"How effectively he performed this duty, and with what success to himself and to the organisation, his subsequent career clearly establishes. We find him in 1865 brought face to face with the law whose jurisdiction he emphatically repudiated. True to himself and to his deep, deep faith in the indestructibility of Irish nationality, he denies the charge of guilt, repudiates the imputation to him of crime, asserts the purity of his motives and then, with calm dignity of manner, he passes from the dock of the prisoner to the cell of convict, willing - ever so willing - to give this new proof of his devotion to Ireland.

"It was down there in the convict prison I first met him. I never saw him till then, but I already learned that Ireland had sent a young art student from Cork to represent her in the convict quarries. He was then in the Invalid Convict Prison of Woking, as the treatment he had received at Pentonville had rendered him unable to perform even the slightest prison labour. For five long, bitter years he endured, with manly fortitude and gentlemanly demeanour, the coarse, repulsive, brutal discipline of an English prison. At last - when persecution had done its work - when the seeds of premature death were sown in his system - the Government, yielding to the oft repeated prayers of the Irish people and to the policy of the time, were gracious enough to send him home to die.

"The sad reality of his death, however, brings us this consolation - that God has called him to Himself: that the pangs of disease were soothed by the tenderest affections and warmest sympathy of his many friends; that the mother who watched over his young life and followed with aching heart his sufferings in the prison pens of England, was at last allowed the great relief of surrounding him in his home with the priceless treasure of her love. Placing the remains of our dear friend in a tomb built of the stones from the very house where he drew the first breath of life, we, from the purity and devotion of that life, may confidently leave him to the esteem of his friends, to the gratitude of his country, and to the mercy of his God."

In 1909 a plaque was unveiled on the house where Brian had lived and died. Eleven years later, on the night of December 11/12th, 1920, a tank-like vehicle raced down Old Youghal Road from Victoria Barracks and demolished the walls of Brian Dillon House and smashed the plaque. It was the night of the burning of Cork. A few years after the end of the War of Independence a new house was built on the ruined site. The builder erected another plaque similar to the one which it replaced except that the opening words were changed to read: "On this site stood the house, burned 1920, where lived and died Brian Dillon, Patriot."

# CHAPTER 25

# RICARD RETURNS TO AMERICA

With his health fully restored, Ricard left Coachford and his brother, Richard, and his many relations and friends and returned to America in 1873 having spent two years convalescing. In doing so he broke the terms of his licence as he could not now report to the appointed person on January 1st. Because of this he could not return to Ireland as he would be arrested and forced to serve the rest of his sentence. Therefore between 1873 and 1922, the year of his death, he returned to Ireland just once.

Like many other Fenians who returned to America, Ricard spent some time lecturing to Irish groups along the east coast. Then he was appointed a clerk in the War Department - Adjutant-General Drum being an old friend of his. He joined the Clan-na-Gael in Washington and remained a member until his death. Though a loyal, respected and steadfast member and a regular attender at rallies and conventions he never occupied a position of prominence within the organisation.

**Clan-na-Gael**

Clan-na-Gael was a powerful organisation among the Irish immigrants. It was founded in New York in 1867 by a group of Irish Americans disgusted with the factionalism of the Fenians. Among its founders was Jerome Collins, scientific editor of the *New York Herald*. The Clan was dedicated to the complete and absolute independence of Ireland by the overthrow of English domination by means of physical force. It was a secret organisation and each camp and club had a number as well as a public name such as *The Napper Tandy Club or the Emmet Literary Society.* At first it was mainly confined to the north-eastern states of America where Dr. William Carroll and John Devoy were very prominent.

The first Chicago Club was established in 1869 - Camp 16 in the Bridgeport area where there was a large Irish settlement. By 1871 clubs had been established in most of the Irish districts in the city. In time, Chicago had the strongest Clan center outside of the north east. From 1881 to 1889 Chicago was the foremost center of Irish Nationalism in the U. S. A. and also one of the most extreme as was the Middle West with little conservative influence. Three of the major personalities in Irish-American politics during the 1880s lived in the same neighbourhood in Chicago on the Near North Side - Alexander Sullivan who was born in either Canada or Maine; in 1881 he was national chairman of the Clan; in 1883 he was elected president of the Irish National League of America, an umbrella organisation for all Irish societies, but which was controlled by the Clan. The second was Dr. Patrick Henry Cronin who was born in Buttevant, Co. Cork in 1846. Sullivan befriended the young doctor upon his arrival in Chicago in 1882 and secured a position for him in Cook County Hospital. Having an outgoing personality and a fine tenor voice, he rapidly became one of the most popular Irishmen in Chicago. He remained on friendly terms with Sullivan up until the end of 1884 when he crossed swords with him and denounced him. The third, Thomas Beach, a British agent and known to his Irish friends as Dr. Henri Le Caron, was born in Essex in 1841. In America he joined the Union army and befriended the Fenians. To gain the confidence of the Irish he pretended to be a Frenchman. Also, a prominent member of the Clan in Chicago was John Finnerty who was born in Co. Galway in 1846. He joined the Clan in the late 1870s and remained a member until his death in 1908. He never had a great influence in the inner circles but was a powerful orator and was much in demand at picnics. He claimed that other ethnic groups were held in greater esteem than the Irish because "all other foreign elements in this country with, perhaps, the exception of the Poles, have strong governments behind them; and they are held in more respect than the Irish who have no government of their own to boast of."

Many priests belonged to the Clan. However, their attitude within the organisation depended on where they were living. In the east they were active in Irish-American constitutional movements and tried to combat the extremist elements within the Clan. With church support, Chicago was completely Clan territory. Here, even Archbishop Feehan championed the Clan in the 1880s.

The extremists in the Clan had set their sights on an uprising in 1882, the centenary of the Irish Volunteer movement. But such a programme required a highly efficient revolutionary organisation at home. To the disgust of the Clan, it was becoming increasingly evident that the I. R. B. did not fit the bill. It suffered from a lack of leadership and internal dissension and lacked the support of the Irish masses. In contrast, Parnell and his colleagues seemed to be the most viable expression of nationalist sentiment in the country. Consequently, in October 1878, came the first public pronouncement of the New Departure when Devoy announced Clan support for Parnell. With regard the Land League, there was not the same support for it among the Clan leaders.

For the rank and file Irish-Americans the Clan meetings served as social gatherings where they could meet their own kind and re-create, to some extent, the atmosphere of life back home. They commemorated all the Irish historic events and held monster picnics where orators like John Finnerty were subject to flights of fancy. The sense of inferiority penetrated deeply into the minds of the Irish-Americans. As a way of compensation these orators created their own racial myths. They waxed eloquent on the Young Irelanders and the uniqueness of Gaelic culture. The Celts were a special people chosen by God from among other nations and other races to achieve His own behests. They reminded Americans of what they had done in the Civil War. They proclaimed they were loyal Americans and their love of Ireland in no way interfered with their duties as Americans. After all they reminded Americans that Ireland only desired what the United States had achieved through violence - freedom from British rule.

In Mount Olivet Cemetery in Chicago, the same cemetery in which Ricard O'Sullivan Burke is buried, there is a burial plot for Clan members. The inscription reads: "Erected August 26, 1888, to

ANNUAL REPORT

# Bureau of Sewers

CITY OF CHICAGO

1900

RICARD O'S. BURKE,
SUPERINTENDENT.

## DEPARTMENT OF PUBLIC WORKS

CITY OF CHICAGO.

L. E. McGANN,
Commissioner.

F. W. BLOCKI,
Deputy Commissioner.

H. LUTZENKIRCHEN,
Secretary.

## HEADS OF BUREAUS.

| | |
|---|---|
| CITY ENGINEER, | JOHN ERICSON |
| SUPERINTENDENT BUREAU OF SEWERS, | RICARD O'S. BURKE |
| SUPERINTENDENT BUREAU OF SPECIAL ASSESSMENTS, | JOHN A. MAY |
| SUPERINTENDENT BUREAU OF WATER, | H. O. NOURSE |
| SUPERINTENDENT BUREAU OF STREETS, | M. J. DOHERTY |
| SUPERINTENDENT BUREAU OF MAPS AND PLATS, | CHAS. J. BUHMANN |
| SUPERINTENDENT BUREAU OF STREET AND ALLEY CLEANING, | F. W. SOLON |
| DEPARTMENT BOOKKEEPER, | L. E. GOSSELIN |

the memory of Departed Brothers. God save Ireland. Erected by the Irish Nationalists of Chicago."

For several years Ricard's activities were confined to the Clan-na-Gael. He was one of the sixty one delegates who attended the Clan-na-Gael Convention in Baltimore in 1874 at which the rescue of the Fenain prisoners in Australia was discussed and at which the executive of the Clan was authorised to go ahead with the planning of a rescue which did take place in 1876 and is known as the Catalpa Rescue. He was one of the Reception Committee which welcomed Charles Stewart Parnell and John Dillon when they came to America in January, 1880, to collect money initially for the Land League but, as news reached them from Ireland of famine and disease, for the relief of the starving people of the west. Ricard was also one of those who secured a hearing for Parnell before the House of Representatives. Though the tour was not without controversy it could be considered successful. In Chicago, for example, extremists like Sullivan and Finnerty co-operated with moderates to provide a rousing welcome for the Irish leader. When Parnell sailed for home in March he had travelled 16,000 miles in the United States and Canada, had spoken in 62 cities and had raised about £60,000 for famine relief and, perhaps, another £12,000 to help finance the Land League.

Always a Republican supporter, Ricard "took to the stump" for Garfield in the Presidential election of 1880. At the Republican convention in Chicago the delegates were sharply divided between the supporters of James G. Blaine and U. S. Grant, neither of whom could command a majority. After 34 fruitless ballots, a break came and on the 36th ballot. Garfield was the unanimous choice of the convention and, at the subsequent election, he became the twentieth president of the United States. However, he only served effectively for four months. On July 2nd, 1881, he was shot and seriously wounded and died as a result of his wounds on September 19th.

In 1884 Ricard was on the campaign trail once again, this time on behalf of James Blaine, a friend of Garfield's. However, he lost the election by a narrow margin to Grover Cleaveland in an issueless and sordid campaign. Blaine was favourite to win and one reason for his defeat is attributed to the loss of the Irish Catholic vote in New York city where Blaine lost the state of New York by only 1,149 votes.

It was during the Garfield campaign that Burke met his wife, Nora Sheehy, in Fort Wayne, Indiana. The pair eloped and married in Washington. He was then forty three years of age and she was only twenty. There were two children of the marriage - Ricard Junior and Nellie. Ricard Junior, a promising young man, died of tuberculosis in 1915 at the age of twenty six. The death of his son greatly affected his father.

About the time of his marriage Ricard left Washington and went to Mexico to build railroads. As an engineer in the employ of the Mexican National Construction Company, he built the railroad from Laredo via Monterey to Mexico city. Returning to the United States once more, he lectured for a while in Colorado and was then appointed Assistant City Engineer in Omaha Nebraska. Leaving Omaha he went to Chicago in 1884 to take up the position of Map Clerk in the County Clerk's office.

He remained in Chicago until his death though he was offered inducements to come to New York. The father of Richard Croker ("Boss" Croker, the famous Tammany leader in New York), a County Cork blacksmith, was veterinary sergeant in Burke's company. He was a very liberal Irish Protestant, a relative of the famous Thomas Crofton Croker, and, while not a Fenian, was in sympathy with the movement. Some time after Burke had moved to Chicago he met the "Boss" Croker, who, in the course of conversation, asked him what he was doing. Burke answered that he was a Map Clerk in Chicago. Croker said: "Do not waste your time in a petty job like that. Come to New York and I will give you a position worthy of your talents. New York is going to be the greatest city in the world and for many years there will be great construction work requiring able engineers. I am sure, from what my father told me of your ability, that you will make good, so you will be fixed for life." Croker was noted for standing by old personal and family friends. Burke was also loyal to his. And as

Michael Ryan, County Clerk of Cook County, Illinois, had sent for him to Omaha and had given him congenial employment, he made up his mind to stay where he was and declined Croker's offer.

Of all the independent forces which transformed 19th century America into a world power there is, perhaps, none so dramatic as the vast migration of peoples from Europe to the United States. Between 1820 and the end of the century over 17 million Europeans reached America. Of these Ireland contributed four million. No other country in Western Europe lost such a high percentage of its population through emigration. The Irish were concentrated in New England and the Mid Atlantic States. Some did settle in urban and rural areas of the Mid West and Far West. But of all the cities outside the Northeast, it was Chicago which attracted the greatest number of Irishmen and sons of Irishmen.

The spectacular growth of Chicago in the nineteenth century was amazing. The city's origins can be traced back to the establishment in 1803 of Fort Dearborn. In 1829 Chicago had only about thirty inhabitants. Work started on the Illinois and Michigan Canal bringing increased prosperity to the town in the form of speculators and labourers. In 1848 construction began on the first railroad into Chicago. During the next twenty years the railway network expanded enormously, climaxing in the completion of the transcontinental railroad in 1869. As a result, Chicago became the railroad centre of the nation. As railways increased, several industries, most notably the meat packing industry, developed in the rapidly expanding city.

The population of Chicago grew very slowly at the outset. In 1833 the settlement had a population of 350. Four years later it was incorporated as a city with 4,000 inhabitants. By the time the canal was completed in 1848 approximately 20,000 people were living in the city. The growth of the population after the completion of the first railroad in 1848 was nothing short of phenomenal. Chicago's 30,000 inhabitants in 1850 increased to almost 300,000 in 1870, to half a million by 1880 and to over a million by the end of the next decade.

Foreign immigration played an extremely important role in the growth of Chicago's population. In 1850, for example, slightly over half the city's population had been born outside the United States. By 1890, however, the figure had dropped to 41%. In 1880 20% of the city's foreign born population had been born in Ireland, compared to 17% in Germany. But the Germans soon surpassed the Irish and by 1890 over one third of the city's foreign born population was German, while only about 16% were Irish. The growth of the Irish population during the four decades between 1850 and 1890 was significant. In that forty years the Irish born population of the city grew from 6,000 to over 70,000. If you include first, second and third generation Irish the figure was about 215,000.

The first great influx of Irish into Chicago came with the building of the Illinois and Michigan Canal in 1836. The Irish had gained a reputation as hard working labourers on projects in the east and a special effort was made to recruit them for work in Illinois. Others were met by agents as they stepped off the boat from Ireland. They lived in uncomfortable shanties all along the canal route. The men worked for contractors who often failed to pay them their proper wages. Many of the Irish settled in Bridgeport and worked in the meat packing yards, brick yards and lumber yards. Living conditions were abominable and lawlessness was a problem. After the Civil War the Irish began to spread into other parts of the city and it is surprising to discover how few Irish were living in real ethnic ghettos. Some Irish, of course did live in good neighbourhoods and in the years after 1890, as the new immigrants entered the city, more and more Irish moved to better areas.

Poor relief statistics provide an indication of the relative poverty of the Irish. In 1870, for example, almost half the 14,000 Chicagoans receiving outdoor public assistance were Irish born. More than half the Irish-born working force was unskilled. Working mainly in such places as meat packing plants, factories, on the railroads or as policeman, bartender and domestic servants, the Irish were poorly represented in the upper ranks of the professions. In the 1880s five out of the 161 physicians in Chicago were of Irish origin; only 30 out of the 494 leading lawyers were of Irish stock; six out of the 222 members of the Board of Trade; two out of the 42 bankers; four out of the 44 building contractors.

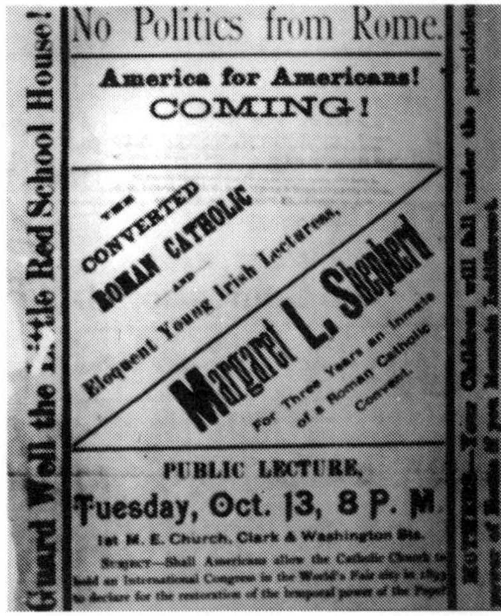


*Anti Catholicism in Chicago*
*(Courtesy Ellis Island Immigration Museum)*

As well as poverty, the most important institution in maintaining a separate Irish identity was the Catholic Church. The diocese of Chicago was created in 1843 and County Offaly born William Quarter became its first bishop. Between 1843 and 1902 all the bishops of Chicago, except one, were Irish born. Catholics established their own school system to provide their children with what they considered a truly Christian education. By separating Catholic children at an early age, these schools served to keep Irish-Americans isolated from the general community.

There were other organisations which helped to preserve the Irish identity. Among these were the nationalists groups like Clan-na-Gael and the Friends of Irish Freedom, both of which Burke was a member. There were the fraternal organisations like the Ancient Order of Hibernians and the United Sons of Erin Benevolent Society. Irish identity was also re-enforced by anti-Irish prejudice. The Irish were the dominant element in the Democratic Party and because of this exerted a powerful influence in the administration of municipal affairs. They looked after their own where jobs were concerned. They were not above taking bribes and kickbacks and they had strong links with gamblers and the saloon element. This angered many of the civic-minded

Protestants and they set up their own reform organisations like the Citizens Association and the Union League Club to combat the Irish influence in politics.

There were several anti-Catholic societies in Chicago in the late eighties. The most important was the United Order of Deputies which was founded there in 1886. There was also the American Protestant Association which was established prior to the civil war.

*Ricard's Home,*
*6311 N Paulina Street, Chicago.*

The American Protective Association, the foremost nativist society, did not become a significant force in Chicago until after 1890.

While the Irish maintained their identity, they also felt a part of the nation and the city in which they lived. Irishmen felt they were far more American than other immigrants. As one Chicago Irishman said: "The're none of them foreigners when they come here, for their hearts and love were in America long before they thought of sailin' for America." Ricard O'Sullivan Burke expressed much the same sentiments in his autobiography. "I was exchanging a land (England) that could never be other than hateful to one of my feelings and antecedents for the country I had read, and heard, and talked, and thought, and dreamt of, until I loved it - my ideal of free government - the refuge of my race - the great Republic of the West."

Ricard later became Assistant City Engineer and did much of the work constructing the Drainage Canal which takes much of the sewage of Chicago to the Mississippi. He was then appointed Superintendent of Sewers, but resigned after some time and resumed the position of Assistant City Engineer. He was later appointed Assistant Harbour Engineer and was in that position when stricken with his last illness in 1917. When he first came to Chicago he lived at Lamont, Illinois, south west of Chicago. Around about 1890 he moved to his final address, 6311 N. Pulina Street, a new development. There was a strong German representation in this area then and is now.

It was while he was Assistant Harbour Engineer an incident occurred which for a time deprived him of his salary. There was then constant "stealing of land" in Chicago through business firms on the lake or river fronts encroaching on the water by putting in slag or other waste material and thus adding to their property. Colonel Burke, whose duty it was to report all such encroachments, did so in all cases, giving full details methodically, but, through political influence, these reports were often pigeonholed. Among his reports was one - and there may have been several - concerning encroachments by one or other of the big harvester companies. A scion of the McCormick family, Medill

Patterson, who was a sort of parlour socialist, was appointed Commissioner of Public Works by Mayor Dunne and in 1903 he made a spectacular tour of inspection (with a lot of newspaper publicity) of the whole waterfront for the ostensible purpose of discovering unreported "stealing of land."

*The Chicago Daily Tribune* of Friday November 10th, 1903, carried banner headlines: NEGLECT BY ENGINEER RICARD O'SULLIVAN BURKE. - SLAG DUMPED INTO LAKE. - CARS OF ILLINOIS STEEL COMPANY ARE SEEN CREATING LAND BENEATH THE WATER. The paper went on to report how the Illinois Steel Company was dumping slag into the lake. The shore along the entire length of the company's property was a steep cinder embankment, eight or ten feet high, the brink of which was laid with a dummy railroad track. The tug on which the city officials were travelling could not be brought close to the shore on account of the shallowness of the lake at this point. This shallowness was accounted for by the steel company's nocturnal operations of filling in the lake. For half an hour the city officials watched the interesting process of making land.

The Commissioner promptly suspended Burke with a great flourish of trumpets to show his own zeal and efficiency as a "reformer." In every case Burke had faithfully made a report, but the reports were put out of sight by *somebody*. The law in Illinois was then very unjust in such cases. It placed the onus of proof of innocence on the dismissed official including the expense of court proceedings. Burke appealed to the courts and eventually was reinstated without any provision for back pay. The veteran Chicago Nationalist and lawyer, Daniel Donohoe, took charge of Burke's interests and never received a dollar in fees.

Burke attended many meetings of Irish-American organisations during his lifetime and was always in demand as a speaker. In a speech in New York on November 24th, 1910, at the Manchester Martyrs celebration, he described the work in the Union Army in detail. "In 1861-2 and 3 the Fenian Brotherhood had in the ranks of the army many members, non-commissioned officers and officers; in the Armies of the West, in the Army of Ohio, the

Tennessee, the Cumberland, the Trans Mississippi; in the Army of the Valley, the Army of the Potomac, the James and the Department of the East. I had the honour to be Center of the division of the Fenian Brotherhood in the Army of the Potomac which embraced the artillery and the engineers. The head of the organisation in the Army of the Potomac was one of the ablest and most gallant of generals of that army, General Thomas A. Smyth of Delaware; and in the last fight of the war - he had a Major General's command and a Brigadier General's rank - but in the last fight of the war, at Sailor's Creek, on the 4th of April, 1865, we lost the head of the organisation in the Army of the Potomac. General Smyth was killed in action and I cannot tell you how grave a loss that was to the cause of Ireland.

"At Gettysburgh we lost many more of our officers. Gettysburgh preceded the action at Sailor's Creek by nearly two years. At Gettysburgh one of the brightest minds of the organisation, Colonel O'Rourke, Lieutenant of Engineers of the United States Army and Colonel commanding one of the Volunteer regiments of New York."

Though Burke was a professed Republican and canvassed for Republican Presidential candidates, he did support the Democratic nominee, Woodrow Wilson, in the 1912 election and later regretted it. (The 1912 election was unusual as the Republican Party was split and two Republican candidates contested the election.) In 1914 President Wilson proposed the repeal of the free tolls provision of the Panama Canal whereby American ships were allowed free passage through the canal. This move was unanimously condemned at a meeting of Clan-na-Gael in the Aeolian Hall, New York on March 4th, 1914 - the meeting had been called to celebrate the anniversary of the birth of Robert Emmet. The resolution of protest which was proposed by Assemblyman, P.J. McMahon, said: "The free tolls provision is necessary for the protection of our coastwise shipping against the competition of the subsidised vessels of Europe, and especially those of England, whose cruisers - carrying the Confederate flag, but built in English shipyards, armed with British guns, manned by British seamen and sent to sea in violation of international obligations, in defiance of the protests of the Federal Government - swept American commerce from the sea, and thus created the monopoly which England now seeks to maintain, to the serious disadvantage and injury of this country.

"The free tolls position is also necessary to protect our coastwise shipping from a combination of American and Canadian transcontinental railroad corporations which want to crush all competition in the carrying trade. It is at the bidding of England and these railroad monopolies that the President is now endeavouring, by undue and improper pressure on Senators and Representatives, to make them sacrifice the interests of the American people, on a false and unfounded allegation that the free tolls provision is a violation of national honour."

Burke, who attended the meeting, said; "For the first time in my life I voted the National Democratic ticket at the last election. I am sorry I did it for I wanted to vote for Taft."

He did not mention President Wilson by name but added: "If I was in Congress I would take steps to impeach him. Our only weakness in this country is 'diplomacy' at Washington."

From the time Ricard left Ireland in 1873 he returned home only once. In his early years in America he could not return as he feared arrest. Presumably family commitments and work prevented him from making the journey in later years. However, in 1915, he made the long journey to Ireland to attend the funeral of his dear friend and former prison mate, O'Donovan Rossa. This must have been a very difficult journey for him as he was now seventy seven years of age and it was only a few months after the death of his son which had affected him greatly. At the funeral he met and spoke with Padraig Pearse thus forging another link between the Fenians and the leaders of the 1916 Rising. He did visit Coachford when he was in Ireland as Kitty Burke, mother of co-author, Mary Lynch, remembered meeting him. She was then ten years of age and described him as a tall, gentlemanly, elderly man.

He returned to America for the last time, suffered a stroke two years later and died in 1922.

# CHAPTER 26

# RICARD'S LAST ILLNESS AND DEATH

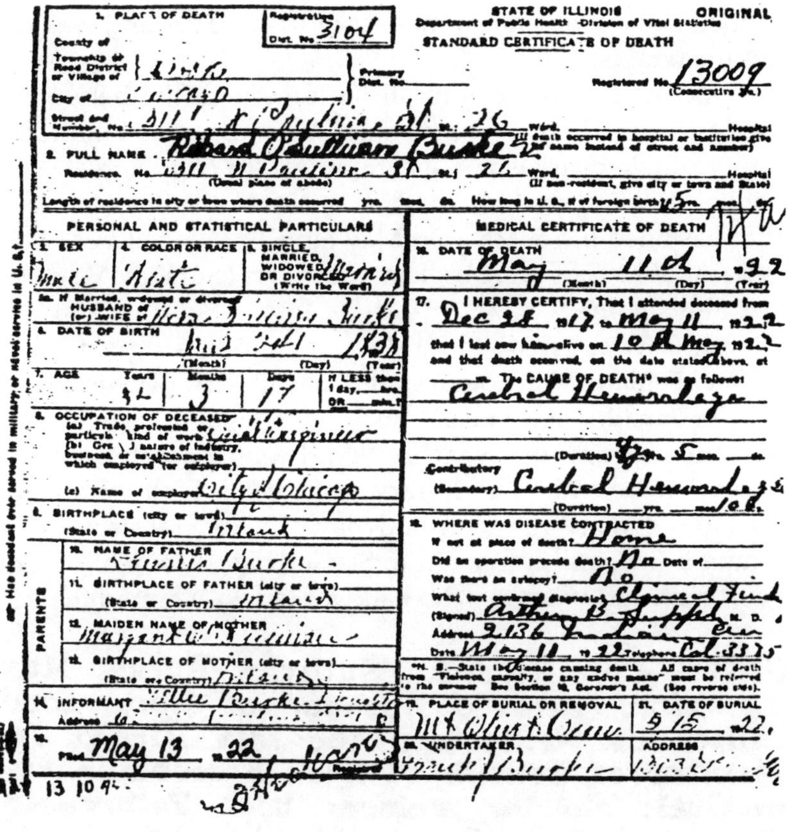

STATE OF ILLINOIS — ORIGINAL
Department of Public Health - Division of Vital Statistics
STANDARD CERTIFICATE OF DEATH

1. PLACE OF DEATH
County of
Township or Road District or Village of
City of
Street and Number, No. 3111 N Pauline St. 26 Ward
Registration Dist. No. 3104
Primary Dist. No.
Registered No. 13009 (Consecutive No.)

2. FULL NAME Richard O'Sullivan Burke
Residence. No. 3111 N Pauline St. 26 Ward (Usual place of abode)
Length of residence in city or town where death occurred ... How long in U. S., if of foreign birth? 45 yrs.

PERSONAL AND STATISTICAL PARTICULARS

3. SEX: Male
4. COLOR OR RACE: White
5. SINGLE, MARRIED, WIDOWED OR DIVORCED: Married
5a. If married, widowed or divorced HUSBAND of (or) WIFE of
6. DATE OF BIRTH: 1838
7. AGE: 84 Years 3 Months 17 Days
8. OCCUPATION OF DECEASED: Civil Engineer
(c) Name of employer: City of Chicago
9. BIRTHPLACE (city or town) (State or Country): Ireland
10. NAME OF FATHER: Burke
11. BIRTHPLACE OF FATHER (State or Country): Ireland
12. MAIDEN NAME OF MOTHER
13. BIRTHPLACE OF MOTHER (State or Country): Ireland
14. INFORMANT
Address
15. Filed May 13 1922
Registrar

MEDICAL CERTIFICATE OF DEATH

16. DATE OF DEATH: May 11th 1922
17. I HEREBY CERTIFY, That I attended deceased from Dec 28 1917 to May 11 1922
that I last saw him alive on 10th May 1922
and that death occurred, on the date stated above, at
The CAUSE OF DEATH was as follows: Cerebral Hemorrhage
(Duration) 4 yrs. 5 mos.
Contributory (Secondary): Cerebral Hemorrhage
(Duration) 10 d.
18. WHERE WAS DISEASE CONTRACTED If not at place of death? Home
Did an operation precede death? No
Was there an autopsy? No
What test confirmed diagnosis? Clinical
(Signed) Arthur B. , M. D.
Address 2136
Date May 11 1922 Telephone Cal. 3375

19. PLACE OF BURIAL OR REMOVAL: Mt Olivet Cem.
21. DATE OF BURIAL: 5 15 1922
20. UNDERTAKER: Burke
ADDRESS

13 1094

*Ricard's Death Certificate*

When Ricard returned to America after O'Donovan Rossa's funeral he enjoyed perfect health for just two years. In the winter of 1916/ 1917, as he was going down the steps from his house, he slipped and fell, hurting himself badly. Shortly afterwards he suffered a stroke which eventually caused his death. For more than five years he made a brave fight for life. For all that time he was confined to bed paralysed, being able to use his left arm and leg a little. His mind was perfectly clear, although his speech was somewhat affected. He was a man of very strong will and fought off death in the hope of living until Ireland became independent. Up to the last he took a keen interest in Irish affairs and was able to read the papers.

His wife, Nora, nursed him all the time with the help of her daughter, Nellie. He was a heavy man and moving him in the bed and other nursing care was a severe ordeal for Nora and she was near collapse when the end came. Coincidentally, it was another fall that hastened his death. On May 8th, 1922, he fell out of bed and several of his ribs were broken. Then, on Thursday May 11th, he died at his home.

The funeral was on Monday, May 15th and was a great tribute to the dead Fenian. Many old friends from all parts of Chicago and some from outside sat up nearly all Sunday night at the wake and among them were many who had been separated by the differences in Ireland. The Rosary was said in Irish by Mathew Harford in the room where the body lay. The funeral started from the family home and proceeded to St. Gertrudes Church. A large crowd of men and women, who had worked with him in the Irish

**BURKE**—Col Ricard O'Sullivan Burke, May 11, 1922, beloved husband of Nora, fond father of Nellie and the late Ricard Jr. Member of Friends of Irish Freedom, Clan-na-Gael; charter member Irish Fellowship club, and Gen. George Meade post, G. A. R. Funeral Monday, 10 a. m., from residence, 6311 N. Paulina-st to St. Gertrude's church, Glenwood and Granville-avs. Interment Mount Olivet. For information call Sheldrake 6114.

*Death Notice from the Chicago Herald Tribune*

movement and many aged veterans who had known and loved him in the stirring days of Fenianism when he was the boldest and most resourceful man among them, packed the sidewalk and filled the street to say their last farewell. The same scene was repeated when the body was carried into and out of the church.

The church was filled with a most representative crowd, practically every old timer in the National Movement as well as most of the younger element and many men prominent in public being present. The celebrant of the Requiem High Mass was Rev. Bernard C. Heeney, Pastor of St Gertrudes; Rev James N. Scanlan, Pastor of Our Lady of Lourdes, was deacon; Rev. Martin F. Kenneally was sub-deacon and Rev. F. X. McCabe, former President De Paul University, Chicago and then of Kansas City, preached the funeral sermon. In the sanctuary was Right Rev. Thomas L. O'Reilly, Bishop of Lincoln.

The pall-bearers were Eugene F. O'Riordan, David P. Murphy, Captain John D. M. McCarthy, Richard T. Hanrahan, John F. Sheridan, John F. Long, John J. Mahony and Charles Callanan. The honorary pall-bearers were: John Devoy, Hon. Edward F. Dunne (Former Governor of Illinois), Hon. Kickham Scanlan (Chief Judge of the Criminal Court), Hon. Daniel Ryan (President County Board, Cook County), Hon. Joseph P. Mahoney, Dr. Alexander Pope, Dr. John M. Murphy, Captain Willian G. Grace, Major J. H. Hyland, Captain P. J. Gibbons, Patrick H. O'Donnell, Richard M. Wolfe, Hugh O'Neill, P.T. O'Sullivan, Daniel J. McMahon, Luke Colleran, John H. Harrington, James O'D. Storen, Major M. H. Enright, Lieutenant M. W. Delany, M. English, Thomas P. Bonfield, Daniel Donohoe, Martin Fleming, John Doody and John A. McGarry.

The coffin was draped with the two flags for which he had fought - the Stars and Stripes and the Green White and Orange Tricolour of Ireland. Interment took place in Mount Olivet Cemetery, which is on the South Side of the city. This Catholic cemetery contains the remains of many of the Irish immigrants and as one walks between the headstones one could be in any cemetery in Ireland so numerous are the Irish names. Father James

*Burke Headstone, Mount Olivet Cemetery, Chicago.*

M. Scanlan, an old friend and colleague, officiated at the graveside, and, as the coffin was lowered into the grave, the vast crowd knelt and offered a last prayer for Ricard.

At the termination of the funeral services the crowd knelt at the grave of the late John F. Keating, which is close to that of Ricard, and Father Scanlan offered a prayer for Burke's old friend and the friend of many present at the funeral. Keating was a Fenian and was one of those who welcomed Burke to Cork when he was released from Broadmoor in 1871. So it was fitting that the two old colleagues should be prayed for at the same time in contiguous graves.

Fr. McCabe's sermon was pronounced a masterpiece by former Governor Dunne and Judge Scanlan. It had a very moving effect on the great congregation.

"I have fought the good fight: I have kept the faith: and now I know there is laid up for me the crown which the Just Judge will give in that day."

*The grave of John F. Keating with Burke's grave in the background.*

*Clan na Gael Memorial, Mount Olivet Cemetery*

"I know of no words, my dear brethren, more suited to the life of anyone who has lived the life of our dear departed than the words which I have just quoted from the Sacred Scripture. Truly his whole life has been in keeping with the words of that text, both from the standpoint of a disciple of Jesus Christ and from the standpoint of loyalty of citizenship to his native land and his adopted country. The two go hand in hand, and one must be founded on the other. For our citizenship is worth nothing unless it is founded upon a recognition of the great responsibility following from our belief in God.

"Our dear departed one believed in God. He got the faith at the baptismal font. He had it nourished by the loving tenderness of a good faithful mother. He had it fostered even in the days of his manhood by the devoted wife and family. He lived it in his life. Notwithstanding human frailty, underlying the character of our dear departed was always that strong determination to adhere to principle and to disregard men. Fundamentally that was his life - a total disregard for the opinion of men, for the personalities of men, but a strong and firm adherence to the principle of a cause, whether it was of his faith or his country, the country of his birth or the country of his adoption. A quiet, unassuming, simple character, with no blaring of trumpets, no beating of drums, but just that simple life of faith in God and faith in his fellow-men, determination to do the thing that he saw was right, so far as in the weakness of human nature he was capable of doing it. ......

"A long life, more than that which is usually allotted to the average man, was given to him, a life spent in devotion to great causes. Coming as a young man into this glorious land of ours, with its great ideals, he devoted himself, as many hundreds of thousands of his fellow men from the same land, to the cultivation of these ideals, to the development of the land that fostered such ideals.

"Hungry for civil and religious liberty, hungry for the liberty that would give the faculties of the soul of man opportunity to expand and develop themselves, the young man threw himself heart and soul into things that stood for the noblest and the best in this land. And when an enemy would defeat this land that it might conquer it more easily, he found that enemy was to be fought even though he had left the heel of its tyranny at home. Therefore he threw himself heart and soul into the maintenance of the Union for which that flag that drapes his casket stands. He was ready to fight at Bull Run and Petersburg, ready to advise and to do all things at General Headquarters, ready on all occasions to risk his life for the principles for which our flag stood here, until he saw a nation saved from the rended garment that might make it an easy prey to the enemy that has ever followed it and follows it to-day. When he saw it secure, like Patrick of old, he heard the voice of his own people calling him back home, calling him to make the great sacrifice over again, if necessary, that it might have that freedom in the throwing off the yoke of tyranny. So he crossed the sea again to fight for the same principles of liberty and the overthrowing of tyranny.

"As a citizen of a land whose sovereignty had been usurped, morally correct he believed that any means that he might use to overthrow that tyranny in fighting for his beloved land were perfectly just and perfectly right. An invader was in the home of his people and he believed that as a member of that home he was justified in hurling him out by whatever means he might succeed in doing so. Therefore, he endeavoured to bring about the freedom of his own native land, having helped to secure the Union of his adopted land. Because he was willing to take the chance, he was willing to lay his life upon the altar of his country, although they murdered others, they tortured him. And he was willing to accept the long martyrdom of fifteen years in a British dungeon, because his country needed him. The term shortened to five years, he returned again to the land of his adoption, to give it his best energies and his best efforts.

"Now, here is a man - we talk of the few that are left of those who followed the flag in the crucial days in the history of our country. Here is one. Where are those who make so much of veterans? Where are they to-day? Where is the display? Here is a man mustered out with the rank of Colonel after honourable service. And none so poor in the land of his adoption as to do him reverence. What cared he for that appreciation? He knew he was right. He sought not the plaudits of men. He sought not the rattle of drums and the blare of trumpets. He saw his work as a man, and because he believed in God, and because he loved that God, and because of his knowledge of that God, he did his work and served his God and served the fixed principles of justice for which that God stood. He cared little for what men thought or what men said. He looked ahead to see the principle, and seeing it and knowing it to be right, he dared to walk the path to that principle, though it led through fire and blood and even death. …

"Let me say to those who were near and dear to him, to those of the family who naturally, even though they saw him on a bed suffering for years, grieve to lose him, although they thank God that he is at last at rest - who would not be human if they did not grieve. Let me say that all we can do is to put you into the arms of Mary, the Mother of Sorrows, standing at the foot of the Cross and offering her Son for the redemption of the world, for the liberty, the spiritual liberty of the entire human race. Mary offered her Son. He who is dear to you gave himself for civil liberty, because he participated in the spiritual liberty of the world, on which civil liberty must be founded - Mary, who offered her Son, will open her arms and gather you into her sacred heart, and into your souls pour the oil of consolation which is drawn from the throne of God, so that you may bow in submission to the Will of God and offer the prayer of faith with all those who have loved him. 'Eternal rest give unto him, O Lord, and let perpetual light shine upon him.'

Ricard Burke was survived by his wife, Nora and by his daughter, Nellie. Nora died in 1939 and the family home at 6311 N. Paulina Street was sold. It was indeed a coincidence that the new owner was also named Burke - no relation. This Burke family still live there. Nellie died in 1966 at Berrien St. Joseph's, Michigan. Both mother and daughter are buried in the family burial plot in Mount Olivet Cemetery. Neither Ricard Junior nor Nellie married and therefore there are no direct descendants of Ricard Senior.

Just a short month after his death Ricard was honoured when Chicago's newest branch of the Friends of Irish Freedom, which was established at a meeting held in Southend Hall, Fifty-ninth and Halsted Streets, was named after the great Fenian. Gathered together were representatives from the old branches in the nearby territories - Thomas Davis, Major John Mc Bride, Mad Anthony Wayne and John Naughton. The meeting was called to order by Dr. John M. Murphy, the President of the Chicago Local Council of the Friends of Irish Freedom. Officers elected were: President: Lieutenant M. W. Delany; Vice President: John J. Hawkins;

Recording Secretary: Elizabeth Leahy; Financial Secretary: P. J. Burke; Corresponding Secretary: Mrs. P. J. Dineen; Treasurer: Mary Ward; Orator: John J. Gleason; Guard: Timothy O'Brien; Director of Organisation: Thomas Fitzpatrick; Director of Publicity: William J. Grace; Trustees: Andrew McSharry, J. P. Dineen, M. McGrath; Delegates to the Local Council: J. Hawkins and Thomas Fitzpatrick.

Dr. Murphy added greatly to the enjoyment of the evening by singing a song in Irish. John J. Hawkins, one of the best known elocutionists in Chicago, recited "The Irish at Marye's Heights." John M. Gleason entertained the huge crowd by singing "The West's Awake" and the "Soldier's Song." Many others were called upon, members of the new branch and visitors who had come to help in the successful inauguration of a new branch on the South Side.

Ricard O'Sullivan Burke spent the last years of his life ill in bed and did not have any income. During these years, besides having to meet his household expenses, he was burdened with many others incidental to his illness. He was a typical Fenian who never hesitated to make sacrifices for the cause to which he had devoted his life. The result was that he never saved money and was wholly dependent on his salary. So to relieve his widow of financial embarrassment Ricard's friends in Chicago set up the Burke Memorial Fund. The following letter appeared in the Gaelic American on June 17th, 1922.

Chicago, June 6th, 1922.

*Mr. John Devoy,*

*Editor Gaelic American.*

*Dear Mr. Devoy — Colonel Ricard O'Sullivan Burke, whose splendid services on behalf of human liberty have been made known through the columns of The Gaelic American to thousands of the younger generation, died as did nearly, if not all, his colleagues in the Irish Revolutionary Movement who have passed away, a poor man.*

*Because of his protracted illness, covering a period of more than five years, the modest little home in which he died is now carrying a mortgage of about four thousand dollars ($4,000). It is the idea of friends here that this burden should be taken away from Mrs. Burke and daughter, the sole survivors of Colonel Burke's immediate family. In order that this may be done, it is proposed to create a fund to be known as the Ricard O'Sullivan Burke Memorial Fund, using, with your permission, the columns of The Gaelic American to acknowledge subscriptions.*

*In view of the fact that the amount required is not large, it is suggested that the maximum individual subscription need not be larger than ten dollars ($10), and, as the Colonel had thousands of friends and admirers in very modest financial circumstances, that a minimum subscription of one dollar, would give us all a chance to subscribe without hardship to anyone.*

*Checks or money orders may be mailed to John J. Mahoney, 155 North Clark Street, Chicago, who has kindly consented to act as Treasurer of the fund and to acknowledge all subscriptions through the columns of The Gaelic American.*

*Sincerely yours,*
*John A. McGarry.*

The Irish from all over America contributed to this fund. Clan-na-Gael clubs in the various cities made collections at their meetings and forwarded the total takings to the treasurer. Donations were small - mainly one or two dollars - but the fund grew and by Christmas of that year it wasn't far short of its target of ten thousand dollars ($10,000). Every week the donations were acknowledged in The Gaelic American and the list of subscribers as published on August 26th, 1922, shows how widespread were the friends and admirers of Colonel Burke.

# BURKE MEMORIAL FUND

The following additional subscriptions are reported by John J. Mahoney, 153 N. Clark Street, Chicago, Ill., the Treasurer of the Ricard O'Sullivan Burke Memorial Fund:

Previously published in Gaelic American .................. $2,672.00
(Published August 12, T. J. Gilmartin $5, should be $2, deduct ........ 3.00

Correcting the above, leaves balance of ........ $2,669.00
Ancient Order of Hibernians . 100.00
John Sheehy, Nat'l Treas. A. O. H. ........ 5.00

Brian Boru Club, New York City.
Daniel Bacon ........ 5.00
Patrick Ferriter ........ 5.00
Patrick Coyne ........ 5.00
John Moylan ........ 5.00
Dennis King ........ 5.00
Michael O'Reilly ........ 5.00
Eugene O'Sullivan ........ 2.00
Frank Flaherty ........ 2.00
Wm. J. Hurley ........ 2.00
Terence McCaffrey ........ 2.00
John McAvoy ........ 1.00
Daniel Neenan ........ 1.00
Edmond Egan ........ 1.00
Patrick L. Ryan ........ 1.00
Mortimer Gleason ........ 1.00
T. J. McCarthy ........ 1.00
P. J. Walsh ........ 1.00
D. W. Lane ........ 1.00
P. Gallagher ........ 1.00
Patrick Walsh ........ 1.00
Patrick Tierney ........ 1.00
Martin Kane ........ 1.00
T. O. O'Herlihy ........ 5.00

Emmet Club, Indianapolis, Ind. 25.00
Napper Tandy Club, New York City ........ 42.00

Wolfe Tone Club, New York City ........ 20.00
James Donohue ........ 5.00
Jeremiah Regan ........ 3.00
M. J. McMahon ........ 2.00

Owen Roe Club, New York City.
Matthew G. Lyons ........ 10.00
James Ryan ........ 2.00
Phillip Dennehy ........ 2.00
Anonymous (New York City). 2.00

Padraic Pearse Club.
John Keane ........ 3.00
Matthew Ebbert ........ 2.00

Thomas Clarke Club, New York.
Peter Mitchell ........ 1.00

Geraldine Club, New York.
M. J. Sherwin ........ 1.00

[illegible] Isle Club, Brooklyn, L. I.
[illegible] Sullivan ........ 5.00
[illegible] Lee ........ 5.00
[illegible] Kavanaugh, Brooklyn ........ 2.00

Garfield Club, Long Island, N.Y. 10.00
Dennis F. Coughlin ........ 5.00
James Murnane ........ 2.00
Daniel Coughlin ........ 1.00

Emmet Club, Youngstown, Ohio.
W. H. Dempsey ........ 5.00
M. J. Foy ........ 2.50
M. J. Carney ........ 2.00
John Walsh ........ 2.00
P. J. Grady ........ 2.00
Rev. P. J. Ferron ........ 2.00
John Collins, Sr. ........ 1.00
James Conlon ........ 1.00
John Holnan ........ 1.00
J. E. Gribbon ........ 1.00

John Boyle O'Reilly Club, West Newton, Mass. ........ 40.00
Celtic Club, So. Boston, Mass.. 15.00
Edward McSweeney, Boston, Mass. ........ 5.00

Mitchel Club, Boston, Mass.
W. P. Rohan ........ 2.00
Bernard McAneany, Fitchburg, Mass. ........ 1.00
James Supple, Somerville, Mass. 1.00

Emmet Club, Torrington, Conn.
John A. Carroll ........ 3.00
Owen O'Neill ........ 2.00
Paul Maroney ........ 2.00
S. J. Cook ........ 1.00
J. J. Gleason ........ 1.00
John Welsh ........ 1.00
Malachi Shanahan ........ 1.00
D. Fitzpatrick ........ 1.00
Michael Walsh ........ 1.00
Lawrence Grasheen ........ 1.00
Patrick Anderson ........ 1.00

Joseph J. Hall, Naugatuck, Conn. ........ 5.00

Celtic Club, Derby, Conn.
John J. Mahoney ........ 1.00

O'Neill Crowley Club, Kansas City, Mo.
J. J. Williams ........ 2.00
M. Hastings ........ 1.00

Mitchel Club, Providence, R. I.
F. J. Finnerman ........ 5.00
James Owens ........ 2.00

Sarsfield Club, Woonsocket R. I.
Stephen Crane ........ 5.00
M. H. Roche, Wolfe Tone Club, Revere Point, R. I. ........ 5.00

Washington Literary Club, Perth Amboy, N. J.
J. J. Ryan ........ 10.00
B. M. Gannon ........ 10.00
J. J. Clarke ........ 5.00
T. J. Burke ........ 5.00
John Kelly ........ 5.00
M. Coughlan ........ 2.00
John Mannion ........ 2.00
Thos. Feeney ........ 2.00
James Murray ........ 2.00
Patrick Bradley ........ 2.00
M. J. O'Hara ........ 2.00

J. J. Deveney ........ 2.00
John Connolly ........ 2.00
Thomas Brady ........ 2.00
C. Carmody ........ 2.00
James Higgins ........ 1.00
P. McConville ........ 1.00
B. McPartland ........ 1.00
Thos. Haney ........ 1.00
Patrick Ryan ........ 1.00
Andrew Finan ........ 1.00
Wm. Maloney ........ 1.00
James McGrath ........ 1.00
P. Burke ........ 1.00
D. Gallagher ........ 1.00
J. J. Dolan ........ 1.00
P. McDonough ........ 1.00
Florence Sullivan ........ 1.00
John Hooley ........ 1.00
Wm. Hallahan ........ 1.00
Richard Ryan ........ 1.00
P. M. Chapman ........ 1.00
A. Garonick ........ 1.00
H. P. McArdle ........ 2.00

McBride Club, Bayonne, N. J.
F. J. Barkley ........ 3.00

Emmet League, Shenandoah, Pa.
P. H. Devine ........ 5.00

Catalpa Club, Pittsburg, Pa.
B. F. O'Connor ........ 2.00

Wolfe Tone Club, Pittsburg, Pa.
John Finn ........ 1.00

William Orr Club, Dover, N. H.
J. W. Lawless ........ 2.00
Dr. J. L. Sweeney ........ 2.00
Michael Harrison ........ 2.00
J. J. Healy ........ 1.00
Michael Duffy ........ 1.00
M. J. White ........ 1.00
B. J. Murphy ........ 1.00
Thos. Loughlin ........ 1.00
Geo. E. Gorman ........ 1.00

Thos. F. Grady, Portland, Ore.. 1.00
J. J. McDonnell, Portland, Ore. 1.00

Emmet Society, Tacoma, Wash.
Lawrence Curren ........ 10.00
Thos. A. Flood, Portsmouth, Va. 1.00
M. J. Cosgrove, Albuquerque, New Mex. ........ 1.00
Joseph Dunn, Catholic University, Washington, D. C. ........ 5.00

A. O. H., Chicago, Ill.
Rev. F. L. Reynolds, County Chaplin ........ 5.00

Mitchell Club, Chicago, Ill.
Timothy Bresnahan ........ 2.00
Dudley McDonald ........ 2.00
William Donovan ........ 1.00

Celtic Club, Chicago, Ill.
P. J. Reynolds ........ 5.00
P. J. McNamara ........ 2.00
William Kelly ........ 5.00
Thos. F. Sampson ........ 2.00
John Morgan ........ 5.00

Total to date ........ $3,250.50

CORRECTION.

Joseph McKeon of the Geraldine Club, New York—not John, as erroneously reported in last week's issue—subscribed $5 to the Col. Rickard O'Sullivan Burke Fund.

*National Monument, Grand Parade, Cork.*

## Great Grand Nieces and Nephew of Ricard's.

*Grace Gleeson Donovan*
*Coachford, Co. Cork*

*Maura Gleeson Murphy*
*Crecora, Co. Limerick*

*Mary Walsh Lynch*
*Coachford, Co. Cork.*

*Thomas R. Walsh*
*Coachford, Co. Cork.*

*The Authors with Jane O'Donovan at Burke's Grave.*

*1867 Panel of Monument Grand Parade.*
*On it Colonel Burke's name is spelt incorrectly.*